LIFE AFTER THE
30-SECOND SPOT

Adweek and Brandweek Books are designed to present interesting, insightful books for the general business reader and for professionals in the worlds of media, marketing, and advertising.

These are innovative, creative books that address the challenges and opportunities of these industries, written by leaders in the business. Some of our writers head their own companies, others have worked their way up to the top of their field in large multinationals. But they share a knowledge of their craft and a desire to enlighten others.

We hope readers will find these books as helpful and inspiring as *Adweek*, *Brandweek*, and *Mediaweek* magazines.

Published

LIFE AFTER THE 30-SECOND SPOT

Energize Your Brand with a
Bold Mix of Alternatives to
Traditional Advertising

JOSEPH JAFFE

WILEY

John Wiley & Sons, Inc.

Published by John Wiley & Sons, Inc., Hoboken, New Jersey.
Published simultaneously in Canada.

For general information on our other products and services please contact our Customer Care Department within the United States at (800) 762-2974, outside the United States at (317) 572-3993 or fax (317) 572-4002.

Wiley also publishes its books in a variety of electronic formats. Some content that appears in print may not be available in electronic books. For more information about Wiley products, visit our web site at *www. Wiley.com.*

Library of Congress Cataloging-in-Publication Data:

Jaffe, Joseph, 1970–
    Life after the 30-second spot: energize your brand with bold alternatives to traditional advertising / Joseph Jaffe.
        p. cm.
        ISBN 0-471-71837-8 (cloth)
    1. Advertising—Psychological aspects. 2. Customer relations. 3. Target marketing. 4. Advertising—Technological innovations. 5. Interactive marketing. I. Title: Alternatives to traditional advertising. II. Title.
    HF5822.J33 2005
    659.1—dc22   2005000050

Printed in the United States of America

10 9 8 7 6 5 4

Dedicated to my beautiful wife, Terri, and gorgeous children, Amber and Aaron — may you all forgive me for living out of a suitcase, exhibiting an exuberantly unhealthy type A personality, and trying to change the world (in no respective order)

Acknowledgments

To my many colleagues in the industry—whom I am privileged enough to call my friends—thank you for your support and belief, and at times for putting your money where my mouth is. Also my gratitude to the thinkers and doers out there who are responsible for some of the exemplary work that I hope I've done justice to in this book.

Thanks to Grant Lyons, creative director and partner at b2fync, who designed my web site and the various lifeline icons depicted in the book.

Props to my man, Richard Narramore, senior editor at John Wiley & Sons, for truly believing in me and my message. Also to Ami Brophy, Executive Director, Clio Awards, for making the introduction which ignited the spark.

And finally, my eternal gratitude to my mother, for pretty much everything.

Portions of this text may have previously appeared as iMedia "Jaffe Juice" columns or in MediaPost's MediaDailyNews.

Contents

16. Communal Marketing   199
17. Consumer-Generated Content   220
18. Search   231
19. Music, Mobile, and Things That Make You
    Go Mmmm   243
20. Branded Entertainment   255

    Epilogue   271
    Index   277

Foreword

Joseph Jaffe and I are about as unlike as any two people you will ever meet. Joseph is an internationalist. I'm an Okie. Joseph has spent much of his time in creative. I have always been a "suit." Joseph has not just embraced new technology, he revels in it. I'm writing this piece using Word 95. Joseph lives in Connecticut. I live in Chicago. Clearly, we are polar extremes.

Yet here I am. A shiny-pants professor suggesting that new knowledge is better than old. That new advertising concepts must replace what we know and love. That tradition must be reinvented. That what lies ahead is more critical than what's behind. All of these are an anathema to what we like to call the "scientific method."

I am writing this foreword because I truly believe what Joseph has said in his columns, speeches, presentations, seminars, and the like. It's what he continues to say from every podium and platform he can find. And he's right.

But the real reason I am writing this preface is that it's a book I wish I had written. And this is the next best thing, being asked to write the foreword. Call it reflected glory if you like.

The reason I think Joseph pursued me for this foreword to his first book is simple: We agree on one basic thing. Media advertising, as we have known, practiced, and worshipped it for the past 60 or so years, is in trouble. Big trouble. And it's not going to get well. Ever.

SOME RELEVANT EVIDENCE OF CHANGE

My own academic research in the following areas shows that traditional advertising isn't working:

- Simultaneous media consumption by audiences
- The synergistic effects of multiple-vehicle exposures
- The uselessness of consumer demographic information for anything much more than determining when driver's licenses should be issued or Social Security payments should start
- The impotence of media optimization models

All these are solid evidence of change, that the old is over and the new has already begun.

Most significant, however, is the massive change in what we cavalierly call *target audiences* or *consumers*. Those nameless, faceless folk who are supposed to respond to what we marketers think is important, interesting, and most of all, very clever and revolutionary.

Being a college professor, I see the future trends long before most marketers. Why? The changes are sitting in my classroom, every day. Changing before my eyes. The class of 2001 has only a slight resemblance to the class of 2004. What takes the trend spotters months or years to identify, I see on an ongoing basis.

The problem is that people in their late teens and early twenties aren't like the rest of us. Certainly not like the advertising experts who pontificate and pronounce and prevaricate about "consumers" or "customers" or "categories." These new people, for they are truly new people, aren't like the demographic groups that we love to lump together into 18- to 34-year-olds or 25- to 49-year-olds. They aren't anything like their parents and certainly not their grandparents . . . the people who grew up and were influenced by the 30-second commercial. And, the problem is, even these folks haven't been the same for some time, no matter how advertisers have tried to treat them in the same old way.

That's the major change Joseph relates in this book: the change in the consumer that is driving all the new concepts, approaches, technologies, and the like that a whole new age of consumers have adapted and adopted. To them, the 30-second commercial is about as relevant as a preview of the next *Lawrence Welk Show.*

The consumer is different and advertising isn't. Certainly, the 30-second commercial isn't. It has a beginning, a middle, and an end. It's a format for a time that no longer exists and for a customer who today refuses to be formatted. That's the problem Joseph addresses in the first section of the book.

BREAKING THE BONDS

Advertising people are still wedded to the 30-second commercial. For an industry that supposedly lives and breathes creativity, advertising people are considerably less enthusiastic about change than accountants, or even tollbooth collectors. Advertising people preach new concepts, new ideas, new approaches, new this, new that. But they are loath to give up what they know and understand and on which they have made tons of money: the 30-second commercial.

Pervasive is too mild a word for how the 30-second commercial dominates the advertising business. Everything we do is based on that fragment of time. Our pretesting research is predicated on a 30-second spot. Our consumer research assumes a 30-second spot as the output, as do the focus group respondents. Our media systems are geared and revolve around the 30-second spot. Our measurement systems all convert everything to the equivalent of a 30-second bit of film or tape with music, dancing, graphics, words, and pictures arranged and rearranged to fit within that arbitrary concept of time. The advertising world revolves around the 30-second spot. It's the standard thinking mechanism that pervades the industry. Ask an advertising person to consider any other time segment and you see a deer-in-the-headlights panic set in.

Yet here is a young whippersnapper named Joseph Jaffe who doesn't just say the 30-second ad is going to die. He says it already has. That's not good news for lots of people, or their livelihoods. Maybe what we are observing today is the wake for the 30-second commercial, with services to follow.

THE END OF DOMINATION

The big media, the big agencies, the big clients, and the big idea are never going to dominate marketing communication the way they did in the second half of the twentieth century. Traditional media advertising, with its myths, traditions, pecking orders, perks, and privileges, is being replaced by gaming, on-demand, communal, and consumer-generated content and the host of other, more relevant approaches. We likely will never, ever see a commercial like Apple's "1984," simply because there will never, ever be a similar venue or a similarly focused audience. While that's a shame, it's reality. So let's move on.

Advertising has already changed, although many marketers continue to try to hold back the tide. But unlike most other texts that "view with alarm" or "challenge the leadership" or "call for new concepts and new approaches," this book provides some solutions and some relevant ways to deal with the traditional areas of media advertising, sales promotion, public relations, and direct marketing . . . the big four of marketing communications. Not tomorrow, but today. That's what makes this book unique. Little time is spent on setting up the problem. Much time is given to suggesting solutions and understanding how to rethink the four fundamentals of marketing (i.e., the consumer, the brand, the advertising, and the agency). Those are the real keys to the future.

Life after the 30-Second Spot is a road map for the present, not a dream world for the future.

EMBRACING CHANGE

We can't put the TiVo back in the box, any more than we can ask people to give up their automobiles or their garage-door openers. Marketing communication has changed. And it will continue to change. The real question is not will advertising change, but will advertising people change? Some will. Some won't. Some are being tugged and pulled and, yes, even manacled and carried into the new world of what media advertising is, could be, and should be. Many of them aren't happy about what they see. They will kick, scream, blog, and criticize what follows in this text. My suspicion is they won't like what they read or the implications for their future.

This book is a road map, not for the future, but for the right now. It's filled with ideas. Lists. Examples. Opinions. Facts. But most of all with truths. Truths about what is really going on in the advertising business. What has changed. What hasn't and what needs to.

About the only thing missing in this book is perforation. Perforated pages so they can be ripped from the text and duct-taped to the cabinet over the work space of every advertising person simply as a reminder that "Toto, we're not in Kansas anymore!"

How long will it take advertisers to change? More important, *can* they change? Joseph and I believe there is life after the 30-second spot. The following pages will show you the way.

Don E. Schultz
Professor Emeritus-in-Service
Northwestern University
Evanston, IL

Preface

This is an opinion piece. That's a good thing. There are way too few opinions out there nowadays. You may not agree with my opinion, but at least you'll be prodded to venture out of that hard, protective shell known as *comfort*.

The book is divided into three sections.

Section 1: The Problem—I attempt to rub salt in the wounds of the ailing 30-second model for two reasons. First, it's fun to kick a bully who's down, and, on a more serious note, I think it's important to articulate the real problem, explain reasons for its cause, and discuss some obvious or not-so-obvious implications.

Section 2: The Solution: Re:think Four Fundamentals of Marketing—I challenge you to rethink four areas—the consumer, branding, advertising, and the advertising agency. This is necessary if we are to reinvent ourselves and our modus operandi: Once we understand how the consumer has changed, it will be easier to find new ways to connect and deepen relationships with them. Then I help you down the path with a look at what's right, what's wrong, and what needs to change in the world of brand building and advertising. Finally, I tackle the giant elephant in the room—the historic keepers of the brand and creators of the communication—the advertising agency.

Section 3: 10 Approaches That Are Transforming the Marketing and Advertising Games—This is the meat and potatoes of the book, where I discuss 10 bold nontraditional approaches that are transforming the advertising game. From the Internet to experiential marketing; from mobile to music; from communal marketing to long-form content. As I am a proud generalist, I've turned to 10 credible specialists from the communications world. They conclude each chapter with commentary on the subject at hand. For their contributions I'd like to thank (in alphabetical order):

- Chris Aldhous, European Creative Director for Hewlett-Packard, Publicis London
- David Apicella, Senior Partner, Co-Creative Head, Ogilvy & Mather New York
- Ian Beavis, former Senior Vice President, Marketing, Product Planning & Public Relations, Mitsubishi Motors North America, Inc.
- Jason Devitt, CEO and President, Vindigo, Inc.
- Robert Greenberg, Chairman, CEO, Chief Creative Officer, R/GA
- Charles K. Porter, Chairman, Crispin Porter + Bogusky
- Jon Raj, Director of Advertising, Visa
- Kevin Ryan, Executive Vice President, Did-it.Com
- Karen Schulman, VP Marketing & Sales, Global Publishing, Electronic Arts (EA)
- Rishad Tobaccowala, President, Starcom MediaVest Group

SOME FINAL POINTERS

You'll notice that several brands—some expected and some unexpected—will pop up throughout the book. These brands have reached a point where the 10 suggested approaches in Part 3 are more of a checklist than a wish list. They have found that once you go "new marketing," it's hard to go back to old marketing.

I believe these 10 approaches are less of a "nice-to-have-if-some-leftover-dollars-from-the-marketing-budget-remain" and more of a lifeline to a struggling industry. If you want to survive, you will need all of these lifelines at some time or another.

Most business books out there take 250-plus pages to make one point 250-plus times. They elaborate and expound on a problem in superficial terms, with few suggestions and solutions.

Most business books are also instant cures for insomnia.

I attempt to tell my story with a strong emphasis on being

prescriptive, proactive, practical, and pragmatic; I zero in on the solution in a way that is engaging, provocative, and above all, not boring. I work hard to keep your eyelids wide open. If I offend you in any way, I wholeheartedly do not apologize. This is tough love. I love and care about this business and the people in it, and this is why I'm telling it like it is.

From a self-serving standpoint, I try to mention some of my clients as often as I can, except I call it *branded publishing* and will charge them to the hilt for doing so.

Finally, I make predictions about the future. In the event these predictions come to pass, I invite you to sign up for my "I told you so" e-mail newsletter, where I will be able to celebrate the successes of being right; in the event my predictions are proven to be hopelessly inept and off base, I invite you to draw on your human nature of forgetfulness and move on.

Ideas Are a Dime a Dozen, so Pay Me My Dime

Many people believe that ideas flow in abundance and *execution* is the valuable component. Phooey! My belief is that ideas are as commonplace as an oasis in a desert—many such appearances are, upon close inspection, found to be mirages or false promises of big potential.

Agencies are forced to produce too many ideas without remuneration, and that's another topic for another day, but for now I want it to be known that this book contains many, many ideas. I encourage you to use them. I don't even mind if you call them your own and take credit for them. But I ask that for every idea you choose to execute, you visit my web site, www.lifeafter30.com and use the honor system to donate $1 (or whatever your heart dictates). If you like, you can even hire me.

SECTION I

The Problem

"Jacksonville, we have a problem."

Not a conversation goes on these days—at least in any marketing industry public forum—that doesn't announce the failings of the Network model. You have probably heard buzzwords, from "audience fragmentation" to "channel proliferation" (I murmur them in my sleep, so I'm told), from "empowered consumers" to "the elusive 18- to 34-year-old male," from "the rise of the Internet" to "TiVo as the Antichrist." All of this is culminating in the clichéd death of the 30-second commercial.

Depending on which talking head or writing hand might be doing the communicating on any given day, you've also heard the resolute and emphatic rhetoric that the 30-second commercial isn't going away anytime soon, although admittedly it is changing. Conversely, if you poked your head into your ad agency's broom closet (aka the new media department), you may even have heard the words, "The 30-second is dead" . . . or was it just the sound of the Swiffer? [Gratuitous product placement number 1.]

A recent AAF study exposed seemingly contradictory opinions from its *2004 Survey of Industry Leaders on Advertising Trends*. Although most respondents felt that the growth of nontraditional ad formats (led by digital video recorders like TiVo) will change advertising, there was also skepticism about these alternatives. This finding could be read two ways: (1) The marketing community is divided into those who embrace nontraditional forms of marketing and those who fear them; or (2), and this second interpretation is more reprehensible, *no one ever got fired for putting TV on the media plan.* In other words, a lot of marketing executives out there still cling to TV advertising because they think they understand the alternatives and therefore that they're safe. *Wrong.* CMOs are being picked off faster than Donald Trump can say "You're fired!" The root of the problem could very well be their reliance on the so-called safer options.

When talking to the New Age marketing zealots, I dance on the 30-second's grave and sing hallelujah; however, when addressing a room with "traditional" marketers and/or media folk, I have been known to feebly parrot that the 30-second isn't going away anytime soon—an act of kiss-ass reassurance and self-preservation (after all, I like being paid and I intensely dislike being attacked).

But now is the time to come out of my closet with this emphatic statement: The 30-second spot—at least as it exists today—is either dead, dying, or has outlived its usefulness. Take your pick.

To be sure, those who believe that the 30-second isn't going away anytime soon might want to scrutinize their definition of the word *soon.* Perhaps we can wager which will go away sooner: the 30-second itself or their jobs.

There was a time when some folk believed that the black-and-white television wasn't going away anytime soon. In fact, there are still some black-and-white televisions out there; I believe they can be purchased on eBay from the antiques section.

The bottom line is that the marketing communication world is in disarray. Client-agency relationships are at all-time lows (both in morale and tenure). Procurement is rife and consultants who run today's new business selection dog and pony show are giving consultants like myself a bad name; Madison Avenue is tarnished and no longer the epicenter of the incestuous world of advertising.

Something gave out a long time ago, but the reality many marketers are still clinging to is a security blanket, embroidered with the letters U P F R O N T, that is soiled, worn, and infested with mold and mothballs.

Now that you're either considering a profession as a volunteer aid worker in Africa or staring upward at that ominous-looking noose, take a deep breath and relax: It's all going to be okay. In fact, it's all going to be swimmingly okay, but it is going to take some time and a lot of hard work. You are going to need to check your ego at the door, and you might even have to work a bit harder to get to a new place, using a new slate, with an entirely new set of possibilities and potential.

The real truth is that there couldn't possibly be a better time to be working in this business. The opportunities are endless, and they're there for the taking, but I stress that preconceptions, political alliances, and fiefdoms have to be summarily dismissed; resistance to change will be futile, and the ability to take risks will prove to be essential to navigate through a brave new world.

1

The End of Mass Media

Whosoever desires constant success must change his conduct with the times

—Niccolo Machiavelli

If there are still people out there who think that mass media is a viable business, please give them this book. The continued fragmentation and proliferation of media touch points and content alternatives makes reaching masses of audiences difficult and aggregating them even more difficult.

Why would you even want to reach a mass audience at a time when there are truthfully very few remaining mass products? With more than 40,000 products up for grabs in an average supermarket (according to MSNBC), the only mass that is present these days is mass confusion, distraction, and clutter.

Even the once revered Coca-Cola is not as mass as it thought it was. The cover of *Business Week*'s December 20, 2004, issue was aptly titled "The Real Problem, or Gone Flat." With C2, Diet Coke, Diet Coke with Lemon, Classic Coke, Cherry Coke, and Vanilla Coke, not to mention Dasani and so on, it is very much a diversified product line against a segmented audience.

Coke is a brand that used to be impregnable. Pepsi would literally prove to consumers that its carbonated sugar water tasted better, but nobody cared. Now for some reason,

Al Ries and Jack Trout spoke about top-of-mind positioning for specific brands, but I don't believe they ever conceived that the *easiest* part of the process might be choosing Colgate and the toughest part would be choosing among Colgate Total Plus Whitening, Colgate Total, Colgate Total Advanced Fresh, Colgate 2in1 Icy Blast whitening, Colgate 2in1 whitening, Colgate 2in1 fresh mint, Colgate Total Advanced Fresh 2in1, Colgate Herbal White, Colgate Sensitive Maximum Strength plus whitening, Colgate baking soda & peroxide whitening with tartar control Brisk Mint Paste, Colgate baking soda & peroxide whitening with tartar control Frosty Mint Striped Gel, Colgate tartar control with baking soda & peroxide clean mint, Colgate 2in1 Kids Toothpaste and Mouthwash, Colgate Barbie* Sparkling Bubble Fruit toothpaste, Colgate Looney Tunes† Bubble fruit, WildMint and Berrylicious, Simply White Advanced Whitening Toothpaste, Colgate Max Fresh, Colgate Fresh Confidence, Colgate 2in1 whitening, Colgate Sparkling White Cinnamon Spice, Colgate Sparkling White Mint Zing, Colgate Sensitive Maximum Strength plus whitening, Colgate tartar control plus whitening gel cool mint gel, Colgate tartar control plus whitening Crisp Mint paste, Colgate Platinum whitening mild mint, Colgate Platinum whitening winter mint, Colgate Max Fresh, Colgate Fresh Confidence, Colgate tartar control with baking soda & peroxide fresh mint, Colgate Cavity Protection Great Regular Flavor, Colgate Cavity Protection Winterfresh gel.

I mean, there's line extension and then there's a one-way ticket to the funny farm.

---

*BARBIE and associated trademarks and trade dress are owned by, and used under license from Mattel, Inc. © 2003 Mattel, Inc. All Rights Reserved.

†LOONEY TUNES and all related characters and elements are trademarks of and © Warner Bros. Entertainment Inc.

they've started to care and Pepsi is breathing hard and fast down Coke's neck. There are many possible reasons for this, but one major point of differentiation could be the way these two brands divide and conquer to connect with their consumers using a combination of old and new marketing approaches.

Is it coincidence that PepsiCo announced in March of 2005 that it would be reintroducing Pepsi One diet cola with one more calorie than the total number of television commercials that would be used for its promotion? (Hint: It has only one calorie.) I think not. Instead, the campaign would include events (see Chapter 14), online films (see Chapters 11 and 15), and other alternatives to traditional advertising (e.g., trading cards). Reads a lot like this book.

Instead of looking at an exploding number of alternatives—from niche programming to mobile marketing to gaming, marketers continue to feel the need, to yield to the urge, to succumb to the tendency to be lazy. For some reason, it just feels better to be able to reach out and touch the largest number of possible people at any given time.

Mass marketing originated from the need to sell mass-produced output following the industrial revolution (e.g., Fordism, started by Henry Ford). Today we are governed by *informational revolutionary* forces—but you wouldn't know it by the way marketing is deployed or by the lack of innovation in the advertising industry. Demand (the consumer) has irrevocably changed. Supply (or the marketing and advertising of it) has not. This gap simply has to be bridged.

The Super Bowl—defined by a self-dated commercial by the name of "1984"—is the only alleged mass-media moment left, and it, too, has slowly degraded to what I would call an act of "desperation marketing," where marketers are going all out in the hope of instant success. In 2005, advertisers paid a record $2.4 million for a 30-second spot—a ridiculously inflated sum that banked on the hope that history or hype would repeat itself.

There is substance, however, for the efficiency of Super Bowl advertising. Although technically it airs only during the game, the actual frequency of a Super Bowl ad may be magnified by several factors, including—but not limited to—the repeat plays that newscasts, newspaper articles, and general PR spikes give to that overhyped Mecca of Advertising. The watercooler effect (recently usurped by HBO— It's not TV, it's HBO!) offers up a refreshing extra-punch cocktail to boot. In recent times, the Web has provided amplification and extension of Super Bowl ads by offering the commercials after the fact and by its ability to forward them to colleagues and friends. CBS and AOL encourage this by driving viewers to the Web to vote for their favorite commercial of the big game in the Super Bowl Commercial Showcase. There's no overstating the value a bunch of tickets to the big game brings to the table on the trade side of the equation. But how do we measure the impact of this spot? In efficiency or effectiveness terms? Should we even attempt to calculate the immediate return on investment (ROI)? How do we monetize and quantify the impact of advertising's annual center stage?

I asked several people to justify why and when a Super Bowl ad makes sense. One of the consistent responses was "continuity." In other words, if this is the beginning of a process, a journey, a means to an end, then how better to introduce a new idea or brand, launch a new product, or introduce a new line extension? Then there's the argument in favor of the message sent out to the market (including Wall Street) when a brand like Reebok took on the creative high ground previously occupied by its archrival Nike with its famed Terry Tate commercial (except it doesn't explain why Reebok did not renew its commitment).

There's a conflict of special interest here. How many times do you think Super Bowl ad agency BBDO sold each of its clients on the same promise: "Hey FedEx, think about the message this will send out to the market and the advantage it will give you over UPS! Let's throw in an alien monster for full effect." (Ka-ching!)

Here are some questions to ponder.

With close to 50 percent of the audience being female,

how does this translate into efficiency for a brand like Gillette, for example? It may appear that even the Super Bowl isn't as super an audience as we've been led to believe.

And from a creative standpoint, is this pinnacle of the calendar year truly the ultimate expression of the promise and potential of advertising? Or is it the biggest overdose of Kool-Aid ingestion? Why is it that we see this kind of creativity only once a year? Shouldn't this be happening all year round? In just one year, we went from a whorehouse in Texas (2004) to a little house on the prairie (2005) — but in both cases, creativity was absent without leave.

An Association of National Advertisers (ANA) report cites that about a third of major marketers polled believe their advertising agencies are infected by "creative arrogance." Does this arrogance translate into inflated production costs — particularly around the Super Bowl?

Think about the Super Bowl spots widely held to be the best of all time. Why is it that most of them are 10 years old or older? (Does the statute of limitations for Apple's "1984" commercial expire in 2084?) What does it say for our industry when a one-off phenomenon like "1984" becomes the best justification for our livelihoods, leaving the other 364 days so conspicuously neglected and barren?

And let's expose the quality of the audience for what it really is. A bunch of intensely inebriated viewers who are about as likely to purchase a car or ship out a package the next day as is Pete Rose to ride the next Triple Crown winner to victory. Under these influences, how effective can this kind of investment really be?

Segue to the heart of the hysteria of mass advertising — the default weapon of choice: the 30-second spot, long protected by a faulty methodology that has survived only because all those who adopt it are too afraid to stick their necks out and say, "Just because everybody goes by the same defective rules doesn't make it okay." But it's actually not okay anymore. It's not efficient. It's not effective. It's time to step aside and make way for a host of alternative solutions.

I'm not sure if there's some deep-rooted psychological mass-media envy that forces us to compare our reach against that of our competitors, but it sure feels good to be able to deliver a feminine hygiene message to males and postmenopausal women . . . just because a given program overindexes relative to some broad-based segmentation based on age.

The implicit assumption is that if everybody plays by the same flawed rules, then by definition the rules are not flawed, because they are generally accepted and practiced by one and all.

Nielsen's ratings and its methodology border on egregious, with 15-minute intervals that conveniently average out the highs of content and lows of commercials. Despite the odd call for minute-by-minute ratings by the occasional agency executive (their version of the machismo game of chicken), the same-old-same-old way of doing business continues to chug along as if nothing were awry.

The following statement appears on Nielsen's web site as an FAQ to potential panel recruits: "We may ask you to fill out a diary, keep a television meter in your home, or just answer some questions over the telephone."

The three methodological approaches conjure up the notion of dumb, dumber, and "dumberer" when conceptualizing the inertial characteristics of the couch potato.

APPROACH 1: THE DIARY

"Dear Diary, today I sat on my royal behind for five solid hours in a comatose state, and at 2 A.M., when I awoke from my trance, I multitasked to perfection as I simultaneously wiped away the hardened drool from the side of my mouth and took a worst guesstimate at what I thought I watched that night on the tube."

APPROACH 2: THE TELEVISION METER

Many of us wonder why TiVo has taken so long to catch on; some argue that it requires too much of a behavior shift too soon. Following on from approach 1, it stands to reason that in a society where the numbers 12:00 flash incessantly on most VCRs, our diligent household members may not exactly be saints when it comes to their reporting duties.

Approach 3: The Telephone Interview

Subject to the same inertia and laziness associated with the first two approaches, with an added bonus: People tend to bias responses to make them appear to be smarter.

Thankfully, there will soon come a day when we are implanted with chips with built-in GPS and proximity locaters to help advertisers determine how truly worthless their messages are. When this day comes, I'll be sure to send you all a postcard from the Galapagos Islands.

2

What's Eating the 30-Second Commercial?

I won't bore you with the usual statistics about how many messages the average consumer is exposed to on a daily basis (it's 3,225, from what I'm told), but suffice it to say that it's pretty difficult to find a place that isn't overrun with marketing messages—from advertising on pregnant bellies to foreheads to even tombstones!

TOO MUCH CLUTTER

The problem is actually worse than the oversimplified predicament of consumers being bombarded with marketing messaging; the real problem is the fact that consumers have lost patience with the implicit mutual agreement between commercials and content.

Slowly but surely, the sacrosanct borders between content and an acceptable level of commercialism have been invaded, to the point where there is no going back as far as acceptability is concerned. The exorbitantly long advertising breaks on morning talk radio practically beg consumers to change the channel; the four-minute-plus[1] pods (groups of ads) and the predictability of ad breaks just after the opening credits or just before "scenes from next week's episode" on television are giant, flashing "bathroom break" signs; the golden goose of search engine marketing, otherwise known as "organic search," has become infested by "paid search."

Marketers have long held that by beating their prospects over the head with the same mundane message, consumers will eventually submit or succumb. Of course the marketers don't explain it that way, preferring to use words like *frequency* or *reinforcement* as substitutes for *bombardment* or *indoctrination*.

Some self-proclaimed media visionaries specifically cite the acute problem of clutter to justify the importance of surrounding consumers with consistent and "integrated" messaging, such as in the following scenario:

> *Wake up:* Clock radio whispers dulcet melodies (interspersed with ads).
>
> ↓
>
> *Cup of coffee:* Consumer turns to newspapers for daily news fix.
>
> ↓
>
> *Morning commute:* Your choice of entrée consisting of more newspaper or radio, with a palate cleanser of out-of-home (billboards) thrown in for good measure.
>
> ↓
>
> *At work:* Background television (sound off) is always on (newspaper score in restroom stalls across America). Internet and radio fill in the gaps.
>
> ↓
>
> *Evening commute:* You guessed it — radio, newspapers, and magazines make the commute home a pleasure.
>
> ↓
>
> *Evenings:* Granddaddy of them all, television prevails with a host of must-see programming.

Warning: If you've been sold on the preceding scenario as Integration, it's not. It's stalking at worst and overkill at best. Here's a different view of the same scenario:

> *Wake up:* Clock radio rudely awakens victim from slumber (snooze button is hit within seconds and/or radio is yanked from nightstand and hurled into wall).

↓

Cup of coffee: Still necessary, but utopian scenario of uninterrupted newspaper quiet time is a pipe dream; television is at best background noise; the Web provides additional source of news.

↓

Morning commute: Radio is consumed, but as soon as commercials begin, channel is changed (that's why radios have presets).

↓

At work: The Web becomes the always-on medium du jour.

↓

Evening commute: See "Morning commute." (To recap, content is good; commercials are bad.)

↓

Evenings: Remote control deftly zaps through 300-plus channels; sadly, there is still nothing to watch, except commercial-free HBO.

According to a Knowledge Networks study released in December 2004, 47 percent of viewers switch channels when watching TV, either because a program has ended or to skip commercials. This is up from 33 percent in 1994. The last bastion of hype—Nielsen—plans to introduce minute-by-minute TV commercial ratings beginning in October 2005. Somehow I suspect this introduction will be conveniently

---

Clutter in each medium (number of ads per viewing, listening, reading, or using session) has become white noise, and when combined with all the surrounding so-called integrated media that agencies are selling you on, things have only gotten worse: it is now gray noise.

Consumers have either built up resistance or have figured out ways to avoid, tune out, or ignore Madison Avenue's obsession with breaking through its self-created clutter.

pushed back, plagued with objections and delays, but in any case, we will soon find out, at least in theory, whether the potential audience actually got to see the commercial. Or metaphorically, *if the tree fell . . .*

. . . did it make a sound? There are no guarantees that the message will register. The same study suggests that the proportion of viewers doing "other things" such as talking, eating, reading, and using the Internet while watching prime-time TV has increased from 67 percent in 1994 to 75 percent.

As Figure 2.1 laments, the likelihood of even remembering an advertised brand is on a sharp and seemingly irreversible decline. Probably just as well for your ticker that my data is only as recent as 2000.

David Poltrack, executive vice president of Research and Planning at CBS television, recently reassured us (Reuters, December 2004) that DVRs are not as much of a threat as once thought because *internal* research (no conflict of interest here) revealed that ad skippers recalled, on average, two commercials and one brand, *which is essentially the same level of recall as with live TV.* This is just insane. For starters, it's a self-serving report basically implying that digital video recorders (DVRs) are no worse than live TV, which would be great if zero multiplied by a million were

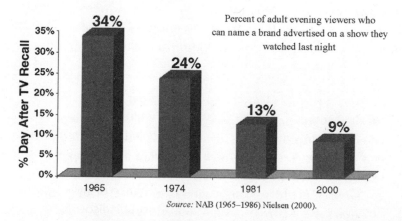

Figure 2.1   Dwindling day-after recall. *Source:* National Association of Broadcasters (NAB), 1965–1986; Nielsen (2000).

anything but zero. Poltrack then essentially concedes that on any given night, it's a crapshoot to determine which singular brand is going to be recalled and which ad will be remembered without any idea of who the advertising brand is. Poltrack should consider changing his title to executive vice president of Betting and Gambling.

Conversely, R/GA's Bob Greenberg talks about media foreground and media background, and when all of this data is combined, he suggests that the first hurdle—namely, getting your message in front of *an* (as opposed to *your*) audience—is not good enough. This is where creativity comes into the picture, but . . .

CREATIVITY (SUCKS)

On the off chance that a "breakthrough" happens, the net result is usually a blob of underwhelming nothingness—a mediocre and feeble attempt at being funny or engaging.

The infamous Super Bowl of 2004 (you know, the one with the "wardrobe malfunction") was Madison Avenue's *one sure thing . . . and they blew that, too.* I bring this up because I believe it represents a tipping point or moment of truth—a fork in the road of the future of advertising and the role that the 30-second commercial will play in it. This was the precise moment in the illustrious timeline of Madison Avenue when I clearly witnessed the beginning of the end.

The takeaways from this 2004 nonevent suggested the following:

- Families—particularly children—were not welcome at future Super Bowls.
- Madison Avenue believed we're all brain-dead.
- Even under the guise of reaching a mass audience, marketers still insist on talking to smaller subsegments, such as the erectile-challenged, which makes up less than 5 percent of the total number of viewers.
- The promise of creative excellence is proving to be an empty one.

Sure enough, 2005 did not prove me wrong, with a mix of banal, ultrasafe, and sickeningly artificially sweetened attempts at pleasing and appeasing both the NFL and FCC.

Double standards prevailed, as it was apparently okay to show "violence and demonic images" (their small print, not mine) for upcoming movie *Constantine* early in the first quarter, or shift the bedwetting from child to parent by having the latter explain to the former what a four-hour erection is after the Cialis commercial, yet Budweiser's "wardrobe malfunction," Mickey Rooney's backside (which looks surprisingly good at his age) for Airborne, or Lincoln's lust (admittedly a bit too much church versus state) were deemed unsuitable for air.

A 2004 American Advertising Federation (AAF) survey underscores how critical creativity (or the lack thereof) is as a top business concern. Figure 2.2 shows how dramatically

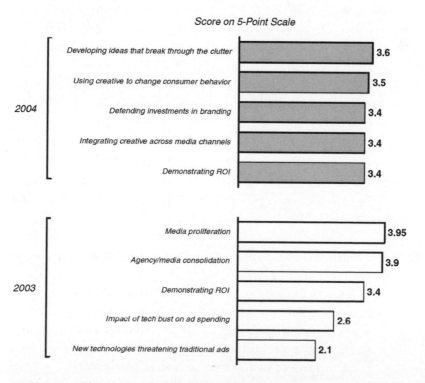

Score on 5-Point Scale

2004
- Developing ideas that break through the clutter — 3.6
- Using creative to change consumer behavior — 3.5
- Defending investments in branding — 3.4
- Integrating creative across media channels — 3.4
- Demonstrating ROI — 3.4

2003
- Media proliferation — 3.95
- Agency/media consolidation — 3.9
- Demonstrating ROI — 3.4
- Impact of tech bust on ad spending — 2.6
- New technologies threatening traditional ads — 2.1

Figure 2.2   Most important business challenges. *Source: AAF Survey of Industry Leaders on Advertising Trends 2004,* prepared by Atlantic Media Company.

the landscape has shifted from 2003 to 2004, with media challenges coming in a distant third to a series of right-brain challenges. Even ROI seems to take a backseat to the all-important task of connecting with the consumer.

This, amid a cold, hard reality where media continues to be separated or unbundled from creative. Go figure.

CONSUMERS AREN'T AS STUPID AS THEY USED TO BE

We're a long way from the secure shores of *Gilligan's Island* (although it's back on TBS as a reality series) and the days when one message could be delivered to the majority of American households through a single episode of *I Love Lucy*—and better yet, *it was taken at face value.*

Today's consumers don't just question, they challenge and flat-out reject the irrelevant, unnecessary, and insulting.

A few years ago, my 10-year-old cousin asked me what I did for a living. At the time, I worked for an agency, so I told him that I worked in advertising. He then asked me what all the small print and fast-talking words at the end of a commercial represented, and I explained to him that these were legal disclaimers and various terms and conditions that were often required. He looked at me thoughtfully . . . paused . . . and then asked me why I work in an industry where I lie for a living.

Interesting insight from a kid who spends more time on the Internet and playing console games than he does watching TV—someone who is growing up in a world of perfect information at a time when marketers are more transparent than ever.

UNACCEPTABLE LEVELS OF WASTE

". . . But it works." Of course it works. Nobody disputes the fact that when hundreds of millions of dollars are poured into television, sales go up. The real question is, *how well did it work or how much of it didn't work?*

John Wanamaker, the department store pioneer who relied heavily on advertising to publicize and merchandise his goods, uttered these famous words: "I know half the money I spend on advertising is wasted, I just don't know which half." More than 100 years later another retailing pioneer, Jeff Bezos, said, ". . . by not spending money on things like TV advertising, we can afford to [*lower prices*]." I wonder how many Fortune 500 CEOs or chief marketing officers (CMOs) would be able to recite Bezos's quote verbatim as opposed to Wanamaker's.

And yet Wanamaker's quote has become a notorious standard at a time when we not only know which half is wasted but realize that it's way more than half. The Wanamaker conundrum is the first part of the knockout punch — the efficiency aspect of piling advertising dollars into a 30-second Hail Mary.

In an age of accountability when consultants (present company excluded) and procurement officers (who, quite frankly, wouldn't recognize a big idea unless it was free) call the shots, one has to question the effectiveness of informing, persuading, and reminding by means of a 30-second mosquito-like annoyance.

3

Mass Murder — Is Advertising Even the Answer?

The quickest way to kill a bad product is with great advertising. These 12 words are common parlance along Madison Avenue. They are uttered every so often by the black-rimmed-glasses-wearing community, usually on losing a key account, or when conducting a postmortem on what was or what might have been.

It's also a classic defense used by the creative community when justifying why a "big" creative idea or execution had the exact opposite effect than was hoped for: Product did not move, although the advertising account invariably did. It's the Pets.com story in a nutshell. But it's also the story of advertising (in a bag of nuts, so to speak).

Every week I skim the "Accounts in Play" section in the trades to see who's hot and who's not. I always ponder what it takes to make the decision to put an account into review. In some cases, it has very little to do with the agencies or their advertising. A new CMO generally means a new modus operandi and, ironically, this is perhaps the one time when the political ideals of client and agency are closest. In the same way that many creatives believe great ideas can come from anywhere (as long as it is from them), CMOs likewise hold (quietly) that great agencies make great advertising (as long as they were involved in the selection process).

Agencies tend to fall victim to the law of succession, but they often fall into a different trap when they utter that aforementioned 12-word phrase — the law of delusion. So I wonder, if you knew the product was bad going into the deal, why did you accept the assignment in the first place?

I also mull over the corollary: If nothing kills a bad product quicker than great advertising, *what about the permutation of great products and bad advertising?* And taking this one step further, what qualifies as *bad* advertising?

Consider the attempt to rename (or reposition) the World Wide Web as the World Wide WOW. AOL recently reached out to sample the fruits of the sexy brand world. AOL utilized the highly recognized Running Man icon in two lead spots that broke around the time of the 2004 Academy Awards. The better of the two spots leveraged the Bionic Man theme and the other, surprisingly, looked to Sharon Stone in an almost uncomfortably suggestive way.

Although AOL's slogan "So easy to use, no wonder it's number 1" needed a drastic shot in the arm, it was cut-and-dried product advertising that served a valuable purpose in appealing to the endless supply of newbies on the Net. Then came the 180-degree shift from 100 percent product-focused to 100 percent brand-focused advertising. The new AOL campaign seemed to ignore the fact that *newbies will always be newbies* as far as their relationship with the Internet is concerned — in the same way that George W. will always be George Senior's little boy.

Arguably, the solution in this case was *not* to employ a feel-good brand campaign, but to return to an emphasis on the product-centric cash-cow approach of the past. AOL's equity lies partially in the user's ability to maintain a screen name or e-mail address, but now its magnetism lies in its branded, exclusive, and proprietary content, whether in the form of offline stalwarts like *People* or in the unique and selective First Look opportunities that seem to be all the rage among the music and entertainment client elite these days. Where was that in the messaging?

Was this a case in which the agency failed to recognize that the warm and fuzzy ways of yesteryear are rapidly drawing to a close, or could the client just not resist the forbidden fruit from the Garden of Broadcast? This had CRM written all over it, not CBS.

All things being equal, advertising should work, and great advertising should work very well. The key word here is *should*, which raises these questions:

- Is traditional brand advertising even/still the answer?
- Is broadcast advertising even/still the answer?
- Is advertising even/still the answer?

So the next time you see an account in play, assuming the law of succession has not been exercised, think a little bit about how it came to be in play—bad product, bad advertising, or just bad approach? Perhaps that well-known saying might one day read: *The quickest way to kill a product is with advertising.* Period.

4

The Vicious Cycle

Clutter, creativity, the changing consumer, and the very efficacy of the 30-second commercial are four major issues that
have separately and jointly made for a complex and challenging communications landscape.

To put it mildly, attempting to build a house on quicksand is highly discouraged. If the 30-second spot is the
house, then the environment in which it is built—as characterized by television, content on television, and the relationship between content and commercials—is the quicksand of
time, into which the 30-second is slowly sinking. Now more
than ever, we're acutely aware of the interrelationship
between the medium (media) and the message (creative),
and where better (or worse) to start an examination of this
than with broadcast television and the 30-second spot?

By analyzing the root of the problem, broadcast television itself—the problem can be seen as a downward spiral,
as shown in Figure 4.1. Fleeting consumers mean fleeting
advertising dollars, which in turn restricts the creative oxygen being pumped into content—that is, fewer dollars are
made available on the production/talent side. This results in
loss of viewers due to the overall lack of quality in programming, which then causes more rats to flee the sinking
ship . . . you get my drift.

According to In-Stat/MDR, the U.S. electronic advertising forecast for 2003 to 2009 (in US$ billions) reflects an
increase from $95.9 billion in 2004 to $114.4 billion in 2009.
This growth will be fueled primarily by Internet advertising,
followed by cable and video game advertising, and it is time
to begin preparing for it. If marketers are still on the fence

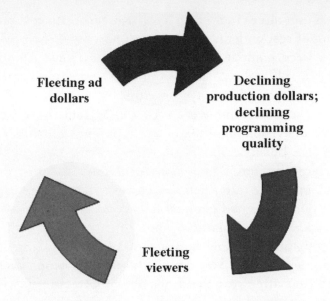

Fleeting ad
dollars

Declining
production dollars;
declining
programming
quality

Fleeting
viewers

Figure 4.1   The vicious cycle of network television.

about whether they should deploy alternatives to traditional advertising, it may be time to electrify that fence of hesitation in the hope that it will spark some immediate action.

TELEVISION HAS "JUMPED THE SHARK"

Attributed to the inimitable Fonz from the sitcom *Happy Days*, this is one of those metaphors that are pretty easy to visualize. I imagine things could only go downhill from the point at which one literally jumped a shark.

Take *Seinfeld*, for example. It might have been when Kramer buttered himself up, or perhaps it was yada yada yada; some sighted that shark during the backward episode. However, many others thought that the shark never jumped in this hugely popular sitcom.

We often talk about cannibalization when it comes to media, but in truth what is happening to network television at the hands of online, satellite radio, and, of course, TiVo is more appropriately described as the painful experience of being eaten alive. In a Lightspeed Research survey, only 31 percent of respondents said network news was their primary news source, compared with 36 percent last year. Among 18- to 34-year-olds, the decline hit double digits, with a 10 percent drop within the past 12 months.

On the entertainment front, things look even scarier. Reality television has begun an economic tailspin as the result of a business model that can best be described as a short-term fix for a mammoth problem. Sitcoms, on the other hand, are anything but funny, and the contrived applause and canned laugh tracks create the impression of being laughed *at* rather than with.

Emmy and Golden Globe awards force the knife deeper into the vulnerable body of network television, as HBO proves year after year that honesty will always prevail over hypocrisy: We all swear; we all look at dirty magazines; we all secretly long to submit to our primal temptations. HBO gives us this in droves, whereas network television chooses to give us "world premieres" for those living in a cave for the past few years who somehow missed the movie, DVD launch, video-on-demand option, or who did not subscribe to a premium channel. These world premieres contain so many commercials that they play out like a backfiring car on its last trip to the scrap heap. Even worse, the networks somehow find gratuitous violence (e.g., *Pulp Fiction*) to be acceptable, but then replace words that most of us use on a daily basis with "shoot," "forget it," or my personal favorite, "Jiminy H. Cricket" (Pinocchio's messiah!).

Declining Quality of Content: The Reality of Television

The once watertight television upfront* process is starting to resemble the *Titanic* in more ways than one, and while the

---

Upfront (TV term) is a method for purchasing TV commercial time well in advance of the telecast time of the programs and generally for a protracted period, such as a one-year schedule.

networks stand on the top railing of the behemoth's bow screaming "I'm king of the world," the rest of the advertising crew is knee-deep in icy water. The first-class arrogance that contends that no iceberg could make a dent in the ironclad broadcast ship was understandable in an era when bigger was considered better.

And yet upstarts are proliferating by the very fibers of their cables, giving network TV a run for its money. Spike TV, Fuse, and OLN are just three of the new entries joining powerhouses like MTV, Discovery, or ESPN as well as stalwarts like Bravo, FX, and even Sci-Fi. Then there are the free spirits of the group—the nonconformists like HBO and Showtime—that remind us (with a nod to Lenny Kravitz): "You've got to pay the price if you want to play."

The bravado of the networks has since been replaced with nervousness and anxiety.

Their solution so far? An epidemic of reality TV so demeaning, insulting, and base that Vanna White suddenly looks like Jackie O. and Bob Barker like Cary Grant.

I would hazard to speculate that Fox's *My Big Fat Obnoxious Fiancé, Boss, Wife, Lover, or Whatever* means we've finally hit rock bottom, but that would be a slight to past jewels such as *Married by America* and *The Will* and no doubt discount a slew of rotters yet to come.

The real irony of reality programming is that the typical man or woman in the street is actually more interesting than the nip-'n'-tucked, artificially inseminated sitcom, which has become more than stale in its present incarnation. All those laughs conjured up through the magical applause button notwithstanding, sitcoms are just not that funny anymore.

What *is funny* is that grown men and women will stick their heads in a bowl of cow intestines in an attempt to pick out pig hearts with their teeth and then wash down their efforts with some liquidized brains in order to win on a reality show. That's hilarious—especially when all but one leave empty-handed, albeit with their "dignity" intact, knowing that "they played the game as hard as they could."

The forces that have been set in motion are too far gone now to be reversed. The passage of time, the inevitability of change, and the power of a ripe idea are such that the broadcast industry's wish to be noticed by the CMO community might be a lot closer to reality than ever before.

WATERCOOLER EFFECT

Let's take a step back for a moment and return to the estranged consumer. Forget about ad dollars for now and focus on why network television's security blanket—the upfront—has remained intact.

If you wonder why things were never the same again after Apple's "1984" commercial, you need only look to the *watercooler effect*—which, in essence, governs the very backbone of the traditional television model—for your answer.

Television's value proposition is quite simple when it comes to big-budget, high-impact, heavy-production, value-laden commercials: When an ad is broadcast, it is likely to be seen by all of those consumers who happen to be watching a specific program at a specific time.

Everybody tunes in to see who the painfully average Joe ends up selecting or which Lord of the Fly gets voted off the island; everybody huddles together to find out whether the bomb goes off in *24*. And the commercials come along for the ride.

If everybody's talking about something they saw on TV around the proverbial watercooler (or perhaps these days across the street in the nearest Starbucks), then chances are they'll be exposed to the commercials that accompanied the attention-grabbing content. And in those special cases, they might even be chatting about the commercials themselves. Go Daddy's buxom spoof might qualify in this category, as would the famous Budweiser "Wassup?" commercials, which certainly have the watercooler effect to thank for becoming ingrained in the very fabric of our pop culture.

Now here's the fly in the ointment. *What will happen to the watercooler effect as network continues to lose audience to cable, amid a frenzy of media fragmentation?*

In 1998, an estimated 76 million people tuned in to the final episode of *Seinfeld*, which represented 58 percent of in-use televisions, according to Nielsen Media Research. This may sound impressive; however, it was significantly less than the 77 percent share, or 105 million viewers, garnered by *M*A*S*H* in its final airing in 1983.

Not many (if any) shows have been able to own the corporate watercooler like *Seinfeld* did. Even so, six years after Jerry and company were mysteriously left in a jail, six familiar *Friends* bid us farewell, but only 51 million viewers tuned in to say adieu. In the 15 years between the *M*A*S*H* finale and that of *Seinfeld*, the share of households watching dropped 19 percent, and another 15 percent from *Seinfeld* to *Friends*, so that's 34 percent in 21 years. . . . Worried yet?

The fact is that besides television's triple crown—the Super Bowl, Grammy, and Oscar ceremonies—it's increasingly challenging to assume any economies of scale associated with the watercooler effect. Seems to me that with only one in five viewers* able to share in last night's unexpected plot twist or shock ending, the watercooler ain't such a fun place to hang out these days.

Unless you are HBO, whose self-reflexive 2004 trade campaign referenced this very insight with the notion that all around America, watercoolers were being removed due to lack of activity—until, of course, the advent of HBO, which is joyously helping return watercoolers to workplaces nationwide. Hallelujah.

---

*Based on current calculations of top-rated programs as a percentage of total television households.

5

The End of the Line

Comedian Steven Wright once said, *"Hard work pays off in the future; laziness pays off now."*

Perhaps that's why, for every industry insider who proclaims that *this* year will be the last TV upfront ever, another 99 say, "That's what they say every year!"

A reverse tipping point is in the cards when it comes to the way television is bought and sold. Numbers will continue to dip until a threshold is crossed, after which advertisers will vote with their dollars—only this time the incumbent will be unseated. In parallel developments, advertisers will soon be able to track and report on completed versus skipped or interrupted views and optimize creative or even entire buys on a 24-hour cancellation clause based on how many samples were requested. When this happens, the upfront will be the least of the market's worries.

We're all familiar with the saying "If it ain't broke, don't fix it." Right now, however, something is definitely broke. It's a huge problem, the size of an elephant occupying the corner office of broadcast, agency, or marketing execs, putting unbearable pressure on those mahogany tables, minibars, designer sofas, and Herman Miller Aeron chairs.

Mainstream media's business model is broken. Thanks to DVRs like TiVo, Prime Time is becoming "My" Time. Time shifting is becoming more pervasive to the point that appointment viewing is being replaced with on-demand viewing. The shift from push to pull isn't just confined to the world of search anymore—it couldn't be more apparent right now than in the world of TV.

In a bizarre catch-22, the "if it ain't broke" philosophy is perhaps the primary reason that the television model still works at all. While television advertising remains arguably the most intrusive and disruptive of all forms of advertising, it is still accepted because it represents the status quo. We were all born into this format and we've come to accept it over time. The consistency of its execution and delivery has conditioned us to internalize and integrate it into our lives. This is not an entirely good thing, though, since many (if not most) of us have programmed ourselves to head for the bathroom when ads come on. But for the most part, there's still the willing or unwilling acknowledgment that this is the way things work.

And yet, facing an ever-fragmenting landscape with an explosive range of choice and the continued hardening of consumers toward irrelevant messaging, the networks' hands have been forced. TV executives are being pressured to seriously reexamine the way they've done business to ensure that they can continue to do business.

There's a fine line between innovation and desperation, if you ask me. Ford is one advertiser that seems to be continually experimenting with new approaches, such as its *24* commercial-free season 2 and 3 premiere sponsorship and *American Idol* support. The former is intriguing but relatively easy to telegraph by suspecting consumers. The latter had promise, but the contrived Ford moments were pretty unsettling to the stomach.

What really takes the cake, however, is the move toward revising the way networks introduce new series and season premieres to America. The transition away from a fall blitz to a more evenly distributed schedule over a wider period of time has got the Big Loser written all over it. It's taken decades to indoctrinate middle America about when they should watch TV, and now in one bold move we're going to try to convince these people that they shouldn't be watching baseball or playing out in the yard with the kids or doing whatever it is that they do when their brains are not being peppered with electrons?

The real issue is to figure out a better business model (which I elaborate on in Part 2). In this regard, I have been fortunate to be a part of an infant industry that has experimented, innovated, and adapted, either by virtue of being in uncharted territory or by force of circumstance (survival can be a very powerful driver) or just because of cultural DNA. Permission (*there's* a wacky idea: actually empower consumers to elect to watch/view/participate) is a pretty common thread in the online advertising methodology; the big portals (Microsoft's MSN, AOL, Yahoo!, and, most recently, Google) use a variety of loss leaders such as Instant Messenger and free e-mail to induce consumers to view their advertiser-supported content. Search engines combine free and paid listings and when sponsored presence is not being responded to, it is given a one-way ticket out of town (can you imagine telling Procter & Gamble that they are being sent to the penalty box?). And then there's the new kid on the block—behavioral targeting, which uses registration and actual behavior to fine-tune and take the guesswork out of targeting.

Whether you have both feet in offline or online, or one foot in both, as long as you continue to fund your 401(k)s by bringing together buyers and sellers through the matchmaking mechanism of messaging, *you'll need to figure out a way to deliver more for less in a world where consumers hold that less is more.*

The decision taken by the networks to pepper in new series at a calculated rate is more likely the manifestation of a divine *Punk'd* than intervention. It will surely fail, as it runs contrary to the one thing that actually worked: consistency. There are so many measures that could work so much better—for example, using On Demand to make sure that a consumer never misses an episode (Time Warner is introducing such a feature), sending a DVD to a consumer to watch while on vacation, or downloading a copy of a missed episode to a PC (the latest rabbit being pulled out of TiVo's hat).

Where Have All the Young Boys Gone?

As consumers continue to depart the shores of network television in droves, they are finding refuge in alternative sources of power, many of which allow them to engage on their own terms and offer a variety of consuming and involving experiences. I want to make something patently clear: Cable is not the long-term solution, either. It is the equivalent of jumping from the frying pan into the fire. Short term, cable icons are reaping the rewards of network's disarray, but in many respects cable is like the toothless, ponytailed, and tank-topped lottery winner on *Jerry Springer*—still a classless piece of trailer trash. Harsh? Perhaps, but it is important to drum something into all of our skulls: Television as an ad-supported medium is undergoing tremendous transitional pains and will continue to be under considerable duress from here on end.

Figure 5.1 offers a perspective and I hope debunks any illusions that cable is the uber-solution to advertising's current problems. The bars on the left represent consumers spending more time with the respective medium compared to 12 months ago. The bars on the right reflect less time being spent compared to 12 months ago. The chart is a good gauge of both the consumption shifts taking place as well as their magnitude.

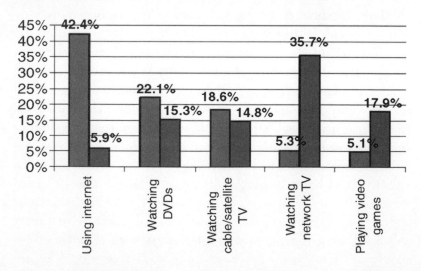

Figure 5.1   Changes in media consumption. *Courtesy:* In-Stat/MDR.

What a difference a year makes and what an endorsement for new marketing and the fact that, particularly if you are in the advertising industry, you made a wise decision to purchase this book! The Web and network television are reverse images of each other. The only other media touch point that finds itself on the wrong end of growth is video games, but this is seen as an anomaly attributable to it being the fifth year of a five-year cycle. With the release of the next-generation consoles, such as PlayStation Portable (PSP) or Xbox 2, video game growth is expected to rise again.

THE END OF INNOCENCE

Traditional marketing, or what I would call "old marketing," is widely held to be a methodology created in direct response to the industrial revolution. Mass marketing was required to address the results of mass production. The efficiency of being able to produce en masse came from the economies of scale generated from doing so; conversely, the efficiencies of communicating en masse resulted from the ability to send one message to all consumers simultaneously.

No longer is any of this babble relevant.

Production has changed from one-size-fits-all to how-would-you-like-your-car-done? Customization and personalization are no longer nice-to-haves but have-to-haves, from the cars you drive to the jeans you wear to the shoes on your feet. *We're not living during an industrial revolution anymore; we are living through a revolution of a different kind.*

Consumers have changed even more (as will be revealed shortly) and have staged a silent but violent coup de grace whereby they have seized control of all facets of the archaic four P's (product, price, promotion, and place)—in pretty much all categories. Occasionally, consumers even flex their newfound freedom to remind marketers that not only are the marketers subservient, but, indeed, they are constantly being scrutinized, judged, and evaluated based on the sum total of their actions.

In one irony-laden case, customization came back to bite a global powerhouse brand in the swoosh. In this case, Nike issued a cease-and-desist against a single consumer (an army of one) who customized his particular pair of sneakers to read: SWEAT (left) SHOP (right). Nike activated its legion of legal eagles to eradicate the unfortunate blot on its squeaky clean record . . . but the damage was done.

Today's consumers, however, have figured out a vital — or viral — component of new marketing: word of mouth, or, rather, *word of mouse.* In the preceding example, e-mail depicting the obtuse chain of correspondence from Nike corporate to the offending consumer circulated the globe several times, in 80 milliseconds as opposed to 80 days. The profound embarrassment caused by just one disgruntled consumer can have irreparable consequences. You can find the actual transcript on www.lifeafter30.com.

The point is that *the truth is out there.* No longer can marketers hide behind the green velvet curtain, pull a combination of levers, flick several switches, and hope that the smoke and mirrors will intimidate consumers into buying their products.

The age of innocence has been replaced with a simple choice: *Embrace change or be consumed by it.* Funny relationship if you think about it: *consumer, consumption, consumed.* Its evolution parallels that of the word *target,* which once reigned supreme through the imperfect science of targeting. Now, however, the "targeter" has itself become the targeted.

Old marketing, steeped in the archaic constructs of reach and frequency, predicates itself on the ability to whack targets over the head until they surrender helplessly. New marketing, infused by the DNA of digital innovation, upsets the imbalance of power to reveal an entirely new paradigm.

6

A Perfect Storm Is Brewing

The concept of the *tipping point* describes how suddenly, as if out of nowhere, a revolution can occur. Often it is caused by the smallest, seemingly most insignificant or inconsequential factor. (Can you say "Atkins"?)

Malcolm Gladwell doesn't need any more money, so I'm going to use another analogy to describe the next big thing in the world of communications. I call it *the perfect storm,* which continues to brew and gain strength, velocity, intent, and momentum.

The perfect storm concerns an ever-increasing digital world governed by the ability to create countless synergies and dynamics owing to the amalgamation of data, information, and communication.

The four ingredients in this recipe for success or disaster (depending on which side of the fence you call home) are covered multiple times in this book, particularly in the chapters dedicated to profiling the various alternatives to traditional marketing (or new marketing approaches) that are energizing brands. These four ingredients are:

1. Broadband
2. Wireless
3. Search
4. Networks

When these ingredients are combined, they create a dynamic that has never been witnessed before (see Figure 6.1).

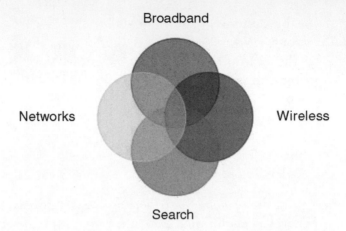

Figure 6.1   A perfect storm is brewing. *Source:* jaffe, LLC.

BROADBAND

The next section discusses broadband in more detail, exam-
ining the realities of a broadband-enabled world. For now, I
want to explain the primary value position that broadband
brings to the table.

It is not speed.

Speed is good, but it is not the most significant attribute
of a postmodem world. The real promise here is that of *ubiq-
uity*. With broadband, consumers are always connected and
never need to log on or defer what they can do today until
tomorrow (let's leave that to the dieters). Broadband enables
consumers to seize the day, to live for the moment, or, on a
less grandiose level, to check the weather, look up sports
scores, book a movie ticket, enter sweepstakes, research a
new purchase, compare notes on a holiday destination, and
so on.

Broadband also reduces and even eliminates the lag or
gap between exposure and action.

Gap = Disconnect

It's 9:25 P.M. You're watching *CSI* (the original—not Miami,
New York, or Timbuktu). You see a commercial for Gap

(humor me by assuming you haven't hit the fast-forward button on your TiVo remote yet), which is instantly recognizable by the gratuitous use of a well-known Hollywood star cavorting against a white background.

Now what?

You have three choices. Should you:

1. Hit the incline button on your power La-Z-Boy, disrobe, de-slipper, and dash out to your nearest Gap store (which happens to be closed)?
2. Live the stereotypical dream of logging on to gap.com and partaking in the cathartic ritual of shopping in your nightgown?
3. Do nothing?

If you selected item 3, you win (and Gap loses).

A fundamental flaw of old marketing is that we *assume* ("ass" out of "u" and "me") we're talking to people in the right place at the right time, but in reality this is just not true. Similarly, expecting someone to log on to a web site, jog in to a store, scroll through a catalog, or execute any kind of action on our command is borderline derisory.

Consumers will choose to do business with you on *their* terms, and the best you can do is to make it incredibly easy for them to do so by offering them a multitude of means to arrive at the desired end.

Broadband helps oodles.

WIRELESS

It took me a while to fully understand that wireless = wire less or *no* wires or unwired if you're trying to brand it like Intel did. The promise of wireless is not fulfilled through a cell phone. It is instead manifested through freedom of mobility. The PC or laptop computer is no longer confined to one particular physical location (where one would, no doubt, log on) but is in fact liberated through *pervasiveness,* or the freedom to move about the cabin that is work, home, travel, or play.

At home, the always-on Internet is truly a virtual experience, with access granted throughout the domicile—from the baby's room to the barbeque, from the porcelain throne to the sofa. The proliferation of multimedia viewing (in this case, the manual, two-screen media consumption of Web and TV) is becoming commonplace in the home, and it is for this reason that a marketer, content provider, or publisher simply must address this phenomenon.

The third wired environment after work and home—on the road—is one of the most underrated and therefore underutilized opportunities for marketers to connect with their elusive consumers.

But it's all changing. Planes, trains, and automobiles are all being wired—make that *wireless*. Consumers will soon be able to connect while on their transportation mode of choice, and smart marketers will follow. Likewise, the promise of WiMax—the technology that promises to bring wireless high-speed connections to entire metropolitan areas—will truly turn all the world into a communications stage.

SEARCH

If by now you haven't heard of the little search engine that forever changed the way we live our lives, I would like to come and visit you in your sanctuary in Shangri-La.

From a pop-culture standpoint, the word *Google* is much cooler than its iconic brand predecessors such as Coke, Apple, or even Nike. Google has become synonymous with life after the 30-second spot, the instant-gratification result of consumers "pulling" (and the death knell of push marketers forcing their wares on the enlightened consumer).

More about search engines later, but for now, the one-word promise of the third variable in the perfect-storm cocktail: *control.*

The rock group Queen once sang, "I want it now," and little did we suspect that Freddie Mercury was prophesying the next wave of consumer empowerment in which they would gain immediate access to information, education, and entertainment on demand and on their terms.

Networks

The term *killer app* (killer application) was often used and abused during the boom and bust of the infamous dot-coms. It has been used to describe pretty much every new medium, technology, and tool. E-mail was once the killer app before it collapsed under its own spammed weight.

My belief—and it's one basket in which I'm confident enough to arrange a good chunk of my eggs—is that *community* is the ultimate killer app. The success stories of both today and tomorrow pivot around a dynamic energy that comes from the ability to tap into, harness, and maximize the power of community.

Community is the only real economy of scale in today's brave new world. It is the next iteration of the legendary watercooler effect.

The promise of community is the *empowerment* that comes from being informed, connected, and unified. Empowerment is similar to—but not the same as—control. The most important difference is that control is exhibited individually, whereas empowerment is ignited or accelerated through the connection between like-minded thinkers.

On one hand, it is the result of "perfect information," brought to you anywhere, anytime, anyplace, on demand, courtesy of your corner search engine and millions of your closest virtual strangers; on the other hand, it is the inevitable venom of the serpent of reality, at a time in which the tree of knowledge has been shaken and its fruits feasted on.

The Ship Has Set Sail. Are You on It?

- The remote control didn't kill the 30-second spot.
- The VCR didn't kill the 30-second spot.

- The Internet didn't kill the 30-second spot.
- The DVR didn't kill the 30-second spot.
- The 30-second spot isn't going away anytime soon (and other urban legends).

On any given day, you'll hear a combination of the preceding statements. Denial is not a river in Egypt; it's a state of emergency, and it is slowly leading to a landmark moment in the illustrious history of the 30-second spot.

The remote control might not have killed the 30-second commercial, but that's really because it ducked and dived within Nielsen's flawed methodology, hiding in between 15-minute intervals of content to the point where it now lives and lurks within content. The VCR is not a disruptive technology—it may be a substitute but it is not a replacement for live content. Because it generally was not possible to watch a recorded program until it was completely finished, the VCR remained unobtrusive and harmless.

The Internet, however, is truly a disruptive technology. Three factors initially slowed or perhaps masked its march on the territory staked out by the 30-second spot: the bandwidth restrictions of dial-up, the dot-com boom, and dual consumption of both television and Internet (via PC). Today broadband has mainstreamed, and more than 50 percent of home users are now wired (and wireless) to the point where they can consume television-quality video through their PCs.*

And then there's the DVR, which one in five advertising industry executives believes will be responsible for the death of the 30-second. With 54.3 percent of consumers from an In-Stat/MDR survey indicating they skip 75 to 100 percent of commercials and 82.8 percent of those intending to purchase a DVR, expressly admitting that they intend to skip commercials, it is plain to see the DVR as both an additive

---

*According to Nielsen/NetRatings, July 2004, 51 percent of United States at-home users connected to the Internet on a broadband connection, versus 49 percent on dial-up—up from 38 percent in July 2003.

stress and surely the final straw that will break the camel's back.

Four forces—broadband, wireless, search, and networks consumers—are accelerating the rate of change that is brewing the perfect storm. At the center of this storm is a most powerful eye. What used to be a collection of faceless eyeballs, blended into an anonymous audience, is now the glaring eye of the empowered consumer, who pulls at will and pushes aside irrelevance and unnecessary clutter and noise. The consumer calls the shots, and the marketers are being shot down—left, right, and center—like sitting ducks.

I'm still not finished. After all is said and done, the biggest contributor to the demise of the 30-second spot is the 30-second spot itself. A once proud and virile icon is now an embarrassed and senile shadow of its former self. The gold standard is nothing more than fool's gold, and the vain fools are those who attempt to perpetuate its reign in the midst of the clutter, mediocrity, and instability that exist in an environment of measurability, accountability, and unforgiving return-on-investment demands.

Is the 30-second commercial dead, or has it just outlived its usefulness? If advertising was once an infant and the 30-second commercial was its diaper, then today advertising is a grown-up who is still wandering around in a diaper. A prime candidate for *Jerry Springer*, no doubt.

The 30-second spot is on the losing end of the efficiency battle. Priced on the *potential* to get in front of a relatively targeted audience (think Always on *Everybody Loves Raymond* or Fixodent on *CBS Nightly News*) that is likely to leave the room, change the channel, tune out, or multitask, it can hardly be intelligently argued that this former powerhouse is delivering either *reach* or *composition* efficiently or effectively—especially when the consumer is likely to remember just two commercials and one brand per night. Sounds more like a game of Russian roulette to me. *Frequency* has become the miserable excuse compensating for the lack of effectiveness, and the bombardment of impressions seems to be the only hope to force home an otherwise contrived and underwhelming message. The lack of ROI echoes this message, according to a Capgemini study focusing on automotive concluding that car manufacturers and their dealers are wasting money on broad-based TV advertising rather than using a direct-marketing approach.

There is no way back. There is only a way forward. Continue with me. Discard and *re:think* everything you thought made sense. Embrace a bold mix of alternatives to traditional advertising that may be the shot in the arm that ultimately saves it.

SECTION II

The Solution: Re:think Four Fundamentals of Marketing

Let's summarize: It's become damn near impossible to break through the clutter; creativity sucks; consumers have wised up and waste is egregious. Television—largely led by the networks but certainly not limited to them—is in a vicious downward spiral. Advertising, the parasite that owes much of its existence to its host, television, is close to the bottom of the barrel in term of its quality, credibility, and even efficacy. Oh, and one more thing: The consumer doesn't care.

Today's consumer has changed irrevocably. He or she (or even you) is devastatingly in control, armed with a whole array of *weapons of the destruction of mass*. While some smarty-pants execs remind us that the first example of interactive weaponry was the remote control, and that neither the remote control, the VCR, nor even the Internet has "remotely" put them out of business, they need only look over the horizon to add a multiplying increment of similar devices including—but not limited to—DVRs and satellite radio that will compound their misery (see Table II.1).

Separately, the devices are causing consternation among the traditional media (I include the Web for now to the degree that it embodies traditional advertising techniques); however, when combined, they are creating powerful negative synergies. In addition, the rate of diffusion of these

Table II.1   Competitive Devices

Medium\Device					
Television	Remote control	DVR	The Internet	Gaming consoles	DVD's
Radio	Satellite radio	MP3 players	The Internet		
Print	TV	Search engines	The Internet		
The Internet	Pop-up blockers	Spam	The Internet		

devices—in particular, those that act in any cannibalistic way—is intensifying.

Without question, television is the one device that has become the sum of all fears. It has the most to lose because it has the most competitive alternatives—many of which use the very same device for their purpose (e.g., gaming consoles).

It is critically important to realize that the television set is no longer synonymous exclusively with either network or cable programming. The fact that Dell sells high-definition flat-screen plasma monitors is an indication of what's happening right now and what's to come.

You're witnessing the introduction of new technologies, devices, and media that are, to a degree, canceling out, replacing, and in some rare cases complementing old mediums. The proliferation of these devices reflects the multitasking proclivities of the average consumer today (I often joke that I am being kept alive artificially, as at any given time I have my BlackBerry, Tablet PC, iPod, and/or digital audio recorder close at hand, and the protruding dangling wires can be somewhat disconcerting), but they also represent overt and conscious decisions to embrace media that do not insult, bore, patronize, and/or invade our precious lives and even more precious disposable time with irrelevant and meaningless commercial content.

Here's the ultimate chicken/egg question: Which came first—technology empowering the consumer, or the empowered consumer necessitating the technology? The question is tough; the answer is easy: Who cares? It's here, so just deal with it.

Whether we subscribe to the belief that mass is crass, whether we are jazzed or jaded by technology, whether we even care about the future of the 30-second, we should nevertheless care an awful lot about the changing consumer, for if we truly understand the changes, their implications, and how to deal with them, then surely we will be in a better position to adapt (which is so much more pleasurable than the alternative: death).

With thanks to my friend Jan Zlotnick (of The Zlotnick Group) for the term *re:think*, it is time for marketers to re:think four primary areas of the business:

1. The Consumer
2. Branding
3. Advertising
4. The Advertising Agency

7

Re:think the Changing Consumer

Step one is inarguably the most important step: Rediscover and reconnect with a consumer who has changed in so many ways for the better. If you demonstrate that you have invested time, money, and empathy in keeping up with the Jonses, Smiths, Wus, Rodriguezes, and so on, you have broken the cycle of an unhealthy and seemingly unbeatable addiction.

A variety of barometers can help you visualize *how* consumers have changed and, specifically, how powerful they have become in the economic sphere in the past decade. From a fragmentation and proliferation perspective, consider the number of cable channels, magazines, and radio stations available for consumption; from a clutter viewpoint, compare the number of marketing messages an average consumer was and is exposed to on a daily basis; from a product choice angle, calculate the average number of supermarket stockkeeping units (SKUs) available to you and me, then and now. The clutter, choice, and overall brand, media, and product chaos have forced consumers to install BS blockers to prioritize, sanction, and weed out the attention invaders from the welcome guests.

Technology has given consumers a means to achieve that end. The multiplicity of consumer technologies today that weren't around 10 years ago include the personal or digital video recorder (PVR or DVR), satellite radio, broadband, and Wi-Fi Internet access, not to mention the explosive growth and permeation of technologies such as the cell phone. In every medium, technological advances have resulted in innovations that give consumers unprecedented power to determine *what* they view, *when* they view it, and *how* they view it.

DVRs such as TiVo have begun to transform "Prime Time" into "My Time." Consumers have tapped into the time-shifting properties that allow appointment viewing to become truly on-demand viewing. Even valuable (meaning "targeted") ads are now, in effect, irrelevant (because they're never seen). Radio has seen the advent of satellite options (XM, Sirius) that offer consumers commercial-free experiences. The heretofore captive audience of drive time has been liberated.

Online has seen its own share of consumer-centric ad balking in the form of pop-up blockers and spam filters that err or skew on the side of caution, which is often unfavorable to legitimate marketers. Capitol Hill is overrun with ignorant, albeit ambitious, politicians looking to use the best promises of the Internet as scapegoats to further their careers.

But again the question begs to be asked: Which came first—the empowering technologies or the empowered consumer? This chicken/egg relationship is a far cry from the days when the American family crowded around Dad on his Barcalounger in the living room for another round of *Father Knows Best*.

Today's consumer household is infused with multiple media devices being used by multiple household members who are rarely in the same place at the same time. It is increasingly common to have a television in most rooms . . . and even in the car. But these televisions are being used for a variety of purposes, including entertainment, communication, gaming, and music.

The old consumer was an easy target at whom the corporate marketers of America could aim and *push* all and sundry. The new consumer, however, is a mobile media maven who *pulls* required content from a variety of resources in a virtual multitasking frenzy.

These days marketers are stumped. Instead of reinventing the process, instead of adapting to their new surroundings, instead of meeting consumers on their own terms, their marketing solution has been to hold on even tighter to the ultimate security blanket: status quo.

Throughout the media age, advertising has been a mirror that reflected the state of the consumer's mind—advertising reflecting life, you might say. A television commercial in the 1960s was met with little resistance on its one-way course to consumers' attention, which was always open for business. The 1980s (1984, to be exact) celebrated brand advertising in its most refined form and constituted a golden age in advertising, when a story could be told in a soft-sell, branded wrapping. Twenty-plus years later, during an era in which every possible life cycle has been accelerated at warp speed—we're still holding on to that past.

The evolution is inconspicuously absent. The revolution, however, is not. Industry after industry has fought and, for the most part, succumbed and been forever altered by the age of empowerment. Banking. Investing. Travel. Dating. Weight loss. Music (remember those weird shiny, circular objects with the hole in the middle? I think they called them CDs, and I'll bet you can pick up some dirt-cheap collector's items on eBay). It is incumbent upon anyone who professes to have any semblance of responsibility for preserving the brand relationship to work aggressively toward understanding consumers, how they've changed, and how best to address their evolving needs . . . on their terms. Delta Air Lines' pioneering suite of empowering tools that use a multitude of digital devices, from the PDA to the Internet to online and kiosk check-ins, is one example of a company listening and responding to consumers.

THE 10 TENETS OF MARKETING TO THE "NEW" CONSUMER

In less than one generation, the entire balance of power seems to have shifted from marketer to consumer. No longer does a marketer tell consumers what they should buy, where they should buy it, or how they should buy it. Rather, it is the consumer who dictates terms and conditions to the marketer.

Indisputably, the digitization of our lives has played a major role in this forced maturation. In a world of perfect information, where cable news stations broadcast blow-by-blow accounts of every sordid or newsworthy event in explicit detail, including reenactments of the Michael Jackson trial, not much has been left to the imagination. And if consumers don't get their fill from the tube, there is always the Internet with its endless supply of opinion, spin, and perspective across the full spectrum of established media properties, community message boards, or blogs.

In Hollywood, the same is true. Practically nothing is left to the imagination, and practically everything is spread out for the pleasure of the consumer voyeur. Care to go back to a more innocent time, when it was left up to the imagination to undress any sultry scenario? Sorry. No can do. This is part of open access and an inevitable loss of innocence.

The uproar surrounding exposure of Janet Jackson's boob was a moment that some feel was long overdue. Shocking, yes; surprising, no. Will it change everything? Yes and no. Departed chairman of the FCC Michael Powell and his cohorts have ridden this puritanical wave (thanks largely to Parents Television Council, a rather vocal minority activist group) to its crest, as was further evidenced in the 2004 elections.

Jackson exposed that which has become commonplace, and surely the natural forces of forgetfulness ebb-and-flow will eventually help things return to "abnormal." However, instead of a complete return to the good old days, there will be a major shift in the distribution of content. Howard Stern will still be yapping away—bigger, badder, and braver than ever before—from on top of the world (and by that I mean a satellite, not the Empire State Building). Walter the Farting Dog and Harry Potter will lead the young person's reading revolution. Grand Theft Auto: Fallujah will be competing with Halo for the coveted award of Most Gratuitous Destructive Sequence in a Video Game at Spike TV's Video Game Awards. In other words, the irreversible sands of time will have sifted through the hourglass. If you don't like it, change the channel, exercise your right to choose, blog until your fingers turn blue, but above all, accept and respect that which has forever changed.

These trends are summed up in 10 behavioral shifts that illustrate and explain the changing nature of the consumer.

1. Today's Consumer Is Intelligent

Superintelligent, actually. Today's consumer exists in a world of perfect information, where corporate marketing defenses are, for the most part, ineffective against the ability of the target audience to see all, know all, and tell all.

The Internet has democratized the flow and dissemination of information, equalized the balance of power between those who have knowledge and those who want knowledge, and created across-the-board parity—pricing parity, product parity, performance parity. If consumers don't know the answer, they can damn well find it out in a matter of seconds—a simple Google search can reveal all.

Brands that don't figure this out lightning-fast are subject to evisceration. Take the lame Pepsi–Apple iTunes promotion, for example. Within hours of the commencement of the promotion, web sites broadcast the fact that if you held a bottle of Pepsi at a 30-degree angle against the light, you could gauge whether that bottle contained a winning cap for a free iTunes download. So, in essence, the one-in-three chance to win (or two-in-three chance to lose) became a sure thing for empowered consumers, and as a result, two out of three bottles sat in the stores gathering dust.

From a completely different angle, companies, brands, and personalities in crisis have turned to the Web to muster loyalty and even mobilize support through the ability to connect with intelligent consumers. A web site such as save-martha.com became a key brand touch point to help keep the Martha Stewart brand alive, despite the travails of the individual behind the brand and behind bars. Today, Martha's comeback, like the Donald's, is assured.

Today's intelligent consumers have built-in authenticity meters to help them navigate between genuine and hyped communications, offers, and promotions. The converse is equally true: A really great initiative, web site, campaign, or community will spread like wildfire when a connection is made between sender and receiver.

Marketers underestimate today's consumers at their own peril. Deny it all you want, but as long as you continue to practice mass marketing, you are condemning your consumer base to a generalized, one-size-fits-all stereotype. A classic rebellion against this type of generalization is revealed by a phenomenon that pretty much all TiVo customers come to discover. They realize that if they delay watching their programs by 10 or 15 minutes, they are able to eliminate virtually 100 percent of the unwanted ads and *still* finish "on time," or at the same time as the rest of the viewing populace.

2. Today's Consumer Is Empowered

Intelligence leads to empowerment. Information and knowledge are actionable—and this action typically takes the form of consumers winning and marketers losing.

Word of mouth has always been the "killer app" when it comes to the way consumers evaluate and purchase goods and services. Using the automotive industry as an example, Figure 7.1 demonstrates an overwhelmingly lopsided snapshot of the perceived effectiveness of traditional advertising against the kings of influencers, you and me.

When comparing the amount spent on the various line items against their perceived effectiveness (e.g., in 2003 automotive spend on television was 43 percent versus the perceived consumer effectiveness of television at 18 percent), it is almost inconceivable, bordering on criminal, that such imbalances are occurring.* Charts like the one shown

*Statistics from TNS Media Intelligence/CMR.

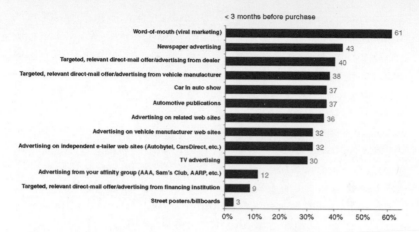

Figure 7.1   Word of mouth versus advertising: There's no comparison.
Source: Capgemini, Cars Online, 04/05, "Driving Growth through Collaboration."

in Figure 7.1 have been around for the longest time, and marketers have come to accept the power of word of mouth as a nonactionable but handy FYI. That was, of course, before consumers figured out how to capitalize on the opinions of their fellow shoppers and before marketers themselves began to realize the possibilities of investing in word-of-mouth beacons—both directly and indirectly.

One of the ultimate effects of being empowered is the ability to see through the facade that is marketing and advertising. Comparison shopping, for example, is just a click or an e-mail away, rendering the same product sold at multiple online stores instantaneously transparent and no longer able to hide behind dancing bears, seminaked cheerleaders, or some combination of bunnies, puppies, and babies.

3. Today's Consumer Is Skeptical

Perhaps yesterday's consumers would accept whatever we told them at face value, but today they question . . . everything.

A book being sold on Amazon.com is subject to several layers of vetting before it is passed into a wish list or shopping cart. Layer one consists of the official reviews; however, this is just the first pass—skeptical empowered consumers demand more and won't accept the publisher's word (or any hired gun's, for that matter). The second layer is your and my reviews, that is, the all-powerful Amazon.com community, and layer three's "was this helpful to you" reality check is built in, to help prospective buyers gauge the worth of the particular reviewer and review.

Sorry, Tom Peters, Peter Sealy, and Sergio Zyman, but your superlatives-for-hire don't cut it anymore.

The same could be said about Tinseltown. No longer do consumers elect to see a particular movie based on the hopelessly out-of-context, truncated version of a critic's review. Moviefone.com and Fandango contain aggregated community ratings that help to balance out the jaded critic's corner. Ebert and Roper's two thumbs up are not what they used to be. A critic's opinion is typically based on a sample size of one—themselves. Their generalist approach might work for a consumer who still clings to the newspaper for showtimes, venues, and reviews, but for the skeptical consumer who has a variety of sources to turn to for an opinion, it just isn't relevant anymore. I don't know about you, but the grammatically incorrect impassioned perspective from another Trekkie is priceless compared to that of Gene Shalit or Jeffrey Lyons.

The perfect antidote to skepticism is trust, and the perfect antecedents of trust are reliability, dependability, and consistency. Smells like a brand to me—or at least what a brand ought to be.

The implications for marketers today are nothing short of catastrophic. If marketing is a window to the soul, then that soul had better visit the confessional—and quick. Corporate scandals, shortcomings, and consistent underdelivery have resulted in an extremely brittle and precarious relationship between consumer and corporation. It is incumbent on corporations to ensure that all touch points are truly integrated, unified, and congruent and that marketing is an accurate and true depiction of the state of affairs as it should be. Anything else is just not good enough.

4. Today's Consumer Is Connected

Today's consumers are always connected—whether at work, using a high-speed connection, at home via an AOL account (yes, there are a few left) or cable modem, or on the road through Starbuck's T-Mobile Wi-Fi hotspots, a BlackBerry, or a cell phone.

But being connected is just the start. It's the immediate access to information on demand, the ability to ask a question and receive an answer in an instant (message) that makes the difference.

Remember *Who Wants to Be a Millionaire?* During the phone-a-friend lifeline, the person called would at times repeat the question out loud and moments later would have the answer with 100 percent confidence. Ever wonder how they did this? The friend repeated the question to a willing accomplice who typed the keywords into Google and, naturally, received the correct answer.

What makes this phenomenon even more interesting is that strangers' opinions are instantly accessible and, through simple vetting processes, very quickly filtered for credibility.

When he was five months old, my son was diagnosed with plagiocephaly—the flattening of the back of his head as a result of continuous pressure from lying on his back. My wife became nothing short of a crusader to acquire all the available information she could on the subject. She discovered a company called Cranial Technologies and within hours was up to speed on the evaluation process, cost, and medical implications.

Cranial Tech is a relatively new company and plagio itself almost unheard of. For this reason, the HMO powerhouses are somewhat reticent to part with up to $3,000 for the treatment. Enter the message boards—a clearinghouse that empowers nurturing and concerned parents with every bit of information they need to find out which HMOs would pay for treatment and which wouldn't, as well as some rare cases in which the same HMO acted inconsistently. The success stories, testimonials, and photo album walk-throughs were equally instrumental in helping nervous parents such as myself decide to move ahead with treatment.

A simple message board. Cost negligible. Returns priceless.

5. Today's Consumer Is Time-Pressed

The number one scarce commodity today is time—or, rather, attention. Today's consumers are being bombarded from every direction by desperate marketers. Clutter is at an all-time high.

Exacerbating this trend are the proliferation and fragmentation of media choices and alternatives. The average consumer today receives 100 channels through cable providers. News Corp. predicts that by 2010 this will rise to as many as 1,000. A thousand channels to choose from . . . and still nothing to watch on TV! If you're in the content-delivery game, don't waste consumers' time with poor content. If you're on the other side of the fence (marketer, agency), you need to rediscover the art of reduction—transforming the complex into the simple, succinct, and profound. Stop wearing your ROI on your sleeves (or stapled to your foreheads) and think about the consumer's ROA: *return on attention.*

This is an attention economy and *time is the new currency.* Anything you do that wastes someone else's time—bullying your way into their lives with an unwanted, unannounced, and unappreciated impulse-purchase yell or insulting their most precious commodity—will be severely dealt with.

The term *permission marketing* was coined several years ago by Seth Godin in reference to e-mail marketing and specifically the process of *opting in* to receive marketing-related materials. I believe that *Permission Advertising* will be coming soon to a consumer near you and that brands will to have to be expressly invited in, as opposed to taking their place for granted. A TiVo showcase is an example of permission advertising. A flexible online advertising unit that comes alive only with the wave of a consumer's magic wand—er, mouse—is another example of an overt vote of confidence for a marketer to begin auditioning for a consumer's attention, mind, and, ultimately, heart.

When the dust settles, we are still dealing with only one consumer and one attention span. Despite the glut of media choices and variety of sources for information and entertainment, it all boils down to a finite amount of time, and every moment of that precious time that a consumer elects to spend with you should be maximized, not reduced to beans counted and valued accordingly.

6. Today's Consumer Is Demanding

Today's consumers feel they are owed something of value and they should receive it pretty much on cue. They have a sense of *media* entitlement, and with that comes the instant gratification of *content*. The consumption of media is no longer viewed as a privilege (was it ever?) but as a right. And the process of controlling, customizing, and personalizing the inflow of content is seen very much as a mandatory, not an optional, extra.

Instant gratification is a serious problem for new marketing and media folk to have to contend with. It comes embedded in the consumer behavior DNA of Gen Y, the wired generation. This is one of those troubles that emerges from Pandora's box of innovation and advancement.

Think about it: How many times have you sent an e-mail to someone and asked them five seconds later, "Have you received my e-mail yet?" Same conversation 30 seconds later and the intended recipient hits the "Send and Receive" button as if it were the Fire button on a first-person shooter game. A minute later, both parties are stumped, completely baffled by what might have happened to the three-megabyte e-mail!

Hooray for cellular telephones and instant messaging — two ways of ensuring that we're never quite out of the clutches of overbearing clients, overprotective spouses, and neurotic parents.

In the CRM/retention realm, the trend is of equal concern. Toll-free customer-care numbers are a joke nowadays. Waits are excruciatingly long, as any attempt to find an elusive human being on the other end of the line is often fruitless. Corporate attempts to cut costs by automating as much of the process as possible are woefully transparent, especially when you juxtapose the waiting time for a sales inquiry (take) with a technical support query (give).

The Web as a customer relationship management (CRM) tool is a dream come true for marketers, but only if they find an optimal balance between saving money and satisfying their customers. FAQs and automated e-mail responders, together with guaranteed 24-hour turnaround, are unquestionably steps in the right direction, but are not good enough. There's still work to be done to accommodate impatient and/or desperate customers, as well as those customers who are still learning how to empower themselves by using this new service paradigm. Here's an interim clue: Instant Messaging.

Instant gratification won't be going away in our marketing lifetimes, but brands and their army of agents who fail to reward consumers for their scarce time may want to start composing their own epitaphs soon.

7. Today's Consumer Is Loyalless

The word is made up, but the meaning isn't.

I consider myself to be the epitome of the loyalless customer. I am loyal to a brand or a company until they fool, disappoint, or let me down once. Thereafter, all bets are off. I'll morph from their best friend to their worst enemy quicker than you can say "Hyde." Instead of "fool me once, shame on you; fool me twice, shame on me," it's more like "fool me once, screw you."

The old marketing world puts a lot of equity into the concept of *lifetime value* when it comes to customers, but perhaps it is time to rethink this utopian ideal in favor of a more pragmatic and realistic paradigm. Rather than "lifetime value of the customer," we should be aiming to contribute to the "time of their lives"—each experience, interaction, or touch point should constitute a self-contained "life," capable of sustaining a relationship and at the very minimum earning the company the right to interact again in the future.

It is both naive and downright foolish to expect customers to stay loyal for the duration of their natural lives—certainly not with so much choice, the proliferation of substitutes, and the competitive parity that exist today. Marketers—largely due to their agency partners' deft skills and brand-building prowess—have been able to transform garden-variety products into larger-than-life brands over decades of careful fertilizing, nurturing, and pruning. But today's consumers have reduced brands to their former product status (or worse still, a commodity) without a second thought. This is perhaps why Pepsi has finally caught up to Coke—lame promotion or not, Pepsi still gave away cool iTunes for free, and according to those taste tests, Pepsi actually *does* taste better! And it is a key reason why the Fortune 50 of fifty years ago looks nothing like the Fortune 50 of today.

Compounding the problem of loyallessness are the decreasing barriers to exit an agreement and the interoperability that make it so much easier to switch cell phone providers without losing your phone number; the Wild Wild West of search engines that allow Davids to play in the same sandbox as Goliaths and kick sand in their proverbial faces; the Priceline model that aggregates all known brands and creates a free-for-all based on the empowered consumer's unique criteria and pricing whims. Even the mightily arrogant Apple had to open up its exclusive club after it realized that it's no fun in an empty orchard. Apple's stock price seemed to think that was a good idea.

A customer relationship is only as strong as its last—or weakest—interaction, whichever comes first. Loyalless consumers are unforgiving SOBs, but at least they're honest about it.

We should follow the lead of professional tennis players, who hit every shot as if it were the only one. A true champion can withstand a 0-40 triple match point situation and battle back to victory. We should treat today's customer relationships as if each transaction is do-or-die. This might sound a bit extreme, but I'll wager my fortitude on it against the alternatives.

8. Today's Consumer Is Always Accessible

Regis McKenna's book *Total Access* (Harvard Business School, 2002) depicts a new world and a new consumer, outlining a reality of "total access" where consumers run the show on their terms. McKenna categorizes mass marketing as the sole remaining responsibility of traditional marketers, which is a far cry from his earlier decree that "marketing is everything" and that every single decision a company makes should have the input, consent, and blessing of the marketing department.

Today, marketing departments have been stripped of their clout by other departments that have seized the initiative. Responsibility for pricing, distribution, and customer service is no longer the domain of the marketing department. Even the process of evaluating and selecting an advertising agency has become a purchasing line item. Marketing has become a joke. It is therefore not surprising that an October 2004 study by the Association of National Advertisers (ANA) and management consulting firm Booz Allen Hamilton found—among other frightening insights—that the corporate marketing function is not aligned with the CEO's agenda.

In similar fashion, consumers who are always connected, always demanding, and always able to get the information they want, when, where, and how they want it, have usurped much of the control from advertisers.

Soon consumers will be able to be "on" anywhere they choose. Entire cities, from Amsterdam to Philadelphia, are being "un"wired with pervasive Wi-Fi access; the John Candy trifecta of planes, trains, and automobiles will likewise be blessed (or cursed) with ubiquitous connectivity. In fact, several airlines, including Lufthansa, Japan Airlines, and SAS, recently introduced in-flight wireless high-speed Internet access. The BlackBerry already delivers e-mail in near real time to the arthritic thumbs of the road warriors of the world.

My hypothesis is a different kind of spin on multimedia. If the consumer is given more avenues to access, connect, research, purchase, and communicate, the result is an always-open-for-business utopia. Media or mediums become essentially transparent, as information is delivered in a seamless on-demand fashion. It spans the gap between physical and electronic worlds through a variety of touch points: from the PDA to the Web; from the telephone to e-mail; from an actual storefront to a virtual one.

Marketers have to meet consumers on *their* terms. One way is to use the "water station" approach, introduced in Jon Berry and Ed Keller's *The Influentials* (Free Press, 2003), whereby a series of metaphorical water stations are positioned on consumers' routes in the hope that the consumers choose to stop off for some water—assuming they're in need of hydration. If they choose not to stop, perhaps you'll get them on the next go-round. Through the provision of a 24/7/365, always-open network of conversion or conversation stations, the probability of success spikes.

In this scenario, no single touch point is more important than another. They are democratized, unified, and integrated—and by *integrated* I mean that when a consumer calls an 800 number, the operator in question has the person's call history on tap, including store visits and Web transactions. Operators therefore do not have to ask consumers to key in their account numbers more than once. They are able to upsell, make offers, and promote, selecting from a palette of perfect information that not only has a full suite of all available products and services from national to regional to local levels, but also can recommend the best choice for a given consumer—thereby eliminating any potential cognitive dissonance.

- How close are you to this fantasyland? Or are you still promising to answer the call in the order in which it was received?
- Are you coaxing your customers to the Web because it's the right thing to do or because it's cheaper? Have you considered that the Web might not be the ideal mechanism for every consumer to interact with?
- When a consumer is ready to talk with you, are you able to respond? Does 3 A.M. = 3 P.M. in your books, or are you still dealing with the "Sorry, we're closed" sign on the door to your virtual storefront?

IBM has always been a pretty good indicator of sea changes in communication and "consumer" behavior. The company royally hit home with the launch of "e-business," coining the industry term and defining the category. In my opinion, they were a little late to the party when it came to the next generation of messaging, which preached to the notion of "on demand"; nonetheless, IBM waved the white flag of voluntary surrender, conceding that the always-on consumer was now in control and their "on-demands" would be met by Big Blue. Smart thinking.

How are *you* similarly reflecting the changes that are occurring right now in your messaging (if you are doing so at all)?

9. Today's Consumer Is ahead of the Curve

Or to put it a bit more bluntly, ahead of *you.*

MARLONB1212: What is the deal with this site: http://www.theheadeddog.com? What is it for? I cannot figure this out, and it's really getting to me. Any thoughts?
GEORGIE GIRL: Dude, it's so obvious you work for a viral marketing company it's painful. I love your use of spelling errors [on a previous posting] to look legit. People, Marlon is a MOLE. He is part of a big paid

company to come on and get you to see advertising, but here the "advertising" is wormed into his postings. So let me guess this post won't go into the packet you submit to the client (MTV2 in this case I'd guess) to show how successful you were at getting the teen graphic interested. Ciao liar!*

Today's consumers are running rings around marketers before they even realize they've been surrounded. The marketing community lost its edge on the communications process a long time ago. The reins of power have been dropped and most likely permanently given over to empowered consumers without so much as a whimper. But make no mistake, blood has been shed in the form of lost market share, market capitalization, and brand loyalty.

Using a combination of most of the preceding tenets, today's consumers use the power at their fingertips to manipulate, finesse, and fine-tune information and knowledge to their unique requirements. Today, consumers will do extensive research before picking up the phone or walking into a storeroom to instruct the salesperson about what they want—including specific make, model, optional extras, and, no thank you, I don't need the monitor replacement plan. Give them half a chance and they'll take you out!

10. Today's Consumer Is Vengeful

The means to harness the network effects of word of *mouse* are just a click away. But this is not always good (for you).

> When given the choice of continuing to allow abusive and even downright offensive telemarketers access into their homes, 62 million consumers (80 percent registered on the Web through donotcall.org) didn't hesitate to vote an entire industry out of their lives.

Source: Business 2.0, Thomas Mucha, February 4, 2005.

Viral success can also very easily become viral disaster. Word of mouth by empowered consumers is what I call WDMs, or *weapons of destruction of mass:* One disgruntled consumer can bring down an empire—or at least make 'em rue the day they forgot that there is a human face behind each transaction or order number.

Consider the Neistat brothers. Casey and Van are two ordinary brothers who made an extraordinary impact by expressing their disgruntlement with a brand that, quite frankly, had set itself up by virtue of its own high standards (perceived or otherwise).

In Casey's words:

> In September of 2003 the battery in my first generation ipod would hold a charge for no longer than one hour. I brought the iPod into the Apple store in Manhattan for repair and was told they did not currently offer a battery replacement program and my best option was to buy a new ipod. I then called the Apple Care 800 number regarding this issue and was told the same. I then sent my ipod to the Apple Executive office addressed to Steve Jobs with a note explaining my situation and requesting a replacement battery. The Apple Executive office contacted me via telephone to explain that Apple does not repair or replace dead ipod batteries and that it was policy of the company to recommend to the customer to purchase a new ipod when the battery fails. I then looked into and purchased a third party replacement battery, which was not endorsed by Apple. After the complicated installation, my ipod did not work at all, even when plugged in.
>
> In response to this experience my brother Van and I made the short film "iPod's Dirty Secret." After we finished production of the film, Apple began offering a battery replacement program for the ipod for a fee of $99 and an extended warranty for the ipod for $59.

> We acknowledge Apple's new battery replace-
> ment policy. Our movie is a documentation of our
> experience.

The short film has now been seen by more than 1.2 million consumers—and that's a conservative minimum based on the Neistats' counter on their web site.

The Neistat brothers were simply expressing themselves in the way they knew how. They stood up for their rights and spoke up for what they believed in. If a consumer has a relationship with a brand, then that relationship takes the form of a dialogue—if it is the least bit healthy (see tenet 7). That dialogue is not always going to be pretty, and if the relationship is at all worth fighting for, both sides will be honest, up front, and fair. The relationship will be great during the good times, but its true test will be during bad or tenuous times. The lesson to be learned here for marketers is to be able to celebrate the good, but certainly to be able to respond to the challenges. Above all, never take it for granted—as Apple found out the hard way.

THE LAST WORD—A DISSENTING VIEWPOINT

> *A man who wants to lead the orchestra must turn his
> back on the crowd.*
>
> —James Crook

Should all product placement be disclosed with "paid advertising" labels? What about guerilla advertising? Or the blurring line between church and state online? Perhaps, and perhaps not. I'm *totally* dedicated to respecting consumers, their time, and attention, as well as catering to their needs. But at what point must we distance ourselves and make tough decisions based on a combination of what's good for us and, ultimately, what could be good for them? Can the consumer truly have it both ways: free, desirable, unspoiled content without any ads?

This is not an easy subject to broach, and I find myself flip-flopping from one camp to the other as I take on the case of either the marketer or the consumer. Whether one believes advertising is a utility-laden valuable service, a welcome distraction, or a necessary evil; whether one believes it is still possible to create needs and change or persuade minds; whether one simply takes the matter-of-fact position that without advertising, all content goes *poof!*—the fact remains: A great consumer or user experience will always be the ultimate goal. However, surely a bad experience is better than no experience at all!

We are entering an era whose hallmark will be a tremendous amount of experimentation. I inevitably return to the dangers associated with being led as opposed to leading. Consumers are beyond vocal nowadays (see tenet 10), and, make no mistake, giving people a chance to be heard is head and shoulders above not doing anything. That said, it is still more important to move beyond what they seem to be saying toward what they really *are* saying, what they mean, and/or what they aren't saying—so we can make the ultimate call that is truly representative of the consumer active minority, silent majority, and, of course, the marketers. We've been focus-grouped to death, and when it comes to innovation, it's time to take risks and trust our instincts. Blink and you may miss out.

Long term, consumers will have the last word. All I'm saying is that marketers shouldn't give them the first word.

8

Re:think Branding

Brands have never been as important as they are today, but branding, as we knew it, has forever changed.

The conversation about the fate of the 30-second commercial really comes down to being about branding. Sure, there's a response arm associated with it, but then again, when was there ever not a component of accountability linked to advertising? The real issue is less about whether it works and more about how well it works . . . or when does it not work? . . . or even, when does it actually do more harm than good?

The case for brands is an easy one. The profusion of noise, distraction, and clutter, complicated by the explosive range of choice, makes for an incredibly confusing and unnerving position for consumers. Fortunately, they can rely on specific products or services that exhibit qualities, attributes, and benefits consistent with their own.

Brands matter for four reasons—the four Cs, corresponding to choice, choice, choice, and choice:

1. Choice—maintaining a firm grip on SKU sanity
2. Choice—a vote of confidence
3. Choice—the aggregation of like-minded people
4. Choice—media communities as filters or brand qualifiers

Okay, brands are important, but what about branding? If branding—the process of building brands—is a shiny Apple, then the core of this apple is infested with a worm in the form of the 30-second spot.

Four simple steps make the argument, drawing a firm line in the sand between old and new marketing:

Step 1.   Branding has long been seen as a primary function of advertising.

Step 2.   Advertising was (and still is) predominantly television-based.

Step 3.   Television (dollars) are generally concentrated on mass opportunities such as network prime time.

Step 4.   The central unit of advertising within prime time is the 30-second spot.

The prosecution rests.

If you need more convincing, may I introduce exhibit A, which I call "the changing face of brands." Figure 8.1 shows the number of brands that were not around 10 years ago but are now considered to be front-runners for brand of the year.

When last I checked, companies like Google, Starbucks, Amazon.com, Pixar, and eBay did not get to this summit by excessive spending on advertising. Contrast that with the declining Coca-Cola (not even on the list!) brand whose only comeback, to quote the new chairman-CEO, Neville Isdell, is to spend more. Don't spend more; *spend smarter.*

THE SEVEN ATTRIBUTES OF NEW BRANDING

If "old" branding is broken, then how exactly does "new" branding provide a solution to the deepening problem? The following seven attributes of new branding should illuminate this.*

1. Brand Experience

Most creative briefs begin with two questions: "What is the product?" and "What is the brand?" Typically, what follows

---

*Thank you to Advertising.com for providing the platform for the development of this framework.

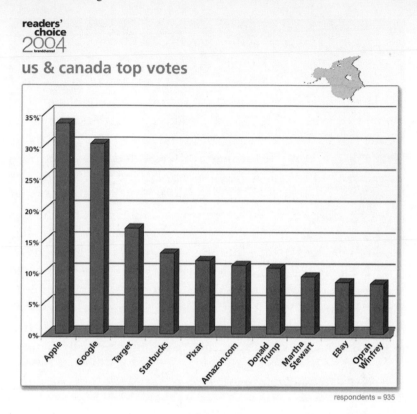

Figure 8.1   Brandchannel's 2004 Readers' Choice Award (North America). *Courtesy:* 2004 Readers' Choice Award, Brandchannel.com.

is an attempt to articulate the core differences between the functional and the emotional, or "what it is" and "what we'd like you to think it is." For example, the *Queen Mary 2* might be documented in terms of *product* as a transatlantic luxury liner, and in terms of *brand* as a transformation portal to Utopia. The product description for a BMW might be "the New X3 Midsize SUV" and the brand description, "the ultimate driving machine for families."

But that's not enough anymore. The problem with brands—or, rather, the way in which they are shrink-wrapped and delivered to our doorsteps—is that they have become ends in themselves, as opposed to means to an end. In addition to *product* and *brand*, it is time for a third dimension to join the mix: *experience,* characterized by its *context.*

Product: What it does
Brand: How it makes you feel
Experience: Where it fits into your life

The acid test to support the case for an additional layer of context or meaning is that the same product and the same brand purchased at the same time and same place by two different people can take on very different meanings. In these cases, those old standbys demographics and pyschographics become contextual identifiers rather than segmentation variables. To Jerry Seinfeld, buying his umpteenth Porsche has far less significance than buying one would to a blue-collar worker who had spent a lifetime aspiring to such a purchase.

I challenge all agencies to work this third dimension into their briefs from now on, asking "What is the experience?" Larry Light, CMO of McDonald's, cautioned that experience (like positioning itself) can assume a variety of forms depending on the specific audience doing the experiencing.

We use products, we buy brands, but we live experiences.

2. Flux Branding

This point dovetails neatly with tenet 7, in the discussion of today's loyaless consumer, in Chapter 7. *Branding—like success—is a journey, not a destination.* Although the ultimate goal might be to reach the destination, the delivery of the brand experience at each touch point should be in a self-contained and independent fashion such that the experience is capable of sustaining itself and keeping the consumer on the brand path. A brand is only as strong as a consumer's last experience with it.

3. The Birth of Antibrands

Google and Priceline are my two favorite antibrands. They represent a new breed of brand, which could be described as *infomediaries.* Amazon and eBay are not far behind in this category. The digitization of our lives has destroyed various

traditional intermediaries—or, specifically, barriers to information—but at the same time has created infomediaries,
which constitute new layers of filtering (as opposed to
increasing complexity). These antibrands trade on data,
information, and knowledge, making the marketing world
particularly tough for conventional brands.

> **Q:** What has traditionally been the only graphical ele-
> ment to appear on Google.com?
> **A:** Google's own logo.

Every day, as millions of searches are conducted on this
search engine, the Google brand receives similar bonus
brand impressions. Not only does Google *not* pay for them,
but they are in fact paid for by Fortune 500, Global 2000
companies, and a bucket load of mom-and-pop stores that
compete on a level playing field for a consumer's click. That's
the antibrand for you—it gets stronger while the rest of the
branding world fights it out for the scraps. If that seems
harsh, it nevertheless reflects the new world of branding
governed by information, consumer control, and democratization.

4. Communal Branding: Branding through Communities

A pattern is developing whereby these attributes of new
branding can be seen to be related to the tenets of today's
consumer. In the case of communal branding (see also the
discussion of communal marketing in Chapter 16), the
propensity for effective branding is closely linked to an
always-accessible and ahead-of-the-curve consumer who
continually reaches out and touches intimate, extended, professional, and global communities, both directly and indirectly. In return, this consumer often receives communiqués
from trusted consumer peers.

Brands that are able to establish communities of interest,
integrate themselves into communities, and contribute to
these communities will be in a position to reap the positive

> We often talk about the consumer as the heart of every marketing campaign, but instead perhaps it is the *idea* that should form the campaign nucleus, with a robust network of connected consumers surrounding it.

effects associated with exponentially growing networks. One stunning example comes from NEC Corporation, which captured the Cyber Grand Prix at the Cannes International Ad Festival in 2004 with a web site that created a virtual tree out of consumers' comments on environmental issues (see Figure 8.2). This represented a breathtaking display of the power of the connected community. Ecotonoha was more than a crude "ad." It was an integrated-cause marketing effort like no other. For every 100 virtual leaves, NEC announced that it would plant one tree in its efforts to contribute to the environment and cope with global warming.

5. Broadband = Broadbrand

Branding online is not only possible; without online, branding itself is impossible.

Too many marketers are not yet convinced about online's role. There are also those who rely on online solely as a quick-fix mechanism for short-term sales. Both positions are flawed, and if they are not swiftly and uncompromisingly addressed, the result could be brand massacre.

Broadband has fostered a ubiquitous culture of open access. It has also created an environment in which video can not only be served up television-style, but also be delivered with a new and improved level of interactivity and control. The result is a mouthwatering array of possibilities.

6. Branding and Direct Response Worlds Have Collided

Once upon a time there was a line. Above the line was a trade called *advertising* (including branding); below the line

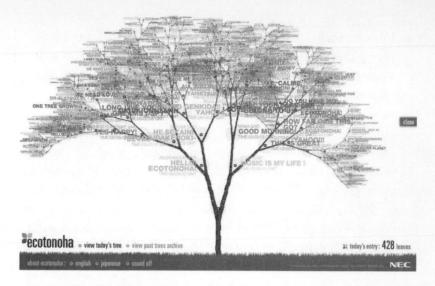

Figure 8.2   NEC's Ecotonoha: Communal branding at its sublime best.
Courtesy: NEC Media Products and NEC Corporation. The Ecotonoha
campaign became NEC's portal and Internet interface through which its
company and brand were introduced to its audiences.

was a discipline called *direct marketing*. And then along came
the Internet, and everything got mixed up.

Sound like an interesting bedtime story to you? Not
unless you don't mind waking up in the middle of the night
sweaty and in disarray. This story is more nightmare than
dream, and I'll tell you why.

The sad truth is that we struggle to make the distinction
between branding and direct response. In traditional forms
of media, the result is a messaging hodgepodge with a gar-
bled look and feel and diluted impact and effectiveness
(jack-of-all-trades). In the Internet space, the industry has
been forced to debate whether the Web is a branding or a
direct response medium. Most think the subject has been
done to death, but I believe we haven't even begun to understand and explain this fundamental conundrum. Those who
contend that "it's both" as well as those who argue the
"branded response" position make valid points; however, I
still think that most of us are reasonably confused about

making the distinction between short-term and longer-term business building.

Whenever I hear someone ask, "Did it work?" or "Was it successful?" about a particular campaign, I have to cringe at the vague criteria employed to determine success. For the most part, campaigns are still being judged on the basis of isolated, short-term metrics.

Branding has never been thought of in terms of sales because branding was thought of as an unaccountable, lengthy process. This is one of the most dangerous traps the industry has fallen into. Ultimately, branding is all about building a business. The goal is to build a business through building a brand. Why should the two be mutually exclusive?

Branding without response is negligent, and response without branding is naive.

Agencies and clients must learn to push back when appropriate, manage expectations, and educate according to what's achievable. *It's foolhardy not to do this.*

Advanced analytics, or *smart metrics,* is our salvation in the mission to redefine what exists above the line and what resides below it—in other words, what constitutes branding and what constitutes direct marketing. (Incidentally, smart metrics is a transferred epithet—please see me after the bell if you need further explanation.)

Perhaps I'm oversimplifying this, but I think it's necessary to reduce the issue to its simplest form: a line. With the birth of the Internet, the line between the two components became blurred—not just on the Internet, but across the board.

In a sense, *branding and direct response are the same thing.* They exist to serve the same purpose—to generate a sale. *The only difference is time:* Branding typically takes longer than direct response.

Smart marketers are recognizing that they now have the ability, probably for the first time, to achieve both goals simultaneously. *Branded response* defines the point at which branding and direct response collide—the "sweet spot." Those marketers who have figured out where that sweet spot will be are the ones to score with today's consumers.

7. Branding by Numbers: Data

Data is the DNA of this business, ROI is the currency, and creativity is the mojo.

I want to take a binary approach when it comes to data. We have an elaborate puzzle before us, which is color-coded and numbered to help us solve it and reveal the hidden picture beneath the surface—and yet somehow we choose not to put the pieces together. We have failed to make the connection between boring data and its ability to invigorate and refresh our brands. This failure is the result of either laziness or stupidity—that's about as binary as I can get to explain why more companies don't use the wealth of data at their disposal to help them better understand consumers, message to them, learn from them, and adapt to their changing needs and the changing constructs of the marketing environment that surrounds them.

The 30-second commercial, as it stands today, is that jock who bullied you at school, stole your lunch, and stuffed you into your locker for good measure—all brawn and no brains, a simpleton. The 30-second commercial could also be an emblem of the traditional advertising agency and the creatives who exert so much power within its walls. But times have changed. The kid with the pocket protector, taped-up glasses, and calculator always at hand is now at the head of the class. He's called "media," for anyone taking notes. As Carat's David Verklin has commented, "It's *Revenge of the Nerds*." However, by connecting the two worlds of data and style sheets, a sort of "GE Profile" emerges: looks good, does good.

But data by itself is meaningless unless it is acted on. It must be continuously fed into a closed-loop process that does not differentiate between data as the input and data as the output as long as the process itself is moving toward a state of actionable knowledge and proprietary wisdom.

For example, here's an illustration.*

What is the definition of *data?*
  The sun rises at 5:38 A.M.
What is the definition of *information?*
  The sun rises in the east at 5:38 A.M. and sets in the west at 7:45 P.M.
What is the definition of *knowledge?*
  If you ever get lost in the woods, follow the path of the sun to determine your direction.
What is the definition of wisdom?
  Don't ever get lost in the woods.

THE NEW BRANDING DIFFERENTIATOR? CRM

If advertising is no longer the answer (and it might not be), then what constitutes ingredient x in the formula for new branding success? If you return to the fundamental principle of branding—the ability to differentiate on a meaningful, *ownable,* and consistent basis—and combine it with attribute 7, which is the ability to solve the puzzle and "color by numbers," then the solution should be right there in front of you: *relationship marketing.* A customer at hand is worth two in the mass.

As long as 80 percent of your sales continue to come from 20 percent of your customers (or in Diet Coke's case, 8 percent of customers are responsible for 84 percent of sales—and my wife probably makes up a good 5 percent of that 84 percent), *you owe it to your stakeholders to invest disproportionately in your most valuable customers rather than your most elusive ones.* As Procter & Gamble's Jim Stengel has remarked, "No P&G

---

*Partial credit goes to the Upstream Group's Doug Weaver.

brand is really a mass brand, not even Tide, whose top 18 percent of consumers drive 80 percent of sales."

What questions should we be asking about branding?

- How are we defining branding?
  How do consumers relate to our brands? To our competitors' brands?
- In what unique ways can new marketing bring consumers closer to our brand?
  How much is art and how much is science?
- How do we measure branding?
  Lifetime or time of their lives?
- Can branding be optimized?
  How about flux branding?
- What determines success?
  When do we register the sale?

9

Re:think Advertising

MAKE ADVERTISING RELEVANT AGAIN

If David Ogilvy, Jay Chiat, and Bill Bernbach were alive today, what would they say about the state of advertising? What would they say about the 30-second commercial? What would they say about new forms of marketing like the Internet? Would they embrace or discard them in favor of traditional media?

Considering that I've worked at both Ogilvy and TBWA\Chiat\Day, the question is close to my heart, but you don't have to have been affiliated with any of these agencies to recognize what Ogilvy, Chiat, and Bernbach brought to the industry. It breaks my heart that advertising has lost its leaders of yesteryear—literally. In their place we have Sir Martin, John, David, and a Maurice, as well as a slew of bean counters who, if they had their way, would replace the term *account executive* with *accountant executive.*

It didn't take me long in this industry to realize that the key to our future could be found in the past. I often refer to *Ogilvy on Advertising* (Vintage, 1985), which should sit in every advertising executive's top desk drawer the way the Holy Bible is placed in every hotel room's nightstand. Many of the legendary Ogilvyisms, uttered some 40 years ago, will still be relevant in years to come:

- "You can't bore your customer into buying your product."
- "Unless your advertising contains a big idea, it will pass like a ship in the night."

• "Bear in mind the consumer is not a moron. She is your wife. Don't insult her intelligence." (And yet we do insult her with the hyperbole of 30-second zingers.)

Chiat was a visionary and a revolutionary. *Status quo* to him was a swearword. How else would he have been able to launch a one-time-only commercial (1984) for a virtually unknown David against the proverbial Goliath using a sporting event, an approach that had never been tested as such? He also revealed his pragmatism when he remarked, *"Let's see how big we can get before we suck!"* —another prophetic statement that could have been written about the day when a handful of companies would control the advertising world.

Bill Bernbach will be remembered as one of the industry's pioneers and foremost leaders, whose words of wisdom included:

• "Safe advertising is the riskiest advertising you can do."
• "Rules are what the artist breaks; the memorable never emerged from a formula."
• "I warn you against believing that advertising is a science."
• "Logic and over-analysis can immobilize and sterilize an idea. It's like love—the more you analyze it, the faster it disappears."

By my count we're 0 for 4.

From a new marketing perspective, some of Bernbach's comments make a strong case for adopting a new suite of tools rather than continuing to use the traditional ones. Note, however, that he also forewarned of the dangers of turning art into science and overcomplicating the issue.

And just when you thought it was safe to go back into the waters of traditional advertising, out came Hal Riney (who was not dead at the time of this printing) with the strongest endorsement yet of a new way to work. All the way back in 2002, Riney pronounced the 30-second television commercial dead, citing consumer apathy and message clutter as reasons for consumer rejection of TV advertising and its relative ineffectiveness compared to the Internet.

When last I checked, the 30-second was still ticking along, but the outcry in favor of its demise is louder than ever. Surely the ticking is that of a bomb ready to explode?

The great leaders and true visionaries of generations past and present have all been risk takers. They dared to dream; they laughed in the face of traditional thinking and scorned conformity. They resided somewhere in the territory between madness and genius—"because the people who are crazy enough to think they can change the world are the ones who do." (Apple's Think Different campaign)

Advertising has not changed, however. Worse, it has lost its relevance. Now more than ever is the time to adopt P&G's new war cry demanding 40 new experiments to reattach some meaning and purpose to the craft.

ADVERTISING DEFINED

Perhaps the place to start is to define advertising itself. What, exactly, constitutes *advertising?*

Take interactive television, for example. Should a client's investment in interactive TV be a job for the agency's digital media guy or for the traditional gal? Perhaps "iTV" should be tattooed on every traditional media planner's forehead. New technology's introduction into the living room poses both the single biggest threat and an opportunity for the medium with the lion's share of every media budget. Then why shouldn't it be taken out of the television budget? The 30-second commercial is alive and kicking—and running rampant online right now. As the standard unit of currency in the television business, should the deployment of this creative format come from the same portfolio as is placing these ads on television?

Then there's search marketing. I'm not convinced that search should *ever* be part of an online media plan. Make no mistake, search should be an integral part of *every single client's core strategy* (digital or otherwise). But how and when did paid search ever become a *media* responsibility?

Perhaps the origin of the term *media,* as defined by the trusty dictionary, can untangle this riddle. I came across three rather intriguing definitions of *media,* using Dictionary.com.

> *Definition 1:* Something, such as an intermediate course of *action,* that occupies a position or represents a condition *midway* between *extremes.*

I love this one. The reference to "action" introduces an argument in favor of a traffic-driving mechanism, which, if you think about it, is the goal of all media communications. The distinction is that with search, the action is immediate. And the result of this action is a potential enhancement to the overall brand experience.

This definition also mentions "extremes." This is a great way of framing the opposite ends of the adoption spectrum: from awareness through action. Quite clearly, it reminds us that it is premature to expect an *intermediate course of action* to be solely responsible for the movement from one extreme to the other—hence, the term *midway.*

> *Definition 2:* An *intervening substance* through which *something else* is transmitted or carried on.

Now we're getting somewhere! An "intervening substance" is half right: Media is intrusive by nature, but to call it substantial is somewhat presumptuous. Then there's the notion of "something else," which, in my mind, speaks to the distractive or superfluous nature of media without targeting and/or contextual relevancy.

> *Definition 3 (the boring one):* A means of mass communication, such as newspapers, magazines, radio, or television.

Personally, I preferred a combination of the first and second definitions that acknowledges media as a necessary evil that intervenes in order to get an inert blob from extreme position A (no sale) to extreme position B (a sale). The third definition infers no real role or purpose whatsoever other than just being a mass communicator.

The "media" label may very well be an insurmountable handicap in today's times—like a bucket that, despite volumes of water being poured into it, has a gaping hole at the bottom.

DESPERATION MARKETING

A man walks outside on a rainy day. He has no umbrella. He carries no hat, newspaper, or other form of protection to shield him from the heavens, and yet not one hair on his head gets wet. Why?

Edward de Bono's pioneering study on lateral thinking originated in his analogy of digging a hole. Vertical or logical thinking is defined as solving problems by using techniques similar to the problem itself, particularly if this approach is based on some past history of success. By simply digging deeper—vertically, logically—one is expected to find the solution to the problem. The rationale is that if we just keep on digging, we're likely to eventually uncover the solution we're looking for. The motivation is that little voice of regret that says, "You've come so far, you can't turn back now."

In truth, the deeper the hole gets, the less likely one will be able to get out of it. Perhaps this is the origin of the saying "You're in too deep."

Lateral thinking, in contrast, promotes looking outside the box for a solution. You can find the means to a solution anywhere along a spectrum that includes digging elsewhere, hiring someone else to do the digging, or dropping a stick of dynamite into the hole.

Hence, the answer to the riddle: "The man is bald." This

might sound elementary to you, Watson, but to the free-spending supporters of advertising as the primary solution, lateral thinking is a skill that is neither practiced nor preached.

Countless marketing and agency executives justify their investment in 2005's Super Bowl based on their unwavering belief that this is the best (and only) way to reach a mass audience. Although Anheuser-Busch was the big winner in terms of driving traffic to its web site (according to comScore), with a 600 percent increase in visits, it required eight spots to do so, and not much beer was consumed in the process. On the flip side, Napster's 30 percent increase in traffic off a lower base compared to iTunes' 170 percent increase was a disgrace.

Such is the desperation of Madison Avenue. Such is the desperation of marketing.

Perhaps this is why, despite the cluttered communications environment, countless marketers are going all-in (celebrity poker has made its indelible mark on me) out of desperation for that big payday.

When IBM created the industry's first eight-page *Wall Street Journal* insert for its e-business launch, it turned heads and made more than an impression—as it should have. First-mover advantage will always count for something and should always reap the rewards associated with innovation, originality, and creativity. Years later, this has become the safe and lazy option, imitated to a fault by all and sundry, with perhaps the only qualifying criterion being "have money, will spend."

Hewlett-Packard's "HP + You" campaign took this desperation ploy to a new low with its 24 (that's *24*) full-color newspaper and magazine inserts to announce that the company was now doing what you already knew it was doing in the first place—promoting digital photography, Web-based print, and printing offerings. The 60-second TV commercials were equally flamboyant. I couldn't help but wonder who laughed loudest on their way to the bank—the agency(ies) responsible for the over-the-top production and exorbitant media placement or the publishers that accepted the dissertations. It certainly wasn't Carly!

HP is not alone. Nissan recently released a 4 × 4 magazine pullout featuring a to-scale cross section of an actual full-size Titan. High fives all around for this achievement — although what was achieved, I have no idea. Was I meant to collect the remaining pieces of the puzzle in order to assemble the whole car myself? (Note to Nissan: There's room for only one Titan in the bedroom.) Or was I simply meant to be overwhelmed to the point where I dashed to my nearest Nissan dealer and asked to swap this titillating teaser for the real McCoy?

If advertising has lost its meaning and has become merely a way to dull the pain and prolong the agony, how do we make it relevant again?

Make Advertising "Real"

The reality of advertising is that advertising is as *unreal* as it comes—from the days of cigarette advertising that always seemed to portray slim, rich, gorgeous people cruising the French Riviera to today's dismal automotive depictions of high-speed racing on deserted highways with the insulting disclaimer that reminds us, "Do *not* attempt this in suburbia."

Talk about misleading advertising.

Will additional doses of make-believe from Madison Avenue be embraced or rejected? If the latter, our creative wunderkinder might want to look to the most unlikely source—reality TV—for something between inspiration and salvation.

Pepsi injected a bit of pop when it invited viewers to vote for their favorite Pepsi television commercial, which would then be screened at the Super Bowl. Coke has experimented with different doses of reality as well. On TV, the brand went out of its way to convince you that it was . . . well, real.

Then there's the story of life after Wylie, the yodeler who sued Yahoo! after earning only $560 for the use of his voice.

To every geek who ever got beat up for yodeling one too many times, Yahoo! offered a chance to be Wylie's heir apparent.

On the Web, reality bites in many different ways. Perhaps the best example of this is the "Ideas Happen" campaign from Visa (which will be covered in greater detail in Chapter 17 in the discussion on consumer-generated content). In this campaign, 13,000 entrepreneurs and visionaries submitted their own big ideas to a like-minded community of more than 1.7 million cohorts in the hope of being voted tops in various categories. Past winners included self-pasting toothbrushes (entrepreneur category), the provision of adequate school transportation for developmentally delayed kids (community), and "cameras for kids" in particular at-risk kids (self-expression).

Develop a New Business Model

Ultimately, the problem for advertising may lie in the reality that it has lost the context that once made it acceptable. Even with the implicit or explicit value proposition about endorsed or subsidized content, consumers just don't care.

Howard Dean Was Robbed

Remember Howard Dean? He pretty much knocked down the political old boy's club with a bulldozer. I followed his rise and subsequent fall and secretly hoped that his eventual selection as president of the United States would serve as the ultimate endorsement of the power of new marketing. It was not to be, and I still wonder whether his demise was a calculated plot to unseat the upstart, the contrarian who cut against the grain, swam against the current, and served himself an extra helping of *change* (hold the conformity).

Dean's story paralleled that of the dot-com boom and bust: a meteoric rise and fall that left everyone with more questions than answers. As some pundits suggested, perhaps the whole Internet strategy was a little too transparent (see the discussion of blogs to come) with its "perfect informa-tion" on display for anyone to access, which telegraphed his every move.

Perhaps there was a flaw in the media strategy. Not all consumers are online and not all online consumers are as actively engaged as the ones who used Meetup.org to con-gregate, distribute bumper stickers, and donate cash. Or perhaps those who constituted this proactive subset were most likely to be Dean supporters from the get-go (in the same way that the audience for *Fahrenheit 911* were already converts to the cause).

And maybe, just maybe, the product itself was not up to standard. As the saying goes, there's no faster way to kill a bad product than with great advertising — or in Dean's case, great new marketing. Whether you voted red, blue, green, white, yeller (didn't vote), or don't even have the right to vote, I strongly encourage you to study what will undoubt-edly become one of the most analyzed campaigns of our time. There were a multitude of ways a Dean supporter could get involved, and this demonstrates one of the most comprehensive uses of the full array of Web possibilities that were available, which included:

- Signing up itself (registration)
- Meetup(.org)
- Take action
- Contribute
- Official blog
- Wireless
- Dean team
- Coalition groups
- Posters and flyers

About the only thing not on the list (which these days every marketer feels compelled to offer on their brand site) was a suite of games.

Dean's efforts were a far cry from "advertising," and each measure individually or in combination created an ever-expanding and more profound layer of involvement, commitment, and loyalty. The implications for brands are obvious.

It will always stump me why John Kerry did not ride the coattails of Dean's efforts. Dean had blazed the way, but the sum total of Kerry's efforts was a suite of ads and the obligatory mention of johnkerry.com. Once again, marketers of today's brands should take note.

In spite of its failure to secure the nomination for its candidate, Dean's campaign made its mark. A four-letter word signifying the difference between old and new media during the 2004 presidential campaign became number one on Merriam-Webster's list of the top-10 words of the year: *blog*.

BUSINESS MODEL REDUX

On a variety of counts we are in dire need of re:thinking the business models that govern consumer access to and consumption of content, and ultimately the role that marketing communications play in that. This, at a time when marketers are required to deliver more for less in a world where consumers hold that less is more.

As someone who has worked on both the so-called traditional and the digital sides of the advertising business, I am certain that in the future, only one of these two scenarios will play out:

1. The offline world will become more like the online world.
2. The online world will become more like the offline world.

Which one do you think will occur?

It is somewhat troubling to see the parallel worlds of television and online struggling to replicate each other when the real goal should be to seek a viable, win-win business model and accompanying revenue stream for publishers and marketers. Instead, television is increasingly infested with crawls, sliders, banners, and picture-in-picture logos that pop up at a moment's notice (recently joined by TiVo itself—sacrilege!), and online is doing its utmost to run repurposed TV spots priced on a glorious CPM basis using the simplified reach and frequency variables as inputs.

The optimal solution is about as obvious as the next combination of numbers in the Powerball lottery. Nevertheless, certain insights about the future are becoming apparent.

1. *Consumers will pay for value.*

Just look at HBO, which could be the way all cable goes in the not too distant future. Recent market noise indicates that we could end up with a model whereby consumers pay only for channels they want. With this model, fortune might favor the Bravo, as the video-on-demand (VOD) model converges with specific programming on specific channels. In this scenario, a micropayment means of fulfillment entwined with a DVR set-top box could easily mesh relevant messaging with corresponding relevant content.

The same approach would (and already does) work, with specific web sites offering premium content on an article-by-article or day-pass basis.

2. *Happy mediums should suffice.*

A combination of subscription and advertising, such as in the print world (however ailing), helps reduce stress on either extreme.

Providing the capability to ante up a nominal fee for some kind of subscription is an instantaneous segmentation of hand raisers who are more likely to be frequent purchasers online. (See insight number 1.)

AOL is an interesting company to watch (and mainly criticize) in this regard, as it plods along, trying to find a happy medium (if, in fact, one exists) between subscription

[handwritten: Internet Service Provider]

(ISP) and subsidized endorsement (advertising). On the one hand, it has its gated Time Warner content, but on the other hand, there is the move toward opening up its proprietary portal to the masses.

One of my core beliefs is that *consumers don't distinguish, differentiate, or discriminate against other, different forms of content, so why do marketers?* You need to aggressively invest in a variety of touch points—from your web sites to mobile devices—in order to "free" or "fee" up content.

That said, consumers want their cake, they want to eat it, and they're not going to give you any (maybe a few crumbs). If you're going to put your content online (which you should), enhance it (which you should), then whatever you do, don't overcharge for it.

3. *If it doesn't smell like advertising, then perhaps it's not advertising.*

[handwritten: —Rotter Foul]

There's a rather putrid stench emanating from the world of advertising right now. And if you can't smell it yourself, then you're either used to it or you've lost your sense of smell altogether (in which case, it's time to consider another career).

Advertising has reacted by integrating itself into the very fiber of content in a curious twist on the saying "If you can't beat 'em, join 'em." Commercial Alert, a group with ties to Ralph Nader, has petitioned the FCC to examine whether the major networks are properly disclosing product placement.

On the other end of the spectrum, Jerry Seinfeld and his pal Superman are currently making headlines BMW-style for their American Express–backed partnership—which assumes the role of meek and mild-mannered advertising by day, but becomes superengaging entertainment content by night.

Is it advertising or not? The answer really depends on the idea itself and the execution thereof. Ken Jennings (and if you have to ask, "Who is Ken Jennings?" then you did well to phrase your answer in the form of a question) was dethroned as

Jeopardy überchamp after 73 glorious days and $2.5 million (a small price to pay for the boost in ratings). This is the answer he missed: *Most of this firm's 70,000 seasonal white-collar employees work only four months a year.*

More remarkable than the fact that I got it right (Question: who is H&R Block?) and Jennings didn't was some of the so-called media commentary that followed, which riffed on the fact that Jennings would no doubt be appearing in a suite of both H&R Block *and* FedEx commercials in the future. "FedEx" was Jennings's incorrect response. (Both companies missed this golden opportunity, and instead, Jennings hawks Cingular Wireless.) The pundits also noted that it was a good thing King World Productions hadn't sold spots to H&R or FedEx to coincide with that particular episode. My correct answer wasn't because I know so much. I think that when advertising is able to smartly and seamlessly integrate itself into content, and to do it in a manner that is unique, original, and not gratuitous in any way, then the result can't be that bad.   *Free/ Costing Nothing*

One other thought: What if (and I know this is a stretch), H&R's Final Jeopardy question was itself a paid placement? When all the bonus impressions are counted, this could be one of the shrewdest media buys of the century (albeit a young century).

4. *When there's writing on the wall, read it.*

Following from the previous point: Instead of continuing down the mass-production line, why don't we just hit the Emergency Stop button and focus our efforts on producing antiwidgets that don't look, feel, or smell like advertising?

In other words, this is our opportunity to stop the rot — to evolve a dying business model, transforming it into a viable and meaningful mechanism for delivering relevance, utility, and entertainment (RUE) (see next point) to the consumer and ROI to the marketer and publisher.

Part one of this process is to focus on the *medium,* to go back to the vicious cycle and clinically address each point:

- Declining production value/quality of content
- Fleeting viewers
- Fleeting ad dollars

Part two is to improve the *message,* to improve the quality of targeting, creative, and utility.

Much of the rest of this book is intended to help with both parts of this process.

5. *Move from ROI to RUE.*

The online world is focused on ROI to the point where success is too often measured by short-term conversion, with an occasional brand-tracking study thrown in to keep the branding folks appeased. The offline world continues to exist at the opposite end of the spectrum. Neither approach should work entirely well anymore.

As we continue to move from an exclusive world of "or" to an inclusive one of "and," I suggest we embrace a principle I call *RUE:* relevance, utility, entertainment. The idea here is to pursue a healthy mix of at least two of the three ingredients, in order to establish a reasonable working equilibrium.

The matrix shown in Figure 9.1 is based on two simple elements: relevance and entertainment (the third would be *utility,* but I can't draw that well). Both are good for business; however, both are not always necessary in order to do business. Quadrant 1 is quite clearly the least desirable and corresponds to a message that is neither targeted nor particularly creative. No medium is exempt from this categorization, but some are more deserving of it than others. Perhaps it's fair to lump mass media into this box. Quadrant 4 is, naturally, the most desirable, and, though all media are capable of playing here, no single medium has come forward yet.

Quadrants 2 and 3 are quite revealing and surprisingly valuable. Quadrant 2, which includes media that are highly relevant but sorely lacking in entertainment value, is more likely to represent a niche medium or one that reaches a local

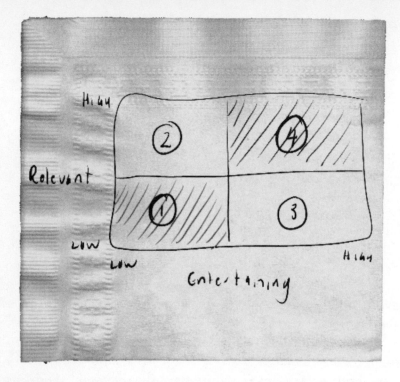

Figure 9.1   Relevance, utility, entertainment (RUE). *Source:* jaffe, LLC.

or smaller audience. It is also likely to represent interactive advertising, which has overdelivered on relevance and utility but struggled with an entertainment quotient. Quadrant 3 is less targeted, but boy, it sure is fun to watch. TV at its best fits into this category, as do new marketing programs such as BMW Films. These media are not so much on the focused side, but they compensate with an aspirational punch and the likelihood that the products and services presented will be thought of as "things I'd like to buy some day."

Quadrants 2 and 3 will be brought together fairly seamlessly with the Internet-protocol-led convergence of the television and computer monitor, which will offer offline the ability to pump utility and relevance into a feel-good, funny, and fuzzy portfolio. Similarly, the increasing supply of broadband will flesh out the tightly targeted rational and functional bare bones of online. Your HDTV DVR DVD-RW PSP will, no doubt, help.

In a perfect world, I'd be able to overlay a third dimension on the grid to represent *utility*—actually bringing something of value to the table (see Discover card example in Chapter 19)—but due to my lack of artistic flair, I'll merely suggest that you consider trying to play up all three aspects (relevance, utility, and entertainment) in order to move closer to the elusive quadrant 4. Perhaps if BMW Films had employed more of the utility dimension, for example, it might have sold a few more cars.

6. *Beware the brands.*

A couple of years back, Steven Heyer (then COO of Coca-Cola) warned the would-be arrogant publishing community to watch over their proverbial shoulders, especially as the year's TV upfront was looming large. He rather prophetically suggested that the world's largest brands were, in fact, the world's largest networks—commanding the broadest and deepest global reach and affinity.

The allusion to the Coca-Cola channel was one expression of this vision, but certainly American Express's Seinfeld-Superman chronicles, the Converse Gallery, "Tiger Trap," and even Burger King's "Subservient Chicken" are expressions of the way brands are essentially bypassing publishers, using their web sites for fulfillment. In some cases, media value is unpaid, through the power of word of mouth. In others, media support comes from the familiar offline world.

This is a strange but true version 2.0 of "If you build it, they will come." The concern of publishers going directly to clients is turned on its head with this ironic twist, whereby brands go directly to consumers.

Implications for the media and agency communities? If you can't deliver the goods, your clients will do it themselves via boutiques.

7. *Everyone has a price.*

Would you willingly watch a 30-second commercial? Nope? What if I gave you one free MP3 download? Still not buying? How about two downloads? At some point I suspect you will willingly concede.

The point is that everyone has a price—and at that particular price point or value level, consumers will entertain almost anything, won't they?

Perhaps we have just been too inflexible and narrow-minded about how we perceive and define the constructs that make up the media business.

8. *Kevorkian those old metrics.*

I'm not sure that *kevorkian* has ever been used as a verb, but if it can work for *Google,* then it sure as hell should be an option for this editor-at-large!

The interactive rating point (IRP) was my early attempt at suggesting an evolved version of the gross rating point (GRP), or even the target rating point (TRP), a rating point that not only built in the target audience, but measured *actual* versus potential delivery and added advanced (and meaningful) metrics such as *time spent, attentiveness,* and *engagement.* These kinds of telling data points are fast becoming realities.

Speaking of old metrics . . . when marketers are able to determine whether their TV ads are actually served (meaning a viewer is watching the specific channel when the first second of the commercial appears) and completed (meaning the viewer does not change the channel or fast-forward the TiVo during the duration of the 30-second interval), do we really think marketers won't completely shift the way they buy, based now on actual versus potential?

9. *Pull my finger.*

The shift from push to pull is in full effect. I no longer have to tell anyone reading this about the role search engines play, but what about the bigger picture—the power of pull? I recall my delusions of grandeur when I registered advertisingondemand.com in the spring of 1999. Not surprisingly, no one approached me with a seven-figure proposal to purchase this domain from me (I let the title deed lapse when it came up for its first renewal, along with the other 50 domains in my possession); however, that doesn't change the reality of a world in which self-selected advertising is no longer a pipe dream.

I fully envision and predict a landscape—sooner than we might expect—where almost every form of media will offer customized and personalized advertising delivered for individual customers. *Advertising on demand* (AOD) is the future of advertising. It's the ability for consumers to pull advertising based on their specific needs, user state, or mind-set. If I'm looking to buy a car, I'm interested in most auto advertising. However, the moment I purchase that car, the same advertising becomes irrelevant. In fact, the utility associated with it potentially drops below zero to a negative value, which often takes the form of cognitive dissonance.

AOD is a way for consumers to have a say in the advertising process. Consumers would register, choose to relinquish some demographic information, and/or opt in to a series of user states, usage occasions, or categories based on their contextual needs, mind-set, and priorities. They could switch a category on or off, assign weights to different verticals, and even order the brands within the category based on some kind of prioritization. In return, a fixed percentage of all available ads would be matched to a particular viewer. This would be a quota and not the entire body of commercials, as the system still must subscribe to a fundamental truism that *sometimes we don't know what we want.* In other words, the lack-of-awareness state still has to count for something.

For example, if you're in the market for a new car, a higher proportion of automobile ads will find their way to you. If you just had a baby, you might see a lot of ads about weight loss and diapers. If this means that I can stop seeing commercials for dentures and feminine hygiene if I'm an

18-year-old male, I'm prepared to belly up to the bar—and I suspect I would not be alone.

10. *The consumer will always have the final vote.*

This might sound like a cop-out or, certainly, an anticlimactic ending to the list of insights about the future, but it couldn't be more important and more appropriate.

Consumers are smarter than we ever give them credit for being. Today's empowered consumer seeks out, and simultaneously obliterates, attention invaders—purveyors of irrelevant advertising. Not only do they demand that propositions be mutually beneficial, but they also expect the scales to be tipped in their favor. The implications for marketers are simple and straightforward:

- Offer consumers options—the more, the better.
- Don't be afraid to try out new approaches.
- Listen.
- Manage expectations.
- Practice consistency to a fault.

But you knew all of that already, didn't you?

The Creative Brief: Discovering a New Purpose for Advertising

Marketing and advertising textbooks consistently teach three primary roles for advertising:

1. To inform
2. To persuade
3. To remind

Combined, they constitute the 30-second's raison d'être— namely, to perpetuate an awareness-biased objective, predicated on mass reach and incessant frequency. I've spent enough time discussing mass reach, so here is a little note on frequency.

If you think about it (and clearly I have), frequency is the ultimate barometer of effectiveness. Most marketers, unfortunately, assume that consumers are so dumb that if they drum their "Buy my crap" message into their minds enough times, the consumers will eventually succumb to the barrage of repetition, come around, and make that purchase.

With branding, impressions are likely to be spread over a longer period; however, with direct response, impressions tend to be compressed into a much tighter window of time. Furthermore, the total number of branding impressions is typically less than the total number of direct marketing ones. This is partly attributable to the higher media cost associated with premium brand placements and partly to the fact that DRTV and infomercials are embarrassingly poorly produced.

What most people leave out of the conversation is that most advertising theory is based on a consumer-packaged-goods underbelly that essentially presupposes a low-involvement, mature (or even declining) category based on *frequently* purchased products. The higher the consumer involvement, the lower the frequency of the ads; the lower the involvement, the higher the frequency of the ads. Stated differently, the less consumers care, the more we try to annoy them into caring. From a creative perspective, the need to employ emotion in advertising follows the same logic: Low-involvement = babies, flowers, and puppies; high-involvement = more factual, utilitarian, and functional ads.

On a third plane, one might infer that the more *effective* a message, the less it needs to be repeated, which is why Apple's "1984" ad is still an all-star with a total frequency of *uno.* On another level, Pine-Sol will keep peppering me with a barrage of messages until the day when I might just need to use it on my floors.

All of this still doesn't explain why Apple's 30-second iPod/iTune commercial featuring U2's song "Vertigo" was repeated so frequently that I was surprised iPod customers nationwide didn't hurl their Pods at the screen to stop the madness. At the very minimum, "Vertigo" gave me vertigo.

What role, exactly, is the oversaturated and overdone commercial performing? The optimal number of impressions is believed to be between 3 (Krugman's Theory, circa 1972/1979) and 12 (according to Jack Myers).* Today's consumer is a lot less forgiving, and although short-term recall may favor repetition, the "if you can't beat 'em, beat 'em again and again and again and again" approach may require a surgeon general's warning about possible long-term damage.

I suspect that any consumer who gives a damn about Apple, its Pod, or its Tunes might have seen that commercial in excess of 12 times. So we know it was no longer "informing"; the "persuasive" element was so oversimplified that it was patronizing, and the "reminder" component, I guess, was just to robotically download more iTunes.

The bottom line is that we've built an entire kingdom on old data, unchallenged theories, and faulty methodologies. We've lost track of the original meaning and purpose of advertising.

This calls to mind the following story.[†]

Four monkeys were put into a room. In the center of this room was a tall pole with a bunch of bananas at the top. One by one, each monkey climbed to the top of the pole and as it got within arm's reach of the bananas, it was doused with a burst of cold water from an overhead shower, which made the monkey give up on the meal and scurry down the pole. After this had happened to each monkey several times, they all threw in the towel.

One by one, each of the original four monkeys was replaced with a different monkey. As expected, a new monkey would start up the pole in search of the prize bananas. But it would be pulled down from the pole by the remaining monkeys who had experienced the drenching firsthand. Soon, all the new monkeys got the message: Don't go up the pole.

---

*Journal of Advertising Research, Nov/Dec 2002, "Beyond Effective Frequency: Evaluating Media Schedules Using Frequency Value Planning."

†A study conducted by Gary Hamel and C. K. Prahalad, as told in Failing Forward by John Maxwell.

> By the end, there were four monkeys in a room who were afraid to climb the pole, although not one of them had ever been sprayed with cold water. This bunch of monkeys was afraid to do anything (to take a risk), but none of them knew why.

If it's not obvious, the monkeys represent a media business that is based on staid assumptions and hypotheses dating back to the ark (or thereabouts). The primary unit of measurement is flawed and outdated, but it is accepted because everyone uses it—which is what makes it a standard, albeit a faulty one. Eventually, the monkeys are going to get hungry. Here's one way to avoid starvation and to help make advertising relevant again.

ADOPT THREE NEW ROLES FOR ADVERTISING

Allow me to introduce three new roles for advertising. In its current form, I have to say that I don't believe television advertising is fully equipped to deliver against these roles, but with a bit of help it could get there sooner than we might think. The three new roles are:

1. To empower
2. To demonstrate
3. To involve

These roles are not awareness-based but purpose-based, presupposing a state of interest and, ultimately, engagement rather than a shot in the dark.

To Empower

M&M's Global Color Vote initiative was one of the best expressions of involvement, but in this case I'd rather call out the act of empowerment, albeit facilitated through involvement. Consumers were invited to vote on the next new M&M's color, which altered the course of marketing history by pooling the global community to influence and ultimately determine the characteristic of a product.

Each advertising medium did its part in a slightly different way to elicit the same end result: directing consumers to register their votes on the Web. Once on the Web—the central depot for the M&M's experience—consumers were greeted with a host of interactive experiences that included playing games, challenging other friends to register their votes (see discussions of communal marketing), and making their voices heard.

The results reflected the community's passion for the brand and the tactic with unseasonable spikes in sales and volume. High involvement in a low-involvement category— nothing short of a miracle.

Advertising that empowers serves a higher purpose in that it actually exists for a reason other than the marketer's self-serving need to meet quarterly sales goals. Target recently launched a campaign that zeroed in on the busiest shopping day on the calendar—the day after Thanksgiving. "Wake-up call" was a rather lavish attempt at lighting a fire under consumers' butts and getting them into the store to shop. Promising a gentle wake-up phone call on Black Friday from a character such as a child diva or a construction worker, or from a B- or C-level celebrity such as Ice-T or Darth Vader, the campaign asked consumers to register at target.com/wakeupcall, where they could customize their preferences. In this case, the empowering act of getting a head start on holiday shopping was a novel way to communicate a retail sales event (are you listening, Kmart?).

To Demonstrate

Mystification has long been the curtain hiding the Wizard of Oz–like 30-second spot. In a world where consumers can proactively raise their hands in an explicit act of compliance and gesture of interest, demystification is equally powerful. The television world, led by consumer package goods (CPG), is full of product demonstrations, but they are caveated to the hilt to force home a point. I always smell a rat when I see a demonstration for a color printer or a camera phone accompanied by the disclaimer "Simulated image. Do not try at home." As someone who was suckered into buying a Sony Ericsson camera phone from AT&T, I can testify to the disappointment, although the images I did get were vaguely reminiscent of a time when I enjoyed a bit too much stimulation from external substances . . .

To this day, the interactive, video-based demonstration, featuring Rick Titus, for the Ford F150 pickup truck has no equal (see Figure 9.2). As I perused this masterpiece, I could only think that Ford's full-view-to-conversation ratio (the success rate based on people who viewed the entire experience and test-drove the truck) must have been close to 100 percent. What better gauge of intent to purchase could there be than a 10-minute voluntary immersion in a detailed and comprehensive demonstration?

The role for advertising that employs demonstration is to present not only a literal depiction of how it works but also

Figure 9.2   To demonstrate: An experiential walk-through for Ford's F-150, like no other. *Courtesy:* Ford Motor Company and Rick Titus, host of *Drivers Talk Radio,* a Division of Jackson-Dawson Communications.

the opportunity to articulate the brand values, promise, and context that are so often missing. The Snickers campaign that warned consumers against the perils of hunger ("Don't let hunger happen to you") with a series depicting the "unfortunate side effects of hunger" including *Survivor*'s Richard Hatch running around naked (side effect: "forgetting to put your pants on") was cute, but what intrigued me was a series of interactive executions such as a saw cutting through a page in order to let a candy bar fall through (side effect: "resorting to desperate measures"). An even more cunning execution teased consumers into clicking to win a chance at a backstage pass and the opportunity to meet their favorite band—except that no matter how hard they tried, they could not click the action button fast enough because it kept eluding them by jumping around the unit. The reveal line for this was "Slowed reflexes: another unfortunate side effect of hunger"—a great message at 4 P.M. when the vending machine is right down the hall.

Advertising as an informing, persuading, and reminding vehicle has offered empty promises for too long. Demonstration—that is, the ability to communicate a "walk" to match the "talk"—is the perfect platform to make good on the hyperbole, innuendo, and euphemism.

To Involve

M&M's involved consumers by inviting them to participate in a program of global proportions. Absolut successfully migrated its iconic magazine back-page ads with a highly involving suite of online executions. Each one relied on the consumer's involvement for the punch line—the reveal of a two-word tagline (see Figure 9.3). By themselves, they functioned much like print ads or wild postings—they sat there and did nothing. However, when consumers interacted and began exploring the creative, they received a payoff for their attention and interest.

In Figure 9.3, the creative starts off as a plain bottle of Absolut vodka. However, once users roll the mouse over the

Figure 9.3   To involve: Absolut involvement. *Courtesy:* TBWA\Chiat\Day
and V&S Absolut Spirits.

creative and come within striking range of the bottle, a series
of lasers immediately appears to "protect" the bottle, which
conveys the message that it is valuable and sought-after. Try
as they might, users only succeed at provoking the warning
indicator until finally steel gates come down and "ABSOLUT
PROTECTION" is triggered.

Thus, the next time you're going through the motions of
penning another creative brief, consider these possibilities to
break the monotony of the mass mind-set:*

- The role for advertising is to demonstrate Embassy
  Suites' promise of two rooms by allowing consumers to
  walk through or explore the layout or a map of a typical two-room suite.
- The role for advertising is to empower potential teach-
  ers to consider a career in a New York City public
  school by communicating the unique characteristics of
  New York City as a place to live, work, and play, and
  by emphasizing the special qualities of the children of
  the city.
- The role for advertising is to involve consumers in the
  very execution of the iconic Absolut advertising
  through a series of smart, subtle, and surprising interactions—all of which are consistent with the core qualities of the Absolut brand.

*All three examples refer to client projects I had the privilege of working on at
TBWA\Chiat\Day. The roles depicted are not the actual ones that penned the creative
brief, but they could have been.

10

Re:think the Agency

FIX THE AGENCY MESS

In true new marketing style, you have a choice to consume the next chapter on the Web in an on-demand fashion, or just to continue with the book.

Advertising agencies are crucial to any conversation about the 30-second spot and therefore the evolution of the communication business. If you are part of an advertising agency or work with an advertising agency, I invite you to the Web, where you can download the chapter, as well as leave your thoughts and opinion on the subject.

You'll find both the PDF and MP3 of Chapter 10 at www .lifeafter30.com/chapter10; in addition at any time, you may join the conversation at www.jaffejuice.com, where I offer my daily new marketing commentary and always welcome your participation.

If however, the advertising agency is not at the top of your agenda right now, read on—uninterrupted. You can always come back to it later . . . it's not going away (on many levels).

Have a nice day!

SECTION III

10 Approaches That Are Transforming the Marketing and Advertising Games

I've outlined a gaping problem and offered some conceptual and self-proclaimed insights into where we're heading and some of the forces that are steering the advertising industry in a new direction.

I bring this baby home by presenting 10 unique approaches that are unmistakably breathing new life into the void left by the terminal 30-second spot.

Most (although not all) of these approaches involve a healthy dose of technology. Do not fear technology—it is your friend. However, it can also be your foe if you choose to ignore it for too much longer.

That being said, recognize that technology is a means to an end; it is no more than a catalyst. I often use the analogy of a rock concert: When is the only time you're ever aware of the sound technician's work at a rock concert? When it sucks. The same can be said about technology.

In-Stat/MDR asked its panel of advertising professionals their perspective on the biggest threats to TV advertising. In order of frequency cited, the responses included on-demand, cable proliferation, DVD, the Web, a dubious "other" category, and gaming (see Figure P.1).

The 10 approaches presented in the following chapters speak to several of these perceived key threats in order to excavate the opportunities and benefits associated with incorporating them in an existing communications mix. The only threat that is not covered directly is the increase in cable channels because it is not the increase itself that is a threat—it just makes the advertising process a little more time-consuming and forces agencies to work a little harder. There's no excuse for laziness.

I affectionately refer to these 10 approaches as lifelines. If you are in the ad business, you can call on them when you are in need of help, but unlike a popular game show that similarly makes use of lifelines, you can use these repeatedly and in various combinations. They don't get old, they just get better with use. The more you use them, the faster they will evolve and grow.

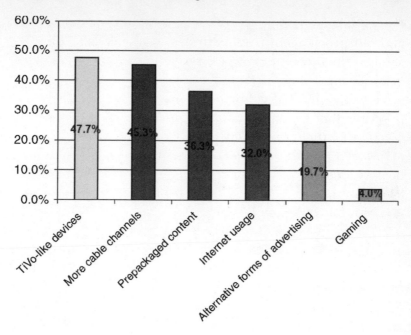

Figure III.1   Biggest threats to TV. *Courtesy:* In-Stat/MDR.

Will any of these approaches completely replace the 30-second as the new gold standard for marketing? That's really up to you, depending on what works for you and your brand and how your consumers respond to them. Some will never completely be able to replace the 30-second, while others already have.

I occasionally throw some stats at you, but for the most part I give you practical examples to illustrate and highlight the main points of each approach, together with a collection of ideas, to-do's, and prescriptive advice. Each chapter concludes with an essay from one of my Justice League of America guest columnists: Chuck Porter, Ian Beavis, Bob Greenberg, Jon Raj, David Apicella, Rishad Tobaccowala, Karen Schulman, Jason Devitt, Chris Aldhous, and Kevin Ryan.

11

The Internet

Let's start with the fastest-growing "medium" of them all: the Internet.

The Internet might still be the best-kept secret in the advertising business today. There are those among us—and you might not suspect who they are—who are hoarding the seemingly limitless fruits of the Net for themselves. It is time to take this conspiracy theory to the masses.

Why do some marketing folk continue to deny the impact of the Internet? It does not make sense to remain skeptical about the potential the Web brings to the integrated table, especially in the face of the evidence that it offers a competitive advantage second to none. There is just too much irrefutable evidence out there nowadays, from case studies to anecdotal testimonials, as well as data, that puts the Web firmly in the top three growth mediums, with . . .

- More people
- Doing more
- Connecting more

- Searching more
- Consuming more
- Sharing more
- Researching more
- Buying more

Three-fourths of all Americans are wired, which suggests that there are those who are shielding us from the truth, namely that the Web is anything but a tertiary or peripheral medium.*

Tim Sanders's book *Love Is the Killer App* (Crown, 2002) suggests spreading the "bizlove" by sharing the triad of knowledge, networks, and compassion. Success in this new technology-driven information economy is predicated on the extent to which professionals share their accumulated knowledge, leverage their network of contacts, and demonstrate their heartfelt compassion.

I'm certainly attempting to do just that in this book, but what about those who keep the stoniest of poker faces and hold their cards tightly to their chests? Should they be obliged to share their love with their colleagues? I am aware of so many success stories that simply blew away the marketers' goals and objectives. So why don't I share these with you right now? Unfortunately, I can't. I don't have approval. And if I were a client, I would probably do the same. Why on earth would I want to give up the one bit of fresh insight to come out of marketing's aging cellar in years? Who could argue that marketers should part with their competitive advantage? I will.

Many marketers exhibit parasitic tendencies. They are takers but not givers, enjoying a limitless supply of premium intelligence, custom research, and proprietary knowledge that comes predominantly from the publishing community, but they offer nothing in return. At a time when one might make a compelling case that the future of advertising is up for

*Statistic is from *The Digital Future Report: Surveying the Digital Future — Year Four,* USC Annenberg School Center for the Digital Future.

grabs, everyone in the industry needs to pitch in and make some kind of a contribution. The closed-door policy to which marketers like Coke adhere is disproportionate to the amount of intelligence they consume in return. PR departments have become corporate bouncers, and speaking engagements are booked in an elitist and self-serving manner.

Such stealth maneuvers won't protect them for long. The transparency of the Internet will propel the knowledge philanthropists to even greater levels of networking and doom the data misers to oblivion.

Tracking and competitive monitoring services are getting smarter by the day. Industry gatherings are fostering an atmosphere of collaboration, industry trades are freely dispensing creative input, and industry initiatives are likewise doing their part to share the wealth.

I suspect that a more accurate assessment of this paranoid hypothesis that marketers are keeping the Internet a secret is that some underleveraged opportunities are still waiting to be pounced on, although there are, nevertheless, those who would keep the Internet to themselves. I only hope to raise enough doubt that you ask this question: Could it possibly be that your fiercest competitors know something you don't?

Here's my take on what has become my adopted child, the Web.

THE TRUTH ABOUT THE WEB

The Internet is the chameleon of modern day marketing. Fifty years ago legendary TV personality Ernie Kovacs referred to television as a "medium," for it was neither rare nor well done. To refer to the Internet as a medium is a misnomer, because it is so much more. In fact, the Internet has been *so* well done that we all got positively charred—and this has clouded our judgment about it. The situation is not helped by the proliferation of fly-by-night charlatans responsible for a slew of pop-ups, unders, spam, and other processed drivel. Nevertheless, the Internet remains a lucrative opportunity for brands and businesses alike.

To help you understand this upside, I need to address the alleged downside—the reasons given by marketers, agency executives, and publishers for ignoring the potential value of the Internet.

The Internet Is Not a Mass Medium

You should care deeply about the Internet for the simple reason that your consumers are there—in droves. The Internet has mainstreamed; it has reached critical mass— and from a media perspective, it is as mass as you could ever wish it to be.

- MSN for example, reaches more people on its home page in a day than the top seven U.S. newspapers combined.*
- iVillage reaches more people (14,819,000) than print publications *Vogue* and *Vanity Fair* (9,480,000 and 4,757,000, respectively) and cable networks WE and Oxygen (11,333,000 and 13,011,000, respectively).†
- Ford reached more than 40 million males ages 25 to 54 with its three-portal online roadblock. (Do I even need to compare this with the alternatives for this demographic?)

The Internet Does Not Deliver Emotion

This statement is moot. As Part 2 of this book suggested, emotion is presupposed to be some kind of a cure-all in advertising, based on the premise that babies, puppies, and

---

*Audit Bureau of Circulation (*USA Today, Wall Street Journal, New York Times, Washington Post, New York Daily News, Chicago Tribune*).

†Statistics are from the following sources: Media Metrix, October 2004; 2004 Fall Mediamark Research Inc. weighted pop. (000), base: all; 2004 Spring Mediamark Research Inc. weighted pop. (000), base: all.

cute combinations thereof will stimulate the ooh-and-aah mechanism in audiences, making them care about something as pedestrian as toilet paper. Using emotion in this way in advertising is not the same as calculating with an emotional quotient that plays a pivotal role in influencing why and how we buy pretty much anything (except maybe toilet paper— you're either a two-ply or one-ply person, it's that simple). Getting people to care about a brand is much more complex than simply tossing in some kitschy clichés.

You've no doubt played the popular advertising party game in which you recall the last beer you drank, car you rented, or watch you purchased and list the features of the product or aspects of the brand that made you select it in the first place. You recognize that there's something amorphous in play and that your buying decision was not made simply on the basis of low carbs, rear airbags, or oyster perpetual motion. Somehow, though, you can't adequately articulate what *really* made you choose Corona, Hertz, or Rolex. That's the emotional quotient. And it's not coming from a cute tagline or a cuddly image being projected.

In fact, the exact opposite is true. There is an emotional disconnect between the highfalutin overpromises of advertising and the harsh reality of experience. Coke's C2 still makes you fat (just not *as* fat); today all cars are reasonably safe; McDonald's cashiers never smile.

Emotion is what you whip out of your go-go-gadget messaging toolbox when you are at a loss for something better. In other words, when all else fails, show 'em the gurgling infant. And quit dogging the Internet.

The Internet Is Not Measurable

The Internet is, in fact, *too* measurable. It does not rely on potential viewers; it is an actualized medium that provides up-to-the-second updates for close anal-retentive, obsessive-compulsive marketers (which is probably about 99 percent of us).

The Internet is measurable in terms of audience delivery; it is measurable in terms of audience interaction; it is even measurable on the transactional/ROI front.

Both David Ogilvy and Mark Twain (I'll let them fight it out) said something to the effect that we must use research/metrics/statistics not like a drunk uses a lamppost for support, but for illumination. Unfortunately, the online advertising prizefighter has been backed "against the ROIpes" by a client community taking out its frustrations from years of receiving limited data.

The Internet Is Limited in Its Ability to Deliver a Message with Impact

The first interactive Internet ad, which contained animation and the ability for a consumer to play along, was 12.3K. This might not mean much to you, but in the context of 10 years of progress, if what is possible today in the online space is the equivalent of a 30-second television commercial, then the first interactive ad was only half a second. Can you imagine trying to communicate in half a second? You should, because that's about all the time that most viewers give television ads today before they hit fast-forward or skip.

We now live in a broadband-enabled world. More than 50 percent of consumers who access the Web at home do so in a dedicated, ubiquitous, or always-on fashion, using a high-speed cable or DSL connection. At work, this number is well over 90 percent. The ability to download entire music albums in seconds or complete movies in minutes is comparable to radio listening or television viewing.

The Internet Is All about Pop-ups

In many respects, you (don't turn around . . . I'm talking to *you*, the advertiser—all of you!) are responsible for the reprehensible scourge of pop-ups, snake oil remedies, spy cameras, and casino advertising online. Pop-ups make up only 5 to 7 percent of served volume, according to

Nielsen//NetRatings' AdRelevance, and about 2 percent, according to DoubleClick, but you wouldn't know it.

The online industry is still populated with things that only come out at night, and if you purvey or promulgate said roaches, then shame on you. Shame on you as well if you are one of the major brands or their agency partners who have, in effect, created this conspicuous void by your absence from Internet advertising. The brand bullies have failed to report for duty, and their AWOL status has allowed bottom-feeders to take their place. A similar circumstance happened with cable television. When the brand bullies showed up and displayed their distended financial clout, they effectively banished the Ginsu knives, Clappers, and Set-It-and-Forget-Its to 3 A.M. on basic cable. The one redeeming feature of network television and its prime time has been the effective separation between the A-list brands and the also-rans.

Much to everyone's relief, the Internet has likewise started to make progress toward this kind of separation.

The Internet Harbors Dot-Cons

Pop-ups are also presumed guilty by their association with spam — scams to rob unsuspecting elderly ladies of their life savings, pyramid schemes, Nigerian royalty desperately attempting to get hundreds of millions of dollars out the country (and they chose *you!*), and the list goes on.

I once addressed a roomful of hedge fund and money managers at a prominent investment bank's investor conference, saying something like this: "If you remember one thing — and only one thing — I have to say today, it would be this: The dot-com boom 'n' bust and the interactive marketing/online advertising industry have got nothing to do with each other. They just happened to start at the same time."

At that time, it was all about greed and cluelessness, and even today some of the dreadful hangover lingers. Back then, so-called marketers decided that it made sense to spend more than 50 percent of their budget on one Super Bowl ad, such as Computers.com, who for some unfathomable reason is no longer with us. Back then, venture capitalists ran the show, not marketers.

On the advertising side, an infant Internet industry was taking its first steps as a medium-in-training. Throughout media history, there has been a logical progression up the advertising food chain. Typically the first category to discover and employ any new form of communication is the rabid direct marketers in the porn and gambling industries. The Internet became a virtual Bahamas for such industries. Is it any wonder that interactive advertising got off to a bad start?

Incidentally, we can learn something from the porn and gambling industries. As much as we might scorn these charlatans, they are the least resistant to change and the most open to trying not only new things, but good things. Of course, by their very nature they typically sour the experience for the sanctimonious Fortune 500, but they nevertheless pave the way for them. Inevitably, the bully brands use their collective clout—financial resources, talent, business acumen, and brand equity—to force out the bottom-feeders, which at that point can no longer financially compete.

The Internet is still too often associated with spy cameras and get-rich-quick schemes that lure the gullible with bells and whistles and empty promises. But things are changing slowly. The Web is becoming like the new Times Square—squeaky clean and family-friendly. It is also quickly becoming a place to which brands such as Nike, IBM, Starbucks, AT&T, and even Wal-Mart choose to donate their leftover dollars (which still amount to quite a lot).

The Internet Needs a Prime Time

One of the realities that marketers are going to have to deal with is that the Internet, as a need-to-know medium, is always going to be a melting pot. When Joe Blog's home page can compete with a multi-million-dollar corporate extravaganza, expect some tricky encounters in the hallway.

With content on offer 24/7/365, it is precarious to apply traditional benchmarks such as appointment viewing or prime time to categorize the open access on the Web.

Current experiments are under way to test this hypothesis, including Yahoo!'s simulcast broadcast of Showtime's pilot of *Fat Actress* or AOL offering exclusive recaps of ABC's *Desperate Housewives*, neither of which have zeroed in yet on a specific time (with a commensurate incentive to tune in at that specific time), but surely this is inevitable.

There is no solution (nor do I think there ever will be) to the problem of firmly demarcating the various tiers of web sites and Internet communication from corporate sources to mom-and-pop operations to the man in the street. From a media perspective, the inevitable consolidation in cyberspace will mean that a select few Web properties will emerge as leaders in their respective classes. This is not that much of a departure from the evolution of television. A big difference, however, is that the Web is not consumed in linear fashion like a magazine or a movie. Instead, it's like a game of pinball where the eye and the ball dart from bumper to bumper. In a single session, a consumer might spend considerable time on an established and reputable site like WebMD, but then jump directly to someone's blog chronicling some personal, contextually relevant experience.

The Internet Is Taking Away Media Dollars

Sorry, not much I can do about this one. The Internet is not only the chameleon of modern-day marketing, it is also the cannibal.

Media multitasking is a significant behavioral phenomenon and the simultaneous consumption of multiple media is a "why can't we all get along" peace offering to all attention contenders, but these are nothing more than medium-term means to stop the hemorrhaging. Multimedia consumption is, after all, a diluted value proposition unless there is some kind of integrating idea to bring the parts together in a meaningful way.

The cannibalistic nature of the Internet is no different from the cannibalistic nature of DVRs or gaming, for that matter. It is not so much a media-consumption variable as it is a function of attention—and therefore the ultimate competitor for arguably the world's most precious commodity (attention).

Media consumption (and ultimately the allocation of dollars against it) is not solely the property of media buyers and sellers: You do not own the consumer's attention, nor do you have any rights to this attention. This is all-out war, and your competition is pretty much everyone—all marketers, brands, media, and even consumers themselves (some people actually like talking to one another).

The first part of this chapter conceded that the Internet is more than just a medium. The Internet is inherently unbiased and presents a neutral array of offerings that consumers can select or ignore as they see fit. The marketing imperative is thus to figure out when to make a grand entrance and make the most of that moment.

I trust I made my points sufficiently about the Internet's alleged deficiencies as a branding vehicle, in integration, and as a creative force.

You Should Be Thinking about How to Use the Web

Any argument against the Internet is really just a short-sighted ploy to stave off the inevitable. The Web is an idea whose time has come and constitutes a sea change in terms of how brands are built, fortified, and preserved. There are several contributing factors that make the Internet such a strong value proposition.

Interactivity

The Internet advertising industry is referred to as "interactive" because of its ability to conduct two-way dialogues that take the conversation to a new level.

Chapter 10 discussed the need to re:think creativity on the basis of four variables that present a powerful value proposition when combined: Sound + Sight + Motion + Interactivity = Full Engagement (see Figure 11.1).

Radio has only sound in its favor, and perhaps this is why its adherents are looking to the heavens (in the form of a satellite) for help.

Print has only sight going for it, and perhaps this is why it is currently devouring itself in a frenzy of paranoia (justified), neurosis (justified), and in-fighting (not so much).

Television has been able to draw on all three variables, and perhaps this is why it has also been able to command its larger share of brand spending.

The fourth variable—a new dimension that completely transforms the sight, sound, and motion proposition into a

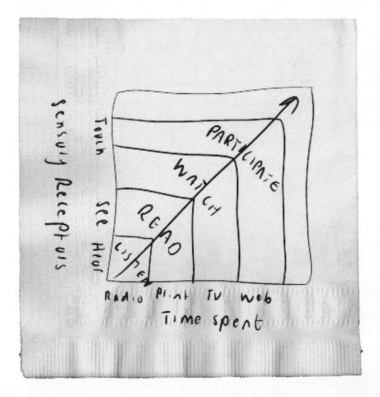

Figure 11.1   A consumer-centric depiction of the evolution of media touch points. *Source:* jaffe, LLC.

mutually beneficial exchange—is that of interactivity. The Internet is the only medium that has been able to draw on all four variables, and perhaps this is why it has been so strongly opposed by those who feel threatened by it and embraced by those who feel liberated by it.

All media predecessors of the Internet could argue that they have in some way injected elements of interactivity into their processes. Some might contend that interactivity began the moment humans were empowered with the means to change the channel using a remote control. (That's too much like the "I never inhaled" argument. I'm not going there. . . .) Regardless of its origins, the ability for the audience to participate has helped to make advertising relevant again. It has brought advertising back to earth and thereby narrowed the gap between marketer and consumer.

Voting for your favorite Pepsi ad or even electing to watch other Pepsi ads after viewing one in particular is a no-frills but meaningful way of giving the consumer some control. The process of clicking has profound implications as an indication of engagement and, combined with subsequent clicks (or "interactions"), an expression of increasing interest.

So-called traditional media as a whole has taken a leaf from interactive's book by introducing the means to "do something about it." The popular game show, *Who Wants to Be a Millionaire?*, allows viewers to participate in the ask-the-audience lifeline through AOL Instant Messenger (see Figure 11.2). Both television and radio involve their audiences by letting callers phone in or e-mail their questions or votes on various issues.

Nevertheless, no other medium to date has been able to inject a pervasive language of interactivity into the commercial advertising process as effectively, comprehensively, and seamlessly as the Internet.

Mind-Set

Three jeers to the generalists (I do not mean the opposite of the specialists here, but merely those who generalize) who

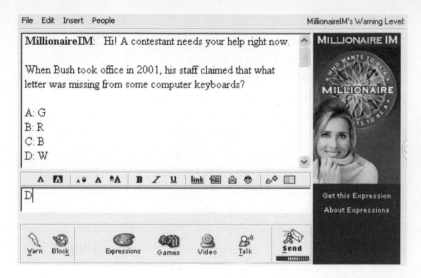

Figure 11.2   Ask the audience . . . or involve them: AOL + *Who Wants to Be a Millionaire* join forces. *Courtesy:* America Online (AOL) Media Networks.

believe that consumers on the Web are somehow different from those who don't use the Web. In reality, they are the same—a conclusion supported by reams of data and, moreover, by common sense. Online consumers are not foreign to you, they *are* you.

The generalists have bought into their own stereotypes—that consumers use the Web purely as a flotation device, a means to conduct robotic functional transactions such as research, fact-checking, shopping, and other pragmatic actions devoid of emotion. That's just one part of the proposition, however. The web has quickly become a means of entertainment as well—for example, the best of ESPN cable on ESPN Motion, made-for-the-Web long-form content on sites like Amazon.com, and some content presented in association with brands such as Reebok and Ford's Lincoln Mercury.

If it seems I contradict myself by talking out of one side of my keyboard about instant gratification (see Chapter 7, tenet 6) and out of the other about being entertained, then keep in mind that consumers can determine for themselves whether they want to lean back and enjoy the endless supply of content or participate in Amazon.com's 1-Click ordering. The consumer mind-set is constantly shifting and ad hoc, and the fine line between leaning forward and leaning back has blurred.

The notorious "lunch hour" (which exists in the media hall-of-fame office clichés just behind the "watercooler" and "drive-time") is now frequently being used for entertainment. For example, the wildly talked-about *Crossfire* segment on which Jon Stewart skewered Tucker Carlson can be viewed in its entirety *without commercials* (at least without the ones that originally appeared on the air). One commercial as a "pre-roll" to the content seems more than reasonable.

Incidentally, more people watched the Stewart-Carlson exchange on the Web (well over 2.3 million views) than watched it on TV (*Crossfire* averaged 550,000 viewers in Nielsen's third-quarter ratings) — a first for a major cable news show.

If the Web offers marketers the perfect context by matching their messages to consumers of the right mind-set, then the converse might be even more disturbing, intensifying what is wrong with the 30-second proposition.

Consumers who are trying to escape the monotony of the daily grind (which includes shopping at Gap, switching from pads to tampons, refinancing a house, or taking the entire family to the Olive Garden) are not necessarily in the right mind-set by 9:30 P.M. Perhaps that is why most consumers immediately change the channel or head for the john when a commercial comes on — it's more than lack of relevance or inaccurate targeting, it's just the wrong place at the wrong time for such advertising, even with the *right* message.

Alternatively, the consumer's mind-set is always in tune on the Internet, since he or she expressly grants permission to participate in the advertising process.

Permission

Permission marketing (term coined by Seth Godin) was a concept that unfortunately got stored away neatly in the file marked "E-mail," with a sticky-note saying, "Tell the IT guys to make sure our double opt-in policies are in order." Permission marketing is far too important to be compartmentalized. It is essentially where all of advertising is heading.

The Internet is the ultimate permission marketing medium, from the time consumers log on to the point at which they request more information. The Internet is young enough and raw enough to be able to rewrite the commercial value proposition and exchange. Although you'd never know it from the proliferation of commercial-free content, some consumers still remember why ads exist in the first place. The Web offers the unique opportunity to reinvent this process, instantly rewarding attention and making advertising welcome again.

Or it could follow the doomed path of the pod people, which crams as many commercials as possible into the buckling belt of an ad break.

Time Spent

Time spent is without question the new currency of advertising, and the base unit is an index of 100, which is the equivalent of 30 seconds. The extent to which marketers can break through the limitations of the 30-second will ultimately determine the extent to which they can bring consumers closer to their brands.

Try to be objective while you complete this exercise (I know you won't be). Jot down what you believe to be the *minimum, average,* and *maximum* lengths of time (measured in seconds) that an *average* consumer spends on the *average* advertising unit in various media.

The "minimum" column really just seems to demonstrate that no medium is completely safe from the apathy of the consumer. You should feel free to be cruel or kind depending on your loyalties; for example, if you're a print sympathizer you can credit print with the fact that a page has to be turned and therefore a brief moment of opportunity exists. Each medium has its own way to tap into those unique moments of truth. Television advertisers have the advantage of being first or last in a pod of ads; print can use inside and back covers; out-of-home signage has bumper-to-bumper traffic; radio has . . . I'll get back to you on this one; the Web has a surprisingly large number of tactics to attract a minimal level of attention and then step back and wait.

The "average" column in this exercise represents the *reality,* and the "maximum" column represents the *potential.*

Because it is still in its infancy, the Web is brimming with possibilities. There really is no ceiling on the amount of time a consumer might spend with a particular piece of communication. An advertisement is just a hyperlink away from a Web experience (in case you haven't checked lately, they're getting awfully good), and the time spent is at the consumer's discretion—unlike the 60-mph drive-by billboard and the "appointment-viewing" television spots. Innovation is integral to the Web, and the opportunity to reinvent a viable advertising business has never been greater.

Here are a few examples of this in practice.

1. *Ultramercial* is an up-front proposition that allows consumers to access premium content by "paying" with either their time or their money (in this case, we'll check the box marked "time." This endorsement message works so well because it explicitly assigns a monetary value to premium content. It respects consumers by giving them a choice and recognizing that they are savvy enough to understand the value exchange. WeatherBug has a similar endorsement model which matches brands to consumers—on the latter's terms.

2. An *Intro Message* (pioneered by MarketWatch from Dow Jones) is a one-a-day full-screen message that resolves within 10 seconds into the regular home page. In plain English, the intro message is arguably the finest format on the Web, since it occurs right before (as opposed to during) the consumption experience. It makes use of the full dimensions of the screen and because it is nonclickable (although consumers can

opt out of the message at any time), it acknowledges the consumer's mind-set of being on the Web to consume content rather than be diverted to a marketer's harem.

3. *Opt-in Intrusiveness* may sound like an oxymoron, but it is not. It can be described by an anecdote about a man who walks up to a woman in a bar (please feel free to substitute genders at your whim). Should he immediately choose to proposition her, he is likely to wake up the next day with pain in certain extremities. (Of course, he might get lucky, but the odds are small. Let's call this *direct response.*)

   However, should he decide to first politely introduce himself, avoid hackneyed pickup lines, and then retire to a quiet corner with the hint that should she wish to continue the conversation she knows where to find him, he may likewise end up in bed, except after a longer interval and with a much higher chance of a meaningful relationship. Let's call this *branding.*

   This second scenario depicts one variation that the Web offers: the ability to attract a consumer's attention in a short period of time and then retreat and await the consumer's subsequent initiation. This is another instance of permission marketing, but it also constitutes smart marketing, whereby every consumer interaction is a quality one and, by definition, implies a degree of interest. This absolutely cannot be said about any form of "push" communication.

   These clicks or initiations may enable sound or other "intrusive" actions, such as enlarging a unit to the size of the entire screen.

TV ON THE WEB

In a bizarre twist of fate, the Internet has rescued the 30-second from certain oblivion by allowing marketers to simply transplant their dressed-up spots to the Web. Naturally, this has raised the ire of purists, who use phrases like "selling out"—and some that would never pass the scrutiny of the Wiley editors.

The always-on capacity and ever-accelerating speed of a broadband world have made this a reality. When entire movies can be downloaded over a latte at your local Starbucks and an album's worth of songs can be purchased (or not) and forwarded across the Web, a lowly 30-second spot can just as easily find its place on the information superhighway. Rest assured, we're never going to reach the point that an hour of viewing is aggressively interrupted by some 23 minutes of commercials (as on network TV), but it is conceivable and, as it turns out, even acceptable to offer up one commercial per viewing experience.

Then again, consumers are armed with a device far more powerful than a remote control—a mouse—and their very proximity to the screen gives them the ultimate "out"—the close button. More important, the elapsed time before this close button is clicked can and does get measured, and surely it is just a matter of time before marketers are paying only for a complete execution. (Don't hate me, media world. It had to be said. You can charge more for the completed views if you like. They'll still buy.)

More than 90 percent of the at-work audience accesses the Internet via a broadband connection; at home, the numbers have recently broken through the 50 percent barrier, which is often referred to as "critical mass." These numbers make a profound statement, especially when combined with the concept of a polite download that takes advantage of idle time to deliver its high-quality, larger-sized files (in other words, when consumers are not using their computers, the commercial is loading quietly in the background).

Broadband triggered the epiphany that television was not the killer app. Video is, in fact, the killer app, especially now that it can be delivered so seamlessly.

Compare apples to apples. If the same video content can be delivered through a wireless device or the Web, then why would (or rather, how could) television be thought of as preferable in consumers' eyes and, thus, marketers' budgets? (This is a rhetorical question. Don't answer. Or if you must, send an e-mail to jaffe@lifeafter30.com, or visit my blog on jaffejuice.com. This book is interactive after all.) Sure, there are differences—the size of the screen, distance from the screen, and posture of the audience—but these are nothing more than red herrings. The content consumed on the Web is becoming more entertaining by the day. The computer screen is getting larger all the time. Dell is in the TV business. Microsoft is banking on the fact that one screen will eventually rule them all (sorry, Frodo), and it will be a digital one at that.

According to the 2004 AAF survey of advertising industry leaders, the four primary benefits of the Web are as follows:

1. The ability to generate ROI
2. New ad formats to break through to and engage consumers
3. Better targeting
4. The ability to complement and enhance the use of traditional media

My two cents on these responses:

1. I am concerned that one in four respondents does not understand how the most measurable medium in history can generate some kind of return on investment. I suspect that these professionals are not doing anything substantial, not doing it well, or just working with the wrong partners. If the Web is anything, it is too accountable in a vacuum (see point 4). Marketers must also make sure that the correct metrics are being applied to the particular strategies and tactics in question.
2. The Internet is itself a "new ad format" and is deploying a host of new approaches, formats, and even business

models to help build a new kind of relationship with empowered consumers.

3. Precise targeting—especially in the form of both behavioral and contextual marketing—is revolutionizing the targeting game. But don't be fooled into thinking that this is just a fragmented play. As focused and diverse as the Web can be, it is similar to other media in terms of being able to aggregate larger audiences. The key for the future is the ability to achieve precise targeting of both quantity and quality audiences. Technology is helping to do this.

4. I've got to express my disdain about the Web's ability to simply enhance traditional media, and nothing more. I find it a little too convenient that the overwhelming consensus is for online advertising to be the icing on top of the traditional cake. This entire book is about the shortcomings of traditional media and old marketing, as led by the 30-second, and if you're looking at online as a gap filler or the line item you fund with whatever is left over, you're ignoring reality. No doubt online will both complement and enhance existing forms, but it will also lead, revive, invigorate, and transform traditional campaigns with traditional media.

The View from the Top

I've always believed that for change to become part of corporate culture, it has to come from the top. Without buy-in from the top, change is extremely hard to implement.

How many CMOs of the Fortune 500 do you think are still on the fence about the Web? How many heads of agencies are biased against the Internet because of a perceived profitability disadvantage compared to other media? How do the heads of the other media conglomerates feel about the role the Internet will play as a branding vehicle?

Things are changing.

On average 8.35 percent of media budgets are currently being allocated to online advertising according to an AAF survey. This number is expected to climb to 17 percent by 2007. More alarming is that a full 17.5 percent of the sample report spending zero on online in 2004. According to projections, about 50 percent of them will have come around by 2007, whereas the other half will be deep into something else. Even so, I fear that the 50 percent who have yet to see the light are going to be so late in the game that their companies will be playing catch-up for a long time after 2007.

A senior marketer recently told me how one of his company's senior executives was fired for making dismissive comments to a panel about the Internet as a means to build both business and brand. In this instance, the company in question had proof to refute the executive's unfounded claims. This company did two things that I would strongly recommend to every client out there:

1. Execute a real campaign in order to gauge true efficacy—put your money where your mouth is. A test campaign will not give you the impact and visibility you need, and therefore won't accurately reflect the power of branding.
2. Field your own proprietary cross-media research to measure both the qualitative and the quantitative benefits and effects of the Web. Speak to consumers who exit the dealership, retail store, arrival gate, or cinema in order to track the full cross-media impact of your marketing efforts.

There is only one true way to gauge the full extent of your marketing efforts: the overall ad-spend-to-sales relationship. The spikes and blips that correspond to injections of communication dollars can be correlated and evaluated accordingly. I'm less concerned about how a budget is divvied up and more interested in how each medium under- or overperformed relative to its allocation.

Think about those few companies that outspend the rest of the pack. What do they know that you don't? Are they still dipping their toes in the water with test campaigns, or have they recommitted themselves to doing full justice to this medium by putting their money where their mouths are?

Some contend that the problem doesn't lie within the ranks of the more junior folks (who tend to be enthusiastic and open-minded), nor does it descend from the executive suites, which are under pressure right now to deliver value, big ideas, and proven results. Rather, the resistance begins and ends with those who have the most to lose from change—the middle-aged middle managers, who are stuck in the limbo.

An Interactive Perspective
Ian Beavis, Former Senior Vice President, Marketing, Product Planning & Public Relations, Mitsubishi Motors North America, Inc.

When Joseph asked me to write a chapter on the subject of "interactive" my initial reaction was sure, why not? I've been working with elements of it for years, including helping get Toyota on Prodigy (really dating myself) if anyone can remember Prodigy. Then I thought, what could I say that hasn't already been said by people a lot smarter than I. Everyone knows its power as a branding tool: At its finest, interactive is capable of capturing customers in ways unheard of in the past. But, I thought, there is something missing on the subject. As luck would have it, there is a lot I could say, but thankfully, I'll be brief and share with you one person's opinion. This will not be a technical chapter and will not contain a single acronym.

A great deal of attention is, quite rightfully, being paid to the interactive environment. It is our present and our future. What I find frustrating are the endless discussions regarding the technology, platforms, and measurement tools by smart people who are missing the point.

Interactivity is not about technology. It is about people and, to a large extent, the human condition. For interactive marketing to truly become the centerpiece of the industry, it must escape from its ugly, jargon-laden, geeky teenage phase and become an adult. The conversation has to move from cubes in trendy lofts or the bowels of IT departments. It has to move into really boring corner offices in large companies in less hip cities. Interactivity has to become a critical part of the discussion among the same people who overanalyze television, radio, and magazine campaigns. The people who work with cultural anthropologists and highly sophisticated research labs. These same people who have the ear of the CEO and all the other Cs in a corporation. It must take center stage in the C level of companies and not be confined to the CRM or interactive advertising manager.

The movement of this discussion further up the organization into what I would call the "real" (although some current practitioners might call it Jurassic Park) marketing department will be scary and take people in both areas outside their comfort zones. It will require collaboration and mutual respect. It will require both parties' realization that to be truly successful, they need each other. More important, it will involve a discussion of the company's marketing objectives, strategies, and tactics. I hope there will be a spirited exchange on the relative strengths of various media and their cost-effectiveness. This must be a holistic approach to how to achieve the company's marketing objectives. The simple fact is, this media-neutral approach to marketing is simply not taking place often enough at clients or agencies anywhere in the world.

So now that we have everyone in the room singing out of the same songbook, what should the song be? This is the most important part of my rant. The discussion of interactivity has to center around people. We need to really understand people and how and why they respond. We need to stop treating them as targets, lumping them into demographic groups, and taking them for granted. We need to find out how to engage them in a positive way. We need to understand that people's motivations and reactions to situations have changed little since we lived in caves. We need to remember that just because you can do something to a person doesn't mean you should. We need to recognize the importance of every touch point and how distracted and suspicious people are. We need to treasure them, not target them. We need to treat them as we would a guest in our own home. Think about it. Would you jump out from behind a bush to surprise someone as they rang the doorbell? Well that is exactly what many marketers are doing with pop-ups!

In this brave new world where we treasure and truly understand our customers, interactivity will quite rightfully take center stage. It will set the tone for every part of the marketing plan.

Treat your customers as you would like to be treated. Allow them to be (pleasantly) surprised and delighted. Allow them the opportunity to discover your company or product in their own way and on their timetable. This is the future of marketing, and interactive media can take us there. We've only scratched the surface. Interacting with our customers in a respectful way will reap huge benefits in terms of their attitudes toward the company and its marketing and, most important, the bottom line. All marketing is about revenue growth, and interactive marketing will provide the strongest growth.

I urge everyone reading this chapter to step away, look in the mirror, and think about the people we market to. If we keep this at the heart of what we do, interactive media will grow up and help our companies grow, too. Thus ends my rant.

12

Gaming

"We will blow past any first-day opening movie that's ever been recorded," said Peter Moore, global marketing chief of Microsoft's Xbox, predicting big things as *Halo 2* was released.

He was right. *Halo 2* hit some $125 million in sales on its first day, according to Moore's own postopening estimates. That made *Halo 2*'s launch bigger than the opening weekend of Pixar's *The Incredibles,* which at $70.7 million was Disney's biggest three-day opening ever (according to Reveries.com).

Take a deep breath and think about this for a while. Now continue this journey with me, keeping your eyes and mind wide open. Gaming is, *without question,* the sleeper of all non-traditional marketing approaches.

The typical Hollywood movie or DVD today launches in tandem with the gaming version for a reason: Gaming magazines have helped maintain life support for the ailing print industry (at least in terms of reaching a younger male demographic). Rock stars such as Green Day and Hoobastank lend their tunes to Madden 2005; movie celebrities (e.g., Jean Reno* in *Onimusha 3: Demon Seige*) have tapped into the power of gaming in order to resurrect, leverage, or cash in their equity.

In many respects, gaming is the convergent utopia of many of the approaches outlined in this book: branded entertainment + Internet + community + music/mobile—are you getting it yet? Nevertheless, gaming has been marginalized and reduced to oversimplification in understanding and practice.

The term *advergaming* is about as misused as Madison + Vine™ (copyrighted to *Ad Age*) and has almost become a token line item to be checked off in the insecure marketer's *Dummies' Guide to Window Dressing the 30-Second Spot.*

Gaming is probably *the* most cannibalistic of all forms of media in play today because it uses the TV screen—the bigger and flatter, the better. There is a certain irony in the fact that the TV set itself is the conduit to and receptacle for gaming experiences, but when the gaming console goes on, the TV (network, cable, other) goes off. According to IDC, 85.8 percent of gamers indicated that their consoles remain permanently connected to the TV.

As gaming consoles continue to drop in price, the capabilities of the games themselves are exploding in value and level of engagement. Virtual reality, network gaming (playing with others via the Internet), customized gaming, and the grandest of them all, premium-priced virtual-world multiplayer games present a mind-boggling array of applications, alternatives, and derivations. Mobile gaming consoles are themselves minicomputers, jam-packed with color, full-motion video, kick-ass sound, and Wi-Fi connectivity. PlayStation Portable (PSP) may very well deal a body blow to the outdoor advertising industry.

---

*Credits include *The Professional* (1994 release), *The Da Vinci Code* (2006 release), and *The Pink Panther* (2005 release).

The ailing 30-second spot is like a veteran quarterback who, quite frankly, should have retired long ago but instead doggedly perseveres despite the fact that his legacy is eroded every time he sets foot on the field. Compounding his bruised and battered physical condition is the sad state that his defense (read: content; see reality TV) is no longer capable of protecting him from the relentless blitz of change in the form of empowered consumers and technology. One and a half mixed metaphors later, the point is that the dearth of quality content on television is as much to blame as any of the factors discussed earlier (clutter, creativity, naïveté) for the pressure being placed on the 30-second, and gaming has very quickly become a worthy and formidable alternative to any form of drama, comedy, or thriller with its original DVD/video programming and elaborate story lines.

In bursts of exceptions, we're seeing the behavioral impact and influence of gaming being used in the 30-second itself. Two examples that come to mind are Volvo and the very impressive Michael Vick Experience. Volvo was so impressed with the way its S40 model played out in Microsoft's "RalliSport Challenge 2," that it used clips from the game to create a 30-second spot (see Figure 12.1). The

Figure 12.1   A cultural marriage between gaming and advertising.
Courtesy: Volvo Cars of North America, LLC.

Michael Vick Experience (so good that it had to be extended to 60 seconds, but should have been 600), brought to you by Nike (who else?), banks on a gaming insight that fans would pretty much do anything to vicariously experience the thrill and exhilaration of being "in the game"—especially existentially, through their hero. Along these lines, Disney created a new theme park ride called the Michael Vick Experience, which lets fans of the National Football League experience the adrenaline rush of passing for 148 yards and a touchdown as the Atlanta Falcons' quarterback. Another example is *Tom Clancy's Splinter Cell Pandora Tomorrow* (published by Ubisoft Entertainment), in which players draw on a suite of Sony Ericsson Mobile phones to achieve their mission. Now that's product placement for you!

Where game designers once had to pay for the rights to showcase a brand, today it is the other way around. In EA's *NASCAR 2005: Chase for the Cup,* P&G had the opportunity to introduce a new product line (Mr. Clean AutoDry) into the gaming space. Integration that included signage, race ticker sponsorship, unlockable Mr. Clean Pit Crew, and a create-a-car feature were all well received by gamers for increasing the realism of the game and aligning well with the game experience (see Figure 12.2). All key metrics, including brand awareness, brand favorability, purchase intent, and specific video game recall, saw significant lifts.

Chances are that you (the reader) don't know what the hell I'm talking about. You haven't played *Riven, Myst, Doom, EverQuest,* or *The Sims*—online, offline, on the road, or in the den. You are doing yourself a disservice, and I have a quick fix for you: Next time your son or daughter is on PlayStation or Xbox, take the time to sit down, observe, and learn.

- You'll see total submission, except that this submission is anything but passive.
- You'll see a kind of attentiveness that has been absent without leave on broadcast television for the longest time.
- You'll experience by association the kind of involve-

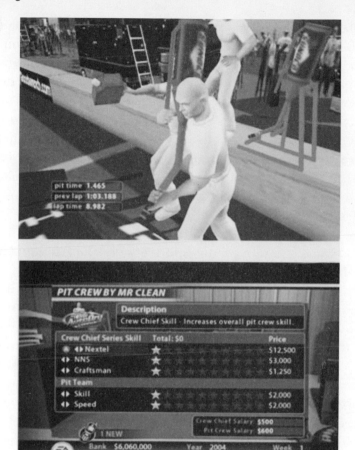

Figure 12.2   NASCAR/Mr. Clean integration. *Courtesy:* Procter & Gamble; NASCAR, Electronic Arts (EA).

ment and loyalty that you fantasize about for your brand but has been elusive to date.

Game playing is nothing new. From the days of pinball to Pong, from Asteroids and Space Invaders to the age of Atari, from the dawn of Nintendo and Sega to now, when PlayStation and Xbox rule the world, gaming has evolved into a viable alternative to all forms of entertainment.

Quite clearly, the active ingredient has been technology, and the exponentially growing capabilities of the technology catalyst have created movielike experiences, breathtaking 3D graphics, Surround Sound, scripted video, and most recently, networked scenarios.

But technology is not the only contributor.

The rise of gaming is as much credited to the consumer as it is to the producer or engineer. The demand has acutely led the supply, and in this case it is the demand for an active viewing or participation experience. In a sports game, a consumer can virtually be the ball; in a new *Star Wars* game, consumers can play either side (good or bad, Luke or "I am your Father") in any battle that has *ever* taken place in the *Star Wars* saga. It is this kind of comprehensive choice that makes the overall proposition so appealing. It is staggering to witness the attention to detail—not only in the inclusivity of being able to fight every battle, but in the design, layout, and nuances of the battle scene as well. Don't kid yourself, these are not the over-the-top products of too-enthusiastic programmers locked away in a dungeon or ivory tower (there's a game idea in there somewhere). They are not equipped with unnecessary and optional extras. Consumers today demand this level of production value. They expect no less than total choice from the purveyors of gaming.

This attention to detail is also applicable to advertising. In an older version of *Triple Play*, Yankee Stadium did not have a Budweiser sign flashing between innings; there were no Fleet (now Bank of America), no Kodak, and no Utz Potato Chips signs. The playing experience was less than believable and seemed artificial. Contrast that with EA's FIFA soccer game, where Sharp, Cannon, and Fly Emirates ads contribute vital touches of authenticity to the playing experience because they replicate reality (see Figure 12.3).

The problem, of course, is that marketers and their Madison Avenue cohorts have yet to recognize the quality and quantity of gaming impressions. And organizations like Major League Baseball or the National Football League, which fined Jake Plummer for wearing a nonregulation

Figure 12.3   Authentic advertising is welcome in gaming. *Courtesy:*
FIFA, Electronic Arts (EA).

decal honoring his former teammate Pat Tillman, who lost
his life in Iraq, are trapped in rights-issue hell (self-created),
preventing the natural distribution of advertising, which for
the first time in its history actually belongs and is welcome.

If you think I'm way too involved, you're wrong. I am a
neophyte when it comes to gaming, but I do recognize the
tremendous impact and potential that gaming can offer
endangered brands. Musicians and actors have already realized this. So have the studios that work feverishly to simultaneously (or very closely) launch movies, DVDs, and
games in order to leverage the obvious brand-extension
benefits.

This state of affairs is sublime: advertising as a welcome
guest. Authentic advertising.

Put gaming and advertising together, and *it's quite conceiv-*
able that sponsorship will be completely renegotiated, redeployed, and
reevaluated based on the gaming visibility rather than mere static

impressions from a series of one-off physical events and/or movie views.

Gaming has become a lot more pervasive on the Web; however, it has simultaneously become a marketer's gimp in the process—a classic example of doing something simply because it *can* be done. Lame (to use game-playing vernacular) "advergames" are created that allow consumers (who are more likely employees of the company commissioning them in the first place) to do things like control the cool dancing man in the Kmart commercials. Yawn.

That being said, simple games, such as the Orbitz three-hole minigolf "ad" are both addictive and absorbing. For some reason, I continue to purchase my air tickets from Orbitz . . .

Other marketers create oversimplified games that would make either of the Mario brothers retch with disgust—positioning a Coke billboard in the background seems to be the "big idea" of the moment. Yeah, that's right, deploy old marketing in a new-marketing format—that's kind of like watching an episode of *Leave It to Beaver* on TV Land in high definition.

Still, anything is better than nothing, and the degree of involvement and interactivity as well as the inherent entertainment and engagement factors that come with gaming are valuable commodities.

Why Gaming? Why Now?

This requires a five-pronged proof point:

1. Your consumers are there.
2. They're spending more time.
3. They're actively engaged (and receptive to *authentic* advertising).
4. They're a quality audience (hint: they pay for content).
5. It's working.

This is not a pimple-faced-geek thing anymore. The skew is still male, but don't be fooled into stereotyping this genre. *Get Up and Go,* a travel profile game on Chrysler's site, attracted 40,000 players in the first week, the average age of a player was 45, and 42 percent of the users were women. In fact, according to a report by Opinion Place, it is women over 40 who spend the most time per week playing online games—9.1 hours versus 6.1 for their male counterparts.

According to IDC research, the average gamer spends 3.7 days a week playing video games and about 2.5 hours playing games on an average day. That's 6.2 hours per week, compared with network television's 7.9 and cable television's 8.8 hours per week.

The average console game takes about 40 hours to complete and, like a good book, once you really get into it, it's pretty hard to stop. The level of undivided engagement is readily evident in the endless message boards, blogs, and community sites dedicated to tips, walk-throughs, cheat codes, and sharing overall experiences.

Their response to old media notwithstanding, consumers are very likely to give up hard-earned dollars to participate in gaming offered by marketers—in addition to purchasing games, at about $50 a pop.

Perhaps the ultimate (not to be confused with Ultima) of all massively multiplayer online (MMO)—I'm not joking, this is real—games is *EverQuest,* the online adventure game that required, in addition to the purchase of the game itself, a monthly subscription of $14.95 to play. The original *EverQuest*—along with its various expansion packs—sold more than 2 million copies, and at its peak had more than 118,000 subscribers playing simultaneously.* *EverQuest II* hit stores just in time (phew!) for the holiday season in 2004.

Even more incredible was a phenomenon in which players created characters in this virtual world and then bartered or sold them in the real world. Here's an eBay listing I found:

---

*Source: Sony Online Entertainment Press Release, July 2004.

Lvl 62 Rogue on BB server. Rogue has epic and nice gear. Has 250 poison making skill. All expansions including LoY. He is flagged for PoV/PoS. Has been unguilded for about 8 months (just exp grinding). Is well liked and is in high demand in groups. You will not regret the investment. Taking buyout $450.00. Thanks and good luck in advance.

Based on a study of thousands of completed auctions for *EverQuest* items and in-game currency, Edward Castronova, associate professor of economics at California State University at Fullerton, concluded that players earn an average wage of $3.42 for every hour they play the game and collectively produce annual gross "exports" of more than $5 million.*

Intel® worked its way into the Sims Online game (which was also subscriber-based). In addition to abundant press coverage, a consumer satisfaction survey from April 2003 revealed that 37 percent of *The Sims Online* (TSO) participants purchased an Intel processor–based computer for their lot, while 66 percent have used an Intel processor–based computer during their *Sims* game play.

The Widening Gap — Plug It or Get Plugged

Madison Avenue stands alone at the pier watching the luxury liner that is gaming disappear into the horizon. The disconnect between branded investment in the space and revenue being generated from it (in terms of unit sales or subscription) is borderline inexcusable and unacceptable.

Let your kids help you see the light. And if you don't have kids (or they won't let you in their room), get some . . . or challenge your agency or marketing partners to set up a demo for you, stat. This is the kind of focus group you need to be conducting instead of the self-serving

---

*EverQuest spins its own economy, January 25, 2002, news.com.

selective-perception-of-cough-syrup claims research group that you so enjoy attending on your multicity tour de force.

You simply cannot afford to be a laggard in this explosive new form of entertainment. And whether you know it or not, you are most likely already way behind. Every other major category has figured out that gaming holds the key to longevity (or at least short- to medium-term prosperity). Musicians, actors, producers, and directors are all clambering to get aboard this ship.

This reminds me of a clip from the old *Benny Hill* show. The billboard reads:

WATERSHIP DOWN

You've read the book
You've seen the movie
You've bought the T-shirt
Now . . . eat the pie

In this case, we should amend this to read: "Now . . . play the game!"

Interactive Entertainment: The New PRIME Time
Karen Schulman, VP Marketing & Sales, Global Publishing, Electronic Arts (EA)

Video games go beyond your children's playground to deliver a universal media platform as pervasive as television, more connected to end consumers, and yet a relatively untapped landscape for marketers. In an era of multitasking media it is time to add interactive entertainment, a platform winning hearts and minds of global consumers, to the marketing mix.

While these are bold statements, the numbers speak for themselves, indicating the interactive entertainment industry (aka video games) plays a significant role in the lives of today's masses. The industry will grow from $23 billion in global revenues and 108 million U.S. gamers over age 13 to $32 billion with more than 126 million U.S. gamers over 13 in the 2009 timeframe (DFC Intelligence, Sept. 2004, and Yankee Group). Gamers as a whole play an average of 75 hours of games per year (PricewaterhouseCoopers, May 2003). Not only does this time and financial commitment stand above other entertainment choices for this consumer, gaming has one unmatched value beyond all other media in reaching this entertainment consumer; interactivity. Just walk into the nearest frat house and you will see the PC on the Web, MP3s playing, five chat boxes in progress on Instant Messenger, the sports game on, and the video game in live action—and the definitive content-winning mind share is gaming!

So what does this mean for the marketer in the future, and how do you get involved? First, the gamers always come first; they purchased the entertainment, and if we hold their experience as the holy grail, the publisher and advertiser alike will reach their goals. Effective marketing in the gaming space requires dropping into the gamers' world—in relevant, impactful ways—while they are in action. We see tapping into this experience via three primary forms: brand integration, opt-in marketing, and online gaming.

First, as it relates to the current generation of technology (Xbox, PS2, and GameCube), gaming offers marketers the chance to immerse their brand and/or product messaging into the game content. Beyond product placement in a movie that finds the actor grabbing a Coke as part of the experience for seconds in what is generally viewed at a frequency of one, brand integration in games is about engagement with the consumer over the life cycle of the game ownership, generally 12 months for, on average, 50+ hours. These integrations include a mix of elements from reach vehicles like signage and broadcast spots to endorsement value from game mode sponsorships. Finally, aspirational features like unlockable characters, tracks, and game levels move a marketer from advertiser to benefactor of unique content with the rare but ever-powerful product integration. Currently, both publishers and advertisers are benefiting from this advertising model that will only grow as the industry continues to introduce greater auditing methods and the ability to dynamically change the messaging within the game after retail launch.

Next, as gaming continues to grow on current and next-generation platforms marketers will have the opportunity to utilize opt-in methods in satisfying the gamers content demand. Given that interactive entertainment products will grow in depth and breadth, publishers will launch games across eight or more platforms, including online and mobile. Gamers will tap into the entertainment at varying platforms, points in time, locations, and currencies, and with this evolves an opt-in advertising model providing advertisers with a direct marketing channel by delivering rich gaming experiences free or reduced in price to the consumer in exchange for permission to direct-market that individual. Not unlike the Pepsi Stuff campaign of years ago or more recently the McDonald's Sony Connect program, gamers will sign up to satisfy the insatiable hunger for unique content and will gladly forgo spending another $1, $5, or $25 for enhanced game content by opting in for marketers' messaging. By interacting with marketer A, the gamer can download the latest game character, receive an invitation to the greatest online live tournament play, or unlock the latest game ring-tone. Ultimately, gamers will become accustomed to paying for these microtransactions and yet are sure to seek out the sponsor-exclusive content and larger subscription-based products offered free of charge by their favorite (or soon to be favorite) brand.

Finally, online gaming includes playing on a console with broadband connectivity, PC-based massively multiplayer role-playing games, as well as Web-based quick-play free games. While each offers varying degrees of advertiser benefit, with Web-based currently most valuable due to sheer size of population and time spent with gaming, it is the connected console that is headed for explosive growth—in addition to serving as a singular space in video gaming that looks more like traditional media. In the current environment less than 10 percent of Xbox and PS2 gamers are connected, and even less than those connected actively play online. This will fundamentally change with Xbox 2 and PS3 technologies, more easily enabling the process, with broadband penetration continuing to grow and online game features advancing. This space, while rather undefined currently, will in the future offer an environment that taps into the lean-forward attraction of games, the community and frequency of fantasy football, and the standard media metrics of the Internet. . . . Keep watching for more to come.

It is clear gaming offers marketers a medium that leverages sight, sound, motion, and interactivity to captivate the masses as a viable addition to the marketing mix. The multitasking consumer will demand marketers reach their target customers, where they want to be reached, with added value and not interruption. With this as the bellwether, we are all sure to succeed.

13

On-Demand Viewing

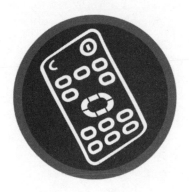

One of the biggest shifts (as described in Chapter 18, on search) is that from push to pull. It sounds simple enough, but in practice it's the equivalent of shifting from drive to reverse while in motion (note to marketers: do not try this at home). The results are catastrophic, and the only viable procedure for changing direction is to call an all-stop, do an about-face (or a three-point turn—i.e., a phased approach), and then shift gears.

In a different but still relevant realm, this is why companies like JetBlue have succeeded where their established counterparts have not. In fact, the gap between JetBlue and, say, Continental or United isn't even about incremental degrees of improvement anymore; it's about the outright difference between success and failure. Marketers, publishers, and agencies that still think the world we live in is governed by appointment viewing are most likely proud US Airways frequent fliers and might want to consider spending their miles real soon.

Prime Time = My Time

The 30-second spot owes its existence to the infamous aggregation of masses of eyeballs. This might sound like an episode of *Fear Factor*, and that comparison is quite prophetic, really. As advertisers, we should have realized we were sowing the seeds of our own demise when we dehumanized our audience and reduced them to nothing but pairs of eyeballs, but that's a story for another day . . .

Some years ago, NBC came up with the ingenious concept of "Must-See TV." Based on ratings success, they determined that Thursday night on NBC = "Must-See TV," and then proceeded to indoctrinate us with this claim at every possible instance. Today, NBC no longer makes this claim, but more important is that no one else does, either (despite what CBS might say).

The oversimplified value proposition that most U.S. households watch as many as six networks (CBS, NBC, ABC, Fox, UPN, WB)—although in reality they only watch 3½—between the set hours of 8 P.M. and 10 P.M. EST Monday through Thursday, with falloff on Friday and even more over the weekend, is in dire need of a re:think. Even demographics, the universal language of the communications business, does not support the fantasy that masses of households huddle around the box in the living room during predetermined hours.

The more affluent subset of the consumer base is more likely to possess multiple media devices, from DVD players to DVR set-top boxes, from gaming consoles to media centers. They're also more likely to be subscribing to VOD services and/or movie subscription services such as Blockbuster or Netflix. Furthermore, they're also not wed to the tube, exercising their appetite for entertainment by going out to the opera, theater, or cinema.

If you're thinking that this range of media options is limited to the upper class, you'd be wrong. It's not. The price of all of these competing options, with the possible exception of the movies, is only going down. A DVD player is available for under $40 at Wal-Mart. A TiVo DVR can be bought on eBay for less than $100. Blockbuster and Netflix are engaged in a war to the death that is causing massive downward pressure on the price of movie rentals.

And let's not forget the real Goliaths out there—the cable companies—which have direct lines and billing accounts to almost every U.S. household that counts (at least in this conversation). Monthly cable bills have incrementally become a whopping expense as a result of bundling in add-on premium services such as HBO, VOD, DVR functionality, cable modems, and very soon, a kitchen sink for sure. All these incremental payments and subscriptions add up, and if you think Americans can't afford these services, you're forgetting that this is first and foremost a media society and an economic culture that is built on the foundation of debt.

At the other end of the spectrum is a populace that is working harder than ever before—especially in the face of widespread layoffs. Many hold down two or more jobs in order to pay the cable bill (I'm kidding, but not really). Compounding this is the fact that consumers are attention-starved, impatient, and suffering from MDD (media deficit disorder), so instead of focusing on one medium at a particular time for an extended period of time, they are now multitasking and engaging in frenetic nonlinear viewing. For example, they might watch three or four programs pretty much simultaneously on their DVRs, all the while keeping the Wi-Fi, broadband-enabled laptop within arm's reach.

Whichever way you look at it, consumers now have the motivation and the tools to consume content and/or media on their terms, whether getting home at 10 P.M. after working a double shift or relaxing on a Saturday morning to catch up on a week's supply of *The Bold and the Beautiful* (which, without commercials, adds up to approximately 60 minutes rather than the 2½-hour on-air running time).

I'll discuss just a few of the more prominent on-demand alternatives that exist today, with some thoughts on their marketing implications (it's not pretty).

The DVR: The Grim Reaper Has Come for the Fat Cats

Trekkies reading this book, please raise your hands.

You can put them down now.

Beware the Borg! And let me just say that when it comes to summing up the seismic shifts occurring in the on-demand landscape, *resistance is futile. You are no longer in control.* The DVR, led by TiVo, represents an entirely new paradigm that already has transformed the way we watch and consume television.

What is more alarming is how marketers have scoffed at the potential devastation that these behavioral changes are going to have on their businesses because the "reach" isn't there.

This is no longer the case.

A Forrester study recently helped put the writing on the wall: When DVRs spread to 30 million households in the U.S., marketers will respond by slashing TV ad spending . . . by as much as 40 percent. This is no Robin Hood fairy tale where the rich (the networks) are robbed to fund the poor (cable)—it's happening pretty much across the board. Everybody—or almost everybody—loses.

Figure 13.1 reveals a crucial mainstreaming in the minds of the advertising community that the niche player has become an industry phenomenon and is being taken very seriously—for the first time.

All in all, 75 percent of the advertising industry leaders surveyed believe that DVR technology will have a *significant* impact on the 30-second norm. One in five now think that the DVR proposition will lead to the outright death of the 30-second commercial (up from 13 percent in 2003). The remaining 55 percent still contend that the 30-second

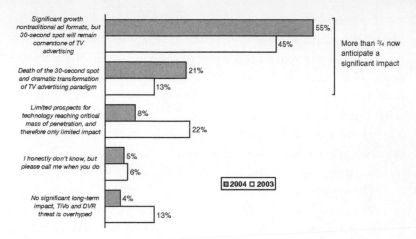

Figure 13.1   Anticipated impact of DVR technology on 30-second TV spot. *Source: AAF Survey of Industry Leaders on Advertising Trends 2004,* prepared by Atlantic Media Company.

commercial will remain the cornerstone of television advertising, but I believe this is at best wishful thinking and at worst foolish bravado.

As shown in Figure 13.2, 54.3 percent of the In-Stat/MDR respondents who skip commercials admitted skipping 75 percent or more of them. All in all, 68.2 percent of the sample admitted (key word is "admitted") to skipping commercials, whereas 82.8 percent of DVR intenders (those

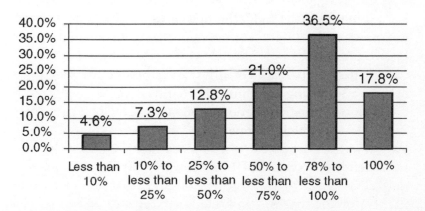

Figure 13.2   Percent of DVR commercials skipped.
Courtesy: In-Stat/MDR.

who indicate that they intend to purchase one) indicated that ad-skipping is on their to-do list. This implies that the intent to skip commercials by the early adopters and mainstream majority (according to Rogers's diffusion/adoption curve) is a bigger priority today than it was with the innovators. That's real scary for marketers.

What you might not be aware of, however, is the fact that digital video recorder (DVR) consumers are *more likely* to watch television—both network and cable—*because* of their ability to control the experience. According to In-Stat/ MDR, there is a causal relationship between ownership of a PVR and the propensity to watch more television, which does not even remotely translate to proportional increases in commercial consumption.

Which Came First? The Egg or the Chicken?

Did technology (in this case, the ability to pause live TV and skip commercials) empower the consumer or did the empowered consumer facilitate the birth of the technology?

The answer is twofold: "Who cares?" and "Both."

The reality is that viewers have been skipping commercials since long before they had remote controls. The DVR has done nothing more than formalize a more efficient process for it and make it possible to measure it.

I think of the TiVo phenomenon as inevitable in a world governed and catalyzed by technology. Consumer reactions to and passion for TiVo are clear evidence that the seed for such a device had been planted long before the box itself arrived on our doorsteps.

A good example of the passion people have for their TiVo can be found at www.tivocommunity.com. The site launches with the disclaimer "Please take note that this site is not operated by TiVo, Inc." But it's hard not to suspect that TiVo is paying the web-hosting fee. The site features a "TiVo Community Meets" area, where enthusiasts can swap stories and experiences with fellow TiVo users and offer tips, tricks, and advice on the viewing experience. But the primary function of the web site is as a meeting place for those with a shared mind-set and a sense of commonality centered around the technology. According to GoDaddy .com, nbccommunity.com is still available!

We are witnessing the birth of a new form of segmentation, whereby consumers, rather than being categorized by demographics or even psychographics, are segmented together on the basis of the very media they consume (TiVo, iPod, etc.). TiVo the technology did not create this segment; TiVo *the brand* did—and a powerful brand it is.

One feature of TiVo technology that unites its users is its de facto 30-second skip button. The manufacturer will tell you there is no such thing, but proud community members discovered a cheat code that enables this function and posted it on the Web. Here's how it works. Punch in the following sequence: Select, Play, Select, 30, Select. Your fast-forward button is now a 30-second skip button, and you can get through an average pod of eight commercials in about one second. (This kind of information is also available from these kinds of books: *How to Do Everything with Your TiVo, High Tech Toys for Your TV: Secrets of TiVo, Xbox, Replay TV, Ultimate TV and More* and, of course, *TiVo for Dummies.*)

In addition to the 30-second skip, TiVo users generally figure out on their own that by viewing any program 5 to 10 minutes after its scheduled start time, they are able to skip *all* commercials and still get to the end of the program at the same time as anyone else.

For example, on NBC's "Must See" Thursday nights let's assume that a consumer "must see" every bit of programming from *Joey* through *ER*—in other words, from 8 P.M. through 11 P.M. Assuming also that there are about 17 minutes of commercials (according to the *2001 Television Commercial Monitoring Report*) for every one hour of programming, this person can begin the "Must See" experience at 8:51 P.M. and still finish viewing by 11 P.M.

For consumers to realize they have beaten the system is the most empowering of all acts. In this sense, TiVo is a virtual time machine because it *gives* consumers back the one thing they need more than anything else: time. The consumer in our example gained almost an extra hour—enough time to talk to your spouse, sit down with the kids to help them with their homework, or watch more—prerecorded—commercial-free TV.

TiVo didn't teach its consumers about its own best feature. Consumers figured it out themselves and then took pride in sharing it with their peers, mostly via the Web.

Farewell TiVo: We Hardly Knew Ye

TiVo could conceivably end up being owned by Apple, Google, Comcast (the street seemed to like the distribution partnership announced in March 2005, which resulted in TiVo's stock soaring by 75 percent in a single day), or a host of salivating suitors. One thing, however, is certain: Whether it continues to beat to its own drum or is absorbed into the belly of a host of beasts, it will have left its mark.

While I love the brand to death and have already added a provision to my will that I wish to be buried with my TiVo box, I think this company has done a lousy job of marketing (as you'll see shortly) and just cannot survive in a market where a powerful few (Time Warner, Comcast, Cablevision, etc.) dictate the terms of the industry. TiVo's decision to introduce "fast-forward banner ads" (that's right, banners à la the Internet, which is sooo 1994) has been greeted with both boos and whatevers. This seems like a short-term fix for a longer-term survival problem, but the average TiVo user will make peace with it, especially if it keeps the company in business. More meaningful is the TiVoToGo™ service that will allow consumers to transfer their TiVo recordings to DVD or their PC.

Ominously for consumers, there are rumblings from Washington to rework HR 2391 (the Intellectual Property Protection Act) and HR 4077 (the Piracy Deterrence and Education Act), which would essentially rewrite copyright law in favor of Hollywood and the record companies, setting back the fair use doctrine to the Middle Ages and proving to us all that special-interest groups really don't exert any pressure on our elected officials. Right.

Legislation to make ad skipping illegal should tell us that we're doing something wrong. As the level-headed senator from Arizona, John McCain, commented, "Americans have been recording TV shows and fast-forwarding through commercials for 30 years. Do we really expect to throw people in jail in 2004 for behavior they've been engaged in for more than a quarter century?" Or we could just do a better job of creating communications that don't scream "*Skip me!*" at consumers.

TiVo has become the standard of the DVR category and is without question a consumers' darling. Not since the introduction of MTV have consumers so emphatically demanded a brand of media. And while MTV changed certain elements of pop culture, TiVo seemed to change the entire landscape. If you're a TiVo user, then you're nodding your head right now in agreement that once you went TiVo, there was no going back.

And yet TiVo is an anomaly. For all the passion and loyalty it generates among its consumer base, the most significant innovation in television history since the television itself has failed to make an indelible mark on the masses. Why?

For starters, some hold that the price point is still way too high for Joe and Jane Public. There are two components to TiVo's pricing: the up-front chunk, which will no doubt continue to drop, and the monthly fee, which is marginal and certainly comparable to the cost of VOD or a premium movie rental.

Perhaps it's not so much the price itself as the incremental cost that puts people off. Anyone checked their cable bill lately? Mine is close to $200 a month (no porn, I assure you). There's also the "box overload" phenomenon, whereby a typical media cabinet nowadays looks more like the screen of an amateur playing Tetris than a home entertainment center.

Beyond these factors, the consensus is that there's a pretty deep-seated inertia that the average consumer must overcome in adopting a new technology like TiVo. The simple switch-on/switch-channel/switch-off triad of the prototypical remote control explodes with a variety of choices that consumers often perceive as too complicated.

These factors would be sufficient to explain TiVo's relative lack of success (and I stress *relative*). But I think there is an additional reason: The company's marketing sucks. Initially, they pursued the most traditional routes of advertising—using television! That's like placing an ad in the in-flight magazine on a prop plane with the message that there's a safer way to fly.

Furthermore, the consumer insight (predicated on an agency team that didn't understand either the technology or the resultant consumer proposition) was all wrong. For the life of me I have wondered why TiVo's many agencies or the marketing genii at head office couldn't figure out that insight instead of using the very rotten commoditized 30-seconds to present an exaggerated unrealistic scenario of a man who has to pause a football game at the death before a vital penalty kick in order to dash to church to pray that the kick is converted. Ironically, sport is the one category that is fairly TiVo-proof. Instead of TV, TiVo should have been investing in a mix of experiential marketing and customer relationship management (CRM)—offering training, on-site installation, in-store workshops, and other simple techniques aimed at overcoming consumer inertia, technophobia, and confusion.

Perhaps the most egregious mistake was that TiVo underestimated its audience, and in doing so, took advantage of their loyalty. Recognizing that TiVo converts were deeply passionate, the company offered dollars-off discounts for qualified referrals from its existing customer base: "We know how much you love your TiVo, now share the love by telling everyone about it." The problem was that they offered nothing in return. No monthly incentive. No discount off a second TiVo box. No trade-in. Nothing. How greedy.

As much as I love TiVo, I just cannot imagine that they will be able to withstand the pressures of the exponentially consolidating media landscape, especially with the cable MSOs starting to resemble Audrey II, from *Little Shop of Horrors,* on a bad day.

The Point of No Return

The ability to time-shift and thereby turn prime time into my time could have irreparable consequences for the business model that powers the 30-second commercial. For starters, if people are watching at different times of the day or different days of the week, how are they being measured and to what extent are they being undercounted?

That's one good way that TiVo can come to the rescue of the ailing network model: by providing the ability to perform this kind of measurement. The bad and the ugly sides of this capacity are a lot more ominous, however. It won't be long before marketers are measuring precisely what was *potentially* viewed (traditional definition of *reach*) and what was *actually* skipped (new marketing definition of *connect*). In fact, this kind of precise measurement and accurate reporting are available today—and TiVo can produce it. That's how we can determine that Janet Jackson's "wardrobe malfunction" at the 2004 Super Bowl was the most replayed moment in TiVo history.

When this happens, how do you think television commercials will be priced? Cost per thousand (CPM), as they are now, or cost per view (CPV)? If I'm a marketer, I'm absolutely going to insist on paying for completed views or calculate some prorated cost for partial views. In other words, a network or cable station will not be penalized for creative that isn't capable of holding a viewer's attention, and a marketer should simply not have to pay for a commercial that essentially never aired.

This is a situation that could make Pandora want to climb into her own box, but it's the reality of doing business in a media world infused with technology.

The good news is that it is conceivable that rates would be boosted by "adjusted inventory" from adding back time-shifting viewers reconciled with the universe of total available or potential impressions. According to CBS's David Poltrack, the addition of time-shifting viewers to a show's live audience would nearly double the ratings for most of the top 20 network series! However, there is no way that this adjustment could make up for the lost revenue from the plethora of impressions that will simply be skipped completely.

Implications for Marketers: Is It Time to Join the Foreign Legion?

Here are five glass-half-empty realities of life in a TiVo- and DVR-led world. They are offered less as a prescriptive guide to help you deploy more efficiently and more as a reality check.

1. If you thought telling a story in 30 seconds was hard, try 3 seconds.

The tried-and-true formula of storytelling in 30 seconds has become tired and blue. The 30-second commercial is now really a story in three chapters: the first 3 seconds, the last 3 seconds, and the 24 seconds in between. The 3-second bookends (and I feel I'm being really liberal here) are about all the time that a brand has to get its proverbial foot in the door of a consumer's attention span.

Another variable that influences the likelihood that a given commercial will even be considered by a consumer is its position in the pod. In the past, the first and last positions in any pod were considered choice. Now, however, the first 3 seconds of the first commercial in a pod and the final 3 seconds of the last commercial in a pod are of paramount interest. These positions function as the bridges between content and commercials, and everything in between risks being a casualty of apathy and/or the skip button.

2. Messaging will have to change to get a foot in the door.

What does this mean for those trusted with creating 30-second commercials? For starters, the creative will need to factor in the first and last few seconds of a commercial. Intentionally ambiguous introductions intended to stimulate intrigue or raise curiosity may disappear entirely. This window of opportunity to deliver an unexpected payoff will require serious tweaking to avoid being skipped.

Likewise, the standard end treatment of commercials will need to be analyzed and addressed as well. The typical fade to black that highlights a logo, tagline, 800 number, and/or web site may not be enough without providing viewers with some reason to rewind in the form of a cliffhanger or a call to action.

Position in the pod will influence success in a DVR-led world as well, and this is yet another case where media and creative will need to work closely together to maximize their chances of success.

3. Advertisers may have to start advertising their advertising.

We've left the comforting shores of the sublime and arrived in the promised land of the ridiculous . . . and it remains to be seen who gets the last laugh.

The stakes—relevance, creativity, and engagement—have never been higher. Where and when advertising succeeds, it will be well received and sought after. However, in most cases, agencies will have to work a lot harder to get consumers to give a damn. A new Nike commercial or a world premiere of a new U2 song in an iPod ad may entice consumers to do the ultimate flip-flop and tune in just to see a commercial, even if they are not tuning in for content at that time. Offering a free iTunes download, for example, to the first thousand people to key in a code released exclusively in a new commercial would add a new and interesting dimension to the mix.

4. Consumers will continue to abandon network providers and the quality of content will continue to deteriorate, leading more consumers to flee, which in

turn will result in further content decay, continuing in a downward spiral.

The business model that is implicitly content-endorsed or subsidized by the presence of commercials is being turned on its head. The domino effect has always been triggered by premium content, which attracts eyeballs and therefore increases demand from advertisers, leading to higher rates. Less advertiser revenue will mean less money to perpetuate Hollywood's lifestyle, unless of course the stars are willing to try out for the $1 million purse on the next *Survivor*.

    5. Abuse of product placement will continue (and get worse).

I'll discuss product placement in depth in Chapter 20, but for now I'll simply state that marketers need to rethink the nature of their communications and stop trying to cut corners by riding the coattails of content. This is like having a minister and a government official barge into your home and start dictating how you should raise your children. In other words, product placement within content is really not welcome.

But enough of the doom and gloom. It's time for the silver lining. Here are some glass-half-full opportunities for marketers as the industry moves forward.

Commercials Frozen in Time

If the fast-forward button is your worst enemy, then the pause button is your best friend.

    If live TV can be paused, then so can commercials. An unexpected twist on this capability is that it can make the 30-second spot into the means to a much deeper and more meaningful consumer experience. TiVo allows marketers to use the 30-second commercial as a launching pad for interactivity.

For example, viewers could be given the ability to request a brochure, enter a sweepstakes, or type in an e-mail address (nothing new to those in the digital space), or they could be offered interesting programming options such as the ability to record an upcoming program or even a commercial. Intel's Blue Man Group productions and Mitsubishi's "See What Happens" chronicles would lend themselves to this. (Remember when I said that advertisers may have to advertise their advertising?)

The ability to freeze commercials and use the 30-second as a portal (Carat's David Verklin would refer to this as "coralling") to a much larger experience will ultimately lead to . . .

The 300-, 3,000-, and 30,000-Second Television Commercials

For too long, marketers have been subject to artificial and contrived 30-second constraints. On-demand viewing—whether through a DVR device or, more likely, a cable or satellite provider—will enable unlimited viewing of brand-endorsed or integrated commercial content. Some of this viewing could even be conditional on a purchase, the way Pepsi used a unique code on its soda containers that allowed consumers to view a worldwide exclusive of a Britney Spears video (instead of that lame iTunes promotion).

Nonlinear Viewing

The advent of "My Time"—viewer control over what is watched when—represents a direct threat to Madison Avenue (or at least to the network providers who prostrate themselves at the feet of those who call Mad Avenue home)—but it could also prove to be an indirect opportunity for the marketing community.

Borrowing a page from the mighty Amazon, the notion of "1-Click Tune In" could revolutionize the way consumers plan for and watch television content. It is passé to regard viewing as a premeditated and linear activity; instead, it is quickly morphing into as much of an impulse experience as it is a planned one. The new technologies allow consumers to find their own balance between on-demand and appointment consumption.

Addressable or personal networks will replace the antiquated "Must See TV" proposition, and consumers will be able to build their own programming based on their needs, beliefs, tastes, and preferences. They will likewise benefit from the ability to share and swap selections with others who are similarly inclined.

Here's an example of how this works: A TiVo Showcase for BMW shows a 2- or 3-minute introduction to a new Beamer model with several related links. One link is to a program titled *Legends of Motorsport and Motorweek,* and another gives the viewer the opportunity to record a 19-minute

---

A few years ago I was home early from work. Back in the days when I actually cared about my stocks, I switched on CNBC and watched an incredibly interesting clip about Martha Stewart. This was at the very beginnings of her unfortunate ImClone dealings. The clip in question was all about companies or brands that base themselves on a person or personality and how that could ultimately harm the company's equity in the case of scandal or negative publicity.

One example given was Steve Madden: while the CEO of the publicly listed shoe company was up to his soles in prosecution for stock fraud, sales of his shoes didn't seem to be affected.

Martha Stewart was thought to be slightly different, as her entire empire was essentially built around her retouched facade, which was thought to be not such a good thing by the brand gurus.

The point of this anecdote is that if I hadn't been home from work early that day I would have missed something pretty relevant for my line of work, and this got me to thinking . . . why miss it at all?

infomercial/demo of the new car, including an extensive review and "inside look" at the vehicle. This demo appears on some obscure channel at 4 A.M. The upshot is that the viewer goes to sleep and wakes up the next morning to find the requested program waiting on the TiVo menu.

Thus, brands can create entire slots, segments, or shows; purchase 30 minutes of airtime on a lesser-known channel at an undesirable time like 3 A.M., and then, using the TiVo link, enable the consumer to automatically record it on demand. I call this *mail-order programming,* and I thoroughly recommend it as an instant cure for the prime-time blues.

The Digitization of Media

What we, knowingly or unknowingly, are witnessing is the complete digitization of media. In the on-demand television world, consumers will soon be able to access pretty much all imaginable content, past and present, all the time. Content will be digitally archived and retrievable by using a series of filters, rules, and search tools. Missing a program (content) will no longer be an issue, and consumption attrition can be managed by advertisers who surround their brands with and inject them into sought-after content.

The following companies may soon be key players in television's digital revolution:

- DoubleClick, third-party "adservers" to the digitally inclined, may soon store, serve, and measure the delivery of your commercials. (You've been served.)
- Advertising.com will dynamically optimize the dispersion and distribution of ads across the 1,000 channels of content based on their "completion" rates (or their propensity to be viewed in entirety).
- Google will power the search functionality of user experiences from TiVo to DirecTV set-top boxes and satellites.
- Microsoft will produce one box to rule them all. (This is already a reality with the introduction of their

Windows Media Center, which—like TiVo and other competitors—attempts to consolidate music, pictures, video, and television content into one screen or interface.)

The next point is not for the squeamish.

Advertising on Demand

Advertising on demand (AOD) is the Grand Poo-Bah. It's the future of advertising, and it suggests a very healthy life for advertising after the inevitable death of the 30-second. I have considered starting a business in this area, and if there are any venture capitalists out there with too much time or money on their hands, they should give me a call.

If you begin with the premise that *given the choice, consumers will actively choose to ignore or skip commercials,* then I believe you are in the best possible starting place. Some marketers and clients believe that advertising is a *right* and that consumers have an obligation to watch it as an expression of gratitude for the content it delivers. Advertising is *not* a right; it is a necessary evil, and our sole mission in this profession is to make our advertising bearable and somewhat appealing. Occasionally, we actually delight consumers, but such times are few and far between.

Jamie Kellner, chairman and CEO of ACME Communications and former founder, chairman and CEO of the WB network is one of those who believe that consumers are spoiled and shortsighted and that it is the duty of viewers to watch commercials. And if ads as they now exist stop working, he calculated that viewers could pay roughly $250 per year, over and above cable and satellite fees. (Uh, isn't that what TiVo is for?)

Kellner's whining focuses on the problem but not the solution. Here's where I take some inspiration from the Golf Channel. I wonder what percentage of commercials are skipped on the Golf Channel relative to the American Broadcasting Corporation? The answer comes down unquestionably in favor of spoiling a good walk, and the reason is contextual relevance. This is what the focused-niche cable

Davids have, and it is what the monolithic network Goliaths have not.

But things might not always be this way. Let's assume there are 20 minutes of commercials per hour of programming. What if 10 or 15 of those minutes could be customized by individual viewers or households?

- What if consumers could preselect specific categories of interest or hobbies, such as outdoor living or music?
- What if they could elect to see ads for certain products or services that they were interested in purchasing, such as cars or home refinancing?
- What if they could use this option to deal with emotional issues such as needing a vacation or finding a gift for a spouse's birthday?
- What if they felt comfortable seeking more information about personal products such as Viagra or wanted specific information on a tech product from Dell?

What if some or all of these conditions could be combined to preselect and organize a hierarchy of commercials that were essentially tailor-made to a viewer's specific needs and demands?

Advertising on demand could be initiated or managed via the remote control, a wireless device, the Web, or even automatically. Companies like Visible World are using algorithms that assess viewing patterns to predetermine which household members will be watching at any given time, so it is entirely plausible that commercial consumption itself will help evolve the quality and mix of advertising. *Commercial intelligence* (CI) — there's an idea for a start-up company.

Now I understand your objection: People don't always know what they want, and AOD presupposes a minimum state of awareness and even some interest (much like search). That's why I specified 10 or 15 out of the 20-minute allotment for commercials. The pre-awareness state will always be a prerequisite for messaging.

The question is whether consumers will care enough to

participate. This is a good question. The answer is that if they don't, then what they will receive will be the status quo. I wager that consumers will take to AOD because it represents a better value proposition. They know it, and you do, too.

Brought to You in Part . . . II

Another form of AOD is a twist on the classic sponsorship of content ("brought to you in part") involving self-selection. A viewer would be given a menu of three or four brands from which to select one they would like to sponsor their commercial-free episode of a particular TV show—there would be four brand impressions, but only the one picked would be charged. Thus, the three other brands get bonus impressions, and the one chosen gets the real value impression because it was picked by the viewer, who is more likely now to view it. Isn't that worth more to a brand? Doesn't it supply the ultimate motivation for creative directors to produce commercials that are desired?

You can see where all this might lead and how technology might play the ultimate transforming role in resurrecting the ailing advertising industry. (*Note to marketers:* It's your money, so you need to challenge your partners—and yourselves—to use the technology that's available to reverse the decay.)

THE DVD

The Family Guy disappeared from prime time a few years ago, seemingly never to be seen again. That is, until a million DVD copies of the first 28 episodes flew off the shelves, making it the top-selling TV show DVD of the year and the fourth-highest selling of all time. It also prompted a media first: The network in question (FOX) decided to bring the canceled show back to prime-time television.

How could the network have missed this? What does this mean for a business model that is already under so much stress?

This fault runs through the bedrock of the TV model: the difference between potential and actual reach. *The Family Guy's* ratings were always a best guesstimate of the number of people who supposedly watched the show but it didn't reflect on the quality and loyalty of that audience. The DVD sales, conversely, were a direct reflection of hand raisers—a statement of interest and intent based on actual purchases. No doubt this is connected to the power of communal marketing (see Chapter 16), although in this case it was not being used proactively but reactively.

The series *John Doe,* on the other hand, seemed to get better with every episode, climaxing in the season finale when John's best friend was revealed to be his archrival. However, we never got to find out what happened next because the season finale became the series finale (without the network bothering to tell anyone in advance).

I Googled my way through the Web to get a sense of how this network stupidity was received. Here's one snippet:

> July 20, 2003: Save John Doe Petition
> John Doe Cancelled :-(
> In case you watch "reality" tv shows and have no soul You can skip this.
> Ok, thinkers and fans of John Doe. I have discovered that John Doe has indeed been cancelled by Fox. However there is a strong following of the show and there is hope if the community speaks out they could bring it back.
> If you enjoyed the show as much as I did then please sign the petition and or write/email the folks at Fox.
> FOX~
> Gail Berman-
> President, Entertainment
> Fox Broadcasting
> 10201 W. Pico Blvd.
> Los Angeles, CA 90035
> Sandy Grushow-President, FOX Television

Fox Broadcasting Company,
P.O. Box 900,
Beverly Hills, CA 90213
E-mail:
stevenm@fox.com
iveyv@fox.com
stevefe@fox.com

The petition contained 11,377 signatures at the time. No, not 14 million potential viewers based on a diary sample, but 11,377 passionate people who represent another sample—one much more vocal and powerful than the average collection of button-pushing couch potatoes. And this is just one virtual assembly; how many others just like it are out there, too?

Masterpieces like *Sports Night* join *Family Guy* on the cancellation scrap heap, as do series with cult followings, such as *Once and Again*.

The networks have too long ignored (at their peril) these pockets of passionate consumers in favor of the bland periphery. It took the DVD to uncover their ongoing lapse in judgment.

Be Afraid, Very Afraid, of the DVD

The average length of time (media consumption) spent watching DVDs is 3.2 hours per week (according to In-Stat/MDR 2004), which is the equivalent of about two DVDs per week and 3.2 fewer hours to watch television. "Prepackaged content" was ranked the third-largest threat to TV advertising by a sample of television and advertising industry professionals (behind DVRs and the proliferation of cable channels).

There is an intense compression occurring right now between the first release of a movie or television program and mass distribution of it via DVD. This time differential is shrinking exponentially.

In an increasing number of cases, the DVD outsells the theatrical release, and at $20 a pop, it's easy to see why—a whole family can watch a movie for the price of just a couple of theater tickets.

The DVD represents the ultimate risk-free trial of entertainment content. In the case of *Family Guy* and *Sports Night*, consumers get to experience some of the best programs that nobody seemed to watch.

Despite consistently glowing reviews for such shows, we advertisers opt to believe Nielsen. Why are we so surprised that Nielsen's methodology often undercounts or misrepresents the viewership for concepts with intelligent and superior writing? Thank the network gods that *Arrested Development* was spared being consigned to similar obscurity.

There are other examples in which the DVD represents the new world order of empowered consumers:

- Consumers avoid the risk associated with becoming involved in a series only to see it canceled.
- They get to watch the series on their terms—be it all episodes in sequence or 15 minutes at a time.
- There are oodles of extra clips, commentary, and supplementary content.
- You guessed it—no ads.

The Ultimate Convergence

The time between original release and DVD will eventually shrink to the point where cinema releases; Internet downloads; on-demand television; aircraft, hotel, and wireless ordering; and DVD purchases will all be available at the same time or, perhaps more realistically, just a few weeks apart.

Attention, Marketers: What You Can Learn from the DVD

The DVD is showing you the future as plain as day. Now open your eyes!

The DVD tells you that consumers don't like commercials. Okay, we know that already. It is also telling you that consumers like outtakes, alternative endings, interviews, and director's cuts. So why not create your next advertising campaign with the same content?

- Who wouldn't like to see the outtakes from the American Express Seinfeld-Superman Chronicles?
- Who wouldn't enjoy watching the "making of" any of the Nike commercials?
- Who wouldn't want to Pytka (as in advertising director, Joe Pytka) the brain of the director responsible for all those pioneering IBM ads?

This is on-demand!

In the television space, look for the compression of time between first look and rerun to create several new opportunities. Programs will be available on demand (perhaps at a premium) pretty much the moment they complete their first run. Time Warner has already announced that viewers will be able to "rewind to the beginning" shows already in progress. Missed the latest episode of *The Swan?* Fear not, it will be available for the next seven days at a nominal cost—and perhaps the nominal cost is the "endorsement" sponsorship model. (How much would you pay to put your message in front of the *right* people—especially if they select you? Start thinking and do the math. It's time.)

On the brighter side, it is encouraging to see the way the broadcast networks and cable brands are using DVDs—in supermarkets, in magazines, or via the Web—to help promote their new seasons and bring new viewers into the picture.

A Thousand Days to an On-Demand Content Economy

Rishad Tobaccowala, President, Starcom
MediaVest Group

Today, half of U.S. households have broadband access. That means more than 100 million people retrieve content pages (billions), download songs (millions), watch videos (hundreds of thousands), and play games (tens of thousands) . . . whenever they want. Nearly 22 million homes access movies and other video content thanks to video on demand. DVRs, the first 3G phones, and a plethora of other devices give millions more the equivalent of an on-demand experience.

By 2008, on demand will be the mode of choice for most U.S. households. The technology will be simpler. The digital rights will be better managed. The costs will be low and plummeting—driven by Darwinian competition. Content will be delivered by servers and databases all over the world to a multitude of screens previously known only as the television, computer monitor, and phone.

What does this mean for marketers and media?

Empowered Era

Predicting the future is a foolhardy venture, especially in an arena where much technology and legislation is still to be revealed. Six years ago the words iPod, Google, and TiVo did not exist. Today they are part of the mainstream vernacular—profoundly changing the music, Internet, and television landscape.

Google, TiVo and iPod empower the end user to retrieve, navigate, and manipulate content, and to do so in ways that are aligned with his or her passions and interests. In this new relationship, the consumer chooses if, when, and how to interact with the content. The manufacturers, distributors, advertisers, and publishers can no longer dictate these experiences. They can only search for new ways to give the end user "godlike power" over his or her environment.

The Environment in 2008

Explore the current broadband society residing in nations like the United States and South Korea, and the future is revealed. Here's a peek at the future.

1. *The end of distribution windows:* It's 2008, and a new movie is opening. In this world, the content hits all channels simultaneously. This satisfies the global demand for content. It is also, by the way, the only sure defense against piracy.
2. *"The rise of the long tail":* Today, the sales at analog entertainment retail stores (Blockbuster, Virgin, etc.) are primarily driven by recent hits and blockbusters. The picture is quite different, however, at places like Netflix or Rhapsody (which provide access to 25,000-plus movie titles and nearly a million on-demand songs, respectively). Inside these digital stores, where a customer can browse huge libraries of content from the comfort of home, niche, classic, and old titles comprise nearly half of all sales. As more customers gain access to online options, (which, by the way, provide search and recommendation engines), content will enjoy a longer shelf life, and purchasers will make decisions based on their unique passions. And just to make it interesting, some of the content will be created by users who share photos, videos, and music mixes with others in their community.
3. *Conquer navigation, conquer the world:* As more and more content becomes accessible on demand, navigating through it becomes more challenging. While search engines provide one path through the content jungles, there are other surprising compasses. Advertising, done well and targeted keenly, can point the way. Brands are a highly effective navigation tool. Word of mouth may be the supreme, eternal navigational tool, leading a consumer quickly to pre-endorsed content locations.
4. *The rise of relevance and fall of exposure:* People don't want to be interrupted with irrelevant content. Blasting messages in consumer-controlled environments doesn't work now, and it won't work in 2008. The only brands getting through will be the ones whose makers figure out the engagement factor. They will mine deep insights and craft carefully tailored messages

that they deliver through carefully selected channels with painstaking attention to timing.

5. *Malleable content:* Analog content has tended to be defined by medium, length, or device. Digital demand content has no such restrictions. It will skip across devices in different forms so sports fans can watch a game on ESPN, see a highlight on broadband Internet, and get scores updated on their mobile phones. How to insert a marketing message into this environment? Carefully.

6. *Consumers as content creators and programmers:* Web logs (blogs) will give rise to independent content-serving companies. In an on-demand world with declining bandwidth and storage costs, there may be new content players—including consumers themselves (see Chapter 17).

The Rise of Marketing

Many marketers panic when faced with an on-demand world. They should not unless they believe that consumers do not want relevant information and products that meet their needs. The on-demand environment allows marketers to better identify and meet the needs of the consumer, and to better target, create, and measure communications. Here is why.

1. *Better targeting and insights:* A person's content behavior in an on-demand world will often reveal his or her interests and passions, which will allow marketers to gain better insights and find new, engaging venues.

2. *Marketers as content and service providers:* Marketers have vast amounts of relevant and valuable information regarding their industries, products, and services. This is vital information for interested consumers who are making purchase decisions. On demand closes the gap between the two.

3. *New forms and economics of value exchange:* Marketers have traditionally underwritten content in exchange for consumers' attention. But intrusion isn't going to work with the empowered consumer. While the cost of engaging consumers will rise, the

investment will yield a higher return with far fewer dollars wasted on ineffective efforts. How to buy engagement? The possibilities are endless, and might start with music, movies, and content-creation tools.

4. *Holistic and virtual marketing:* People will not live only in the digital world. At times, even their digital consumption (e.g., downloading music) will occur in place-based locations such as next-generation music stores. The intelligence we gain from on-demand behavior will inform the other marketing components, including content like live news, sportscasts, and reality shows.

Moving Forward

Change is inevitable, and will be as long as human beings stay attracted to power and control. The best marketers accept this. They seek to meet the needs of consumers as opposed to controlling them.

We have nothing to lose but our fears. And on the other side of fear is invention.

14

Experiential Marketing

Experiential marketing is the very antithesis of the 30-second commercial, and by virtue of its stature, it very much deserves to be in a book about alternatives to traditional marketing.

Experiential marketing is oftentimes synonymous with event marketing, but to limit it to that would be a grave injustice. It is at times the holistic intersection between brand and event marketing and, on another level, the evolution of brand marketing altogether. Experiential marketing is one of the new tools in the alternative toolbox—one more weapon in the fight against clutter—categorize it alongside the Internet, new music formats, and long-form content (to name a few). I would take this one step further and contend that experiential is the *only* option to marketers today—at least those who base their business on brands.

Brands have become ends unto themselves rather than means to an end—that end being some kind of an internalized and personalized consumer experience. The term *contextual relevancy* is the key in any discussion about the role that brands play and the value they bring to the table.

In some ways, experiential marketing is the logical extension of marketing as we used to know it. The old marketing formula predicated itself on the ability to talk *at* people, whereas the new marketing approach centers around—and prides itself on—the ability to walk and talk *with* people—be they suspects, prospects, customers, clients, or loyalists.

Event Marketing

Event marketing is in actuality a subset of experiential marketing. It is the nontechnological or "offline" expression of the ability to involve. This is becoming one of the hottest touch points today, offering to consumers a tangible and sustainable experience. Where once a series of messages (or promises) was used, marketers now have the ability to demonstrate the promise, to make good on it, and thus to deliver the goods.

Though similar, event marketing is not quite the same thing as experiential marketing. There are certain times when events do not constitute experiences—for example, sales events or gatherings that are not strategic, are not tied to any form of sustained messaging or brand value or expressions, and are not differentiated or consistent with previous initiatives. I'm, of course, making a pretty obvious play for why "keepers of the brand" have a right to sit at the event table—particularly if they have the means to help transform an event into an experience.

Take Chrysler's partnership with Celine Dion, which seemed doomed from the start. This marriage was not successful, but I wonder how much work really went into making it an experience to remember. The automotive category plays an important role in family life, but somehow this campaign didn't convey that. The disconnect between the singer and the intended audience was cited as one of the many reasons for the failure, but arguably the real reason was the inability to capitalize on an idea. The Celine Dion fiasco was all about advertising, when the opportunity to deliver an *experience* was practically presented on a silver platter.

We look back at the dismal sales of the Pacifica model and deem Chrysler's marketing efforts a failure. Correct description, but incorrect assessment of the reasons for this failure. Did new car owners get a limited-edition Celine Dion CD (perhaps even autographed)? Did they get two tickets to the Chrysler-sponsored Celine Dion concert in Las Vegas? Did they enter a very elite competition to have a romantic dinner for two at their home with a private performance by the Canadian diva?

DEHYDRATED EXPERIENCE, JUST ADD BRAND

It's a lot easier to execute against an experience—event-driven or otherwise—when it is identified as such. In the case of Jeep (another Chrysler brand), BBDO helped create an experience that, on a strategic level, was bang on target for the brand and the type of consumer who would likely want to own and drive one. Part of the Jeep advertising code is that the car must always be shown off-road. In a recent departure, a campaign showed the Jeep in a suburban situation, but it was covered with dirt, revealing its heritage.

This is all good . . . but, realistically, the best it could ever be is a snapshot of the aspirational qualities and benefits of buying a Jeep. Isn't a better way to bring this promise to life through reproducing a live Jeep experience?

Enter the *Jeep Experience,* a bimonthly magazine that markets the experience. Other consumer experiences included the Jeep Jamboree, Jeep games on Yahoo!, and my personal favorite, Camp Jeep (see Figure 14.1).

The campaign was masterminded by Gary Topolewski, BBDO Detroit's chief creative officer, and he summarized the philosophy behind it: "If a picture is worth 1,000 words, then experiencing the vehicle is worth 1,000 pictures." I

Figure 14.1   Jeep's Experimental Marketing Panacea. *Courtesy:* DaimlerChrysler, BBDO, Detroit.

think this captures the promise of experiential marketing to perfection.

When I was at TBWA\Chiat\Day, I came up with an idea for our then stumbling client, Kmart. I share it with you in this book with pride and without shame for two reasons:

1. I still think it's a great idea.
2. It never saw the light of day because it never got in front of the client.

To set the context: The discount retail category is fascinating. There are many players in the market, but I'll focus on three in particular: Wal-Mart (the ubiquitous giant, aka the Antichrist); Target (a thorn that quite brilliantly repositioned itself as a rose, coining the phrase "cheap chic"); and Kmart (sentenced to a "living" hell in a schizophrenic purgatory of a nonwinnable price and quality war with the aforementioned players).

Back then, whenever I suggested the Web as an alternative mode of communication, I was told how the average Kmart customers would never figure out the whole PC/Internet thing-amabob.

This got me to thinking. Inspired by Robert Kennedy's exhortation to see things that weren't and ask "why not?" I came up with a hybrid cause and experiential marketing solution that aimed to rectify the MRI numbers suggesting that not enough Kmart shoppers paid attention to the Internet. Similar to the concept of in-store real estate being dedicated to fast food (McDonald's, Dunkin' Donuts, et al.), my plan was to create a section dedicated solely to empowering moms to embrace the Web, maximize the possibilities and benefits it makes available, and even connect with their kids by better understanding how they use the Net.

The insights behind this concept were twofold:

1. There is a digital divide between kids, who have grown up with the Internet, and their parents, who are virtual strangers to the technology.
2. Parents have a critical responsibility to be aware of the dangers kids may encounter when using the Web.

The proposed Cyber Kafe would naturally sell computers, accessories, Internet subscriptions, and additional services, but more fundamentally it would be dedicated to providing a service to Kmart's customers—doing its part to "wire America." In addition, guest lectures and presentations on topics such as "countering spam" and "how to protect your kids from degenerates online" would be scheduled throughout the week. This alone would help drive store traffic and make a visit to Kmart something to look forward to.

But it didn't stop there. By joining a loyalty program, shoppers could earn points that they could exchange for one-on-one instructor time to further tutor, train, and educate them.

Come to think of it, this would have been a pretty obvious cross-marketing tie-in with a certain slumbering Internet service provider, who likewise opted for a series of ads rather than experiences. Come on AOL, get it done with the new hybrid Sears, Kmart, or whatever they're calling it nowadays.

Branded Experiences

Oprah's car giveaway (more on this in Chapter 20, on branded entertainment) is a perfect example of experiential marketing—certainly for those who received a car in exchange for attending a taping of *Oprah*, definitely for GM's Pontiac, but also for all those invited to share the experience. Was it worth $7.7 million? That's another story.

One company that opted for the experience quotient was arguably the most unlikely candidate of them all: Amazon.com, the company that pioneered 1-Click ordering and the classic e-tailer that knows a thing or two about the art and science of "conversion." The holiday season 2004 launch of Amazon.com Theater premiered on a "network" with an audience of 32 million registered consumers (according to the Minneapolis–St. Paul *Business Journal*, November 2004)—their own. I'll return to this example later, as it leverages most of the new marketing approaches mentioned in this book, but for now let's focus on the experiential variable in the equation.

This series of five short films included the recognized brand names of Chris Noth, Minnie Driver, and Darryl Hannah, and the directorial prowess of Tony and Ridley Scott. There is a fine line between genius and madness; likewise there is a rather subtle dividing line between "huh?" and "a-ha!" Amazon's tactic was no different to a "Santa's Grotto" booth, book reading, or in-house Starbucks. While some people prefer to get-in get-out get-on with life, others prefer to linger. Amazon catered to both.

Would you be surprised if I told you Fallon Worldwide, the agency behind BMW Films, was also responsible for Amazon.com Theater? You probably shouldn't be. Fallon is a shining light for the rest of the agency world to follow. According to Fallon's chief marketing officer:

> What we want is to get millions of people in a busy frame of mind to stop, pause and be left with a good entertainment impression and be enlightened to everything available at Amazon. When people go the extra step to get involved with a piece of entertainment or communication and have a good experience, they will keep coming back for more.

Although this statement is strategically sound, tactically there were too many loose ends that needed to be tied together for this marketing effort to be considered completely successful. The product placement tied to Amazon's e-commerce engine (which I believe was the whole point of the exercise) seemed contrived and tangential, and the almost inconspicuous Chase logo at the bottom of the viewing screen prompts me to ask, How much did *they* pay for their "special thanks." Nevertheless, this was a good example of experiential marketing — I only hope the Amazon.com execs will see it that way when they evaluate the ROI. That said, there was no paid media component (read: old marketing) and according to reports, traffic doubled to the site, and that can only be good for business. (See Chapter 16, "Communal Marketing.")

For the most part, agencies are just not structured to deliver against an event-led experiential scheme — not unless it involves a bucketful of 30-second spots to help sell it. Fallon had a useful case study under its belt to apply to similar undertakings. (This might be why BBDO snatched David Lubars from Fallon.) So take this as a rather blunt call to action: If you aren't geared to conceptualize, develop, and implement experiential solutions, you're buying a one-way ticket to oblivion — or you could just hire a creative director who has recently been initiated into new marketing and hope for the best.

HYPE: The Brand Experience as Product Showroom, or How We Built an Art Escalator to HP

Chris Aldhous, European Creative Director for
Hewlett-Packard, Publicis London

HYPE was going to be a press ad. That's what the brief asked for. That's what the client expected. So there was a sharp intake of breath at the first presentation when we said we didn't want to do a press ad. In fact we didn't even want to do advertising. Not in the conventional sense anyway. We had a better idea; we wanted to build an art gallery. A brand space, a product experience in brick and stone.

And it wouldn't be a run-of-the-mill art gallery. We wanted to open an art gallery that started off completely empty. We'd throw open the doors and usher our visitors into a totally blank space. No art on the walls. No movies showing in the film bunker. No content at all.

The opportunity we were looking for came along in the form of a brief for HP Imaging and Printing Products. What really got us excited was a client brave enough to say he didn't want short-term sales, he wanted a long-term predisposition to his products. We didn't have to deliver a sales spike in three months. It was our job to go out there and deep-seed some goodwill.

HP wanted to make an impact with the graphics audience and there was one particular part of that audience we thought it would be interesting to reach; the young artists and filmmakers who, if not exactly hostile to HP, certainly were indifferent.

So we had a clean slate. We could define the terms of the relationship. We could take the conversation out of all the traditional media and find a way to connect directly with them.

Context moved ahead of content. We wanted the right environment for our messages. So we moved over to the artist's side of town. We decamped to Brick Lane E1 and sat around in coffee shops reading arcane local self-publications like the *Shoreditch Twat.* Magazines photocopied and put together in the back rooms of pubs and clubs. A DIY culture of self-promotion.

HYPE seemed like a good word for it. And the fact it also contained the letters *H* and *P* was even better.

First we decided to hook up with a Mancunian multimedia artist called Moose. He introduced us to clean graffiti, a totally legal way to inscribe your message across the surface of the city. We did it on the steps of all the art colleges in London. We did it on the old corrugated metal beside the local coffee bars. On the wooden floors of obscure fashion shops.

HYPE became the word on the street. But that was all we said. No information. No explanation. Just HYPE. The word was good. We liked it because it was knowing. Sly, but somehow honest about itself and what it stood for.

And that's what we wanted. We wanted to be straight with this audience. But in a crooked sort of way. HYPE gave us that twist. Enough of an unexpected angle to intrigue them, but once you got past that crypticism, there was a simple idea waiting for you.

We wanted to give them the truth and proof of what HP had to offer.

HYPE might be what got their attention but HP would be there at the heart of the idea, proving its relevance to their artistic lives and ambitions. There was no dissonance between HYPE and HP. Both offered partnership, collaboration. Empowerment. We were just creating the right context in which to forge that connection.

We didn't want to make a big deal out of the corporate reveal, so the client agreed to no logos. The only branding would be on the technology. The HP badges that sit on the front of the printers and the side of the projectors.

The low-key approach worked spectacularly. In the exit interviews we did at the end of the exhibition, 19 out of 20 artists understood the HP connection to the HYPE project. Every one of them endorsed the idea, but more important, they started talking about how the HYPE experience had made them reconsider the relevancy of HP mainstream advertising.

HYPE had become a way into HP for a group of people who had never seen a reason to make that journey before. More than a passive, look-at-me brand space, HYPE was a corridor, a connector, an escalator. It carried people up to the front door of HP and we trusted that the legitimacy of the products to be in an art gallery, to help create the art that filled the gallery, would be sufficient to pull those people in.

The gallery was a transaction. Content would be the powerful persuader—because the content would be theirs. We were at the mercy of what they created. The quality of the communication message relied on the quality of the work they contributed.

Our message was simple: "Without you, HYPE is nothing."

The idea became passive, almost submissive. We surrendered control to the audience. The control freakery of the archetypal corporate big brand evaporated.

If no one turned up, the communication chain broke. And we would have a very large empty space in which to rewrite our CVs. There was no question this was high risk.

On January 22, 2004, at precisely 6 P.M., we threw open the doors to HYPE. People were waiting outside. More important, artists were waiting outside. Young artists with their work on digital files ready to hand the disc over to a HYPE technician and see their art roll off an HP Designjet 5500 in an immaculate 3 × 4 foot print that was then mounted and hung up on the wall of the gallery.

That first evening about 120 artists turned up with their images. The first digital films also arrived and we uploaded them to the projectors in the Film Bunker.

We'd synchronized the third phase of the hypegallery.com web site to go live at exactly the same time the Truman Brewery doors opened, so the online community could wander round a virtual version of the gallery and see its art at the same time.

Over the next four weeks HYPE spread around the world. The web site had 4.5 million hits with 90,000 unique users from 142 different countries; 2,500 pieces of digital art were uploaded to the site. In the East End of London, the physical space that was the HYPE Gallery had 1,193 artists submit their work.

And this is where another unique feature of HYPE came into operation: The Gallery refreshed its content three times. As soon as we had the first 400 pictures up and every frame was filled, we started taking the first submissions down, posting them online and putting up new artists' work (see Figures 14.2 and 14.3).

The idea proved a hit. In the four weeks of the exhibition, HYPE had 9,021 visitors. When we closed the gallery, we invited all the

Figure 14.2   Hype interior. *Courtesy:* Hewlett-Packard; Publicis, London.

contributing artists to return and collect their prints; 1,050 came back and took away their HP print sample. HP hadn't known what to expect at the outset, but the reaction to HYPE London spurred the company on to further commitments: HYPE Paris opened in November 2004 and attracted 32,000 visitors.

What was the secret to HYPE's success? It was simple: Everything linked together. All fed in and out of one another, carrying people from one channel of experience to the next. *Holistic* is a devalued word these days: It does the job of putting the matching-luggage mentality of *integrated* in its place. But we never felt it was adequate for HYPE. We tried transdimensional advertising.

The project picked up awards across the board. Interactive, integrated, direct marketing, precision marketing, new media, Web design.

We made 13 no-budget films to run in art house cinemas, every one of them directed by the sort of filmmakers we wanted to attract to HYPE. We evangelized the project round the London postproduction houses, and everyone helped out, donating editing and mixing time for free.

Again, we surrendered control of content. The directors were given the freedom to shoot whatever they wanted as long as it was inspired and titled with a word or phrase containing the letters *H* and *P.*

Figure 14.3   Hype interior 2. *Courtesy:* Hewlett-Packard; Publicis, London.

You can still see the films on the web site. Including *Hairy Pooches*. Or *Hedonistic Penguin*. Every film as inventive as HYPE. As inventive as HP. And the only information they carried was the hypegallery.com web address.

We applied the same principles to the art we commissioned for the flyers, postcards, and press ads that followed the clean graffiti campaign. We created a series of posters that used hypertag technology to interact with mobile phones and text opening details of the gallery. And wherever the work appeared we gave the artist a credit and printed their e-mail address. Radio, PR, and events worked just as hard.

All the time we had to remind ourselves: HYPE was going to be a press ad.

15

Long-Form Content

Eric Hirshberg, managing partner and executive creative director at Deutsch LA, recently said something profound, after which you could hear the sound of a penny dropping as the enormity of the epiphany sank in. (How's that for a setup?)

He was talking about the 30-second spot and said something to the effect that, "If I'm in the advertising business right now, I'm not as concerned as if I were in the network television business." What he meant was that as a creative director and agency executive, he'll be where the consumer is and where he's needed—he'll focus on the Bernbachian "how" to deliver the message, regardless of which medium is used to do so.

The advertising and television businesses have been willing (and sometimes unwilling) bedfellows thus far, and now that the 30-second is arguably no longer the star of the show, it has become clear that this relationship was mainly one of convenience.

As already mentioned, television never was the killer app—video was. Suddenly agencies have been emboldened to create stories that are not just functions of the time allotment, but of an *idea*. Frustrated copywriters who went into the advertising business because no producers would return their calls are now in the driver's seat—and are no longer frustrated.

Long-form content is the embodiment of "life after the 30-second spot," and it *will* save the advertising business.

BMW Films has become the gold standard for long-form content, but depending which side of the fence you sit on, you will view it as either the messiah or a false god. For one thing, it is not scalable, evidenced by the fact that BMW Films was not extended or "renewed" beyond a reduced "second season." And hiring a roster of Hollywood directors is cool, as is employing James Brown or Gary Oldman, but this is more ego play than brand imperative. From the standpoint of production values, BMW Films delivered the goods—from the quality of the programming to the "making of" and "driving techniques" segments—but it may have fallen victim to its own success, especially when the reductive assessment is along the lines of "But how many cars did it sell?"

Make no mistake, BMW Films was way ahead of its time (which is often the problem in such cases), and the dearth of quality programming (TV, Web, or otherwise) as a logical successor has led to somewhat of a void, which conveniently left BMW Films as the default king of long-form content. I've heard both endings to the story. Here is some of the anecdotal evidence about whether it worked:

- Jim McDowell, BMW's vice president of marketing, commented before the launch that if 1 million viewers logged on to watch the films, the campaign would be a "home run." Within two months of the launch, the company reported that more than 3 million visitors had watched at least one film.
- Over the course of the campaign, there were 13 million film views and 2 million registrants, with 1.2 million

opting in to receive more information from BMW via
e-mail (according to MarketingProfs.com).

- BMW Films launched in May of 2001. Coincidentally,
  BMW had its best May and June ever in terms of car
  sales, exceeding 40,000 vehicles, amid a turning economy (according to WebDev IQ).

One estimate, from Business 2.0, put the cost to produce
the films at a minimum of $14 million (not confirmed by
BMW). Using the estimate of 13 million film views, it is
likely that about 4 million unique consumers watched them
(i.e., some watched more than once), putting the cost per
view to BMW at $3.50 a head (versus a prime-time TV com-
mercial view of 13 cents). Keep in mind that a BMW Films
view was an actual view (compared to a potential view for a
30-second spot), and because viewers opted in or gave permission, it is also likely to have been a fully attentive,
engaged view. The 13¢ cost for prime-time TV is based on a
30-second commercial, versus the 7 minutes spent (on average) with Films, which really means we're comparing $3.50
to *at least* $5.46 (the 13¢ per 30-second spot multiplied by 14
spots to give you an equivalent time spent (7 minutes), then
multiplied by a conservative 3 to compensate for the two-
thirds of television viewers who never see the commercial
because they're on another channel, out of the room, or
focused elsewhere). This calculation does not factor in attentiveness or engagement, which would make the Films view
even more favorable against the 30-second spot.

BMW remained tight-lipped about whether it was able
to establish a direct link between sales and its films. And
unless it is possible to isolate and measure every contributing
factor—from media to marketing touch points, from promotions to point-of-sale, from word of mouth to local dealer
personal selling—it is at best inferential to attempt to reduce
the input of BMW Films and the output of sales to a direct
relationship.

That said, recall my earlier argument for applying a *net
present value to ideas*. The same applies to ROI. Put it this way:

In 7 to 10 years, thousands of Beamers will be sold to consumers whose first, and maybe most significant, impression of the brand came from BMW Films. How on this green earth can you put a price tag on that? At what point must we make a leap of faith and cease merely plodding along with certainty?

Ultimately, this comes down to a fundamental new marketing question about *qualitative reach:* Are you reaching the most people or the *right* people? In the case of BMW Films, according to BMW's Teller (of Penn & Teller), Jim McDowell let on that the median visitor was 31 years old and earned $91,000 a year. Furthermore, 50,000 visitors volunteered that they were thinking about buying a car. This brings up a third concept I'd like to plant in your noggins—the notion of *productive reach*—in other words, closing the loop from reach to ROI and back again. Reach. Connect. Effect.

Many marketers shrug off the idea that they should be using long-form content—because of its big budget; perhaps because the hype around branded entertainment implies that big stars, producers, directors, and agents have to be involved. In fact, all long-form content really represents is anything greater than 30 seconds that is capable of engaging and entertaining.

Most of the best TV commercials of all time are 60-seconds long. What is this telling you?

There are many examples of long-form content at its best:

- Christopher Walken was awesome in *Ripper,* a PC-based game I played over 10 years ago. Interestingly, Ripper appears on Walken's long list of film credits.
- Terry Tate, the office linebacker, became a cult hero in a series of Web-based movies for Reebok that ran the gamut from the sublime to the ridiculous.
- Tiger Woods was a hero in Buick's "Tiger Trap" ads.
- Mercury launched "The Lucky Ones," an esoteric and episodic storyline reminiscent of the film *Memento*

involving the destinies of 10 interrelated characters and aimed at 20- to 30-year-olds.

- American Express brought together Jerry Seinfeld and Superman in its much-talked-about Web-only Seinfeldian tales.
- Mitsubishi's "See What Happens" created 50-second vignettes with cliffhanger endings to follow up its 30-second teasers.
- Ford created 3-minute "bookends" as part of its commercial-free sponsorship of the TV show *24* in one of the raw first attempts at deploying long-form content using network television as a distribution mechanism.
- Napster used a series of classically described "web-isodes" to announce the relaunch of its legitimate download service.
- TiVo Showcases are awash with long-form content.

Consider what this means to the advertising industry and what it means to network television. Advertising is essentially liberated by the ability to return to its roots and tell stories again, whereas network TV has effectively been banished from the kingdom as a disgraced monarch. (I may have gotten carried away there.)

I'm not sure that conventional television is capable of responding to the impact of long-form content because of its currently entrenched content and commercial programming legacy system.

That's not to say that they will be hapless hitchhikers on the *Autobahn* of change. Indeed, the extent to which they are able to integrate their Web personas, play nice with the DVR and cable companies, and for the most part subscribe or concede to the paradigm of consumer control and empowerment will determine how well they survive and even thrive.

The raw materials are all in place for the networks to build their new model. Groundbreakers like P&G, with its "40 Experiments" initiative, will lead the way for the others. Nike's "Whatever" was one of the first attempts at a Web strategy using the cliffhanger tactic to motivate viewers to visit whatever.nike.com to complete the commercial. Leveraging popular sports stars like Marion Jones and Mark MacGuire didn't hurt. Web viewers were not only able to follow the storyline, but were allowed to choose one of several endings. There's no reason why this shouldn't already be happening on television. NBC's *The Apprentice* is doing elements of this reasonably well with extended scenes and unaired clips online.

Long-form content begins at the thirty-first second and runs as far as the imagination will allow or the consumer will permit. It's the single biggest messaging shift and will truly converge the worlds of Hollywood and Madison Avenue (banishing the practice of paying large sums of money to insert Absolut bottles into *Sex and the City*).

A Sting in the Tail for Media

Creative purists are celebrating. Media professionals, however, might want to take a moment to detach their clip-on ponytails and take a deep whiff of the winds of change (again).

For a while now, media folk have been enjoying explosive growth and savoring the fruits of being the new client darlings. The traditional and creative agencies have become the walking wounded, while the media independents are basking in the glory of no longer being confined to the back office and the final five minutes of the conversation. Currently they are living large and becoming more like traditional agencies by the day as they shore up their offerings with fast-depleting planners, client service managers, analysts, mathematicians, rocket scientists, and even creatives.

But there's a countermovement occurring, which is very much under the radar. In the future, however, it's going to be inordinately powerful. It's related to long-form content, but it also draws from several of the other new-marketing buckets including interactive, consumer-generated content, and communal marketing.

The Honda "Cog" commercial is a good example. It has been seen by more people in the United States for the grand old media cost of $0 than have most likely viewed all paid Honda commercials. Although the car advertised is not available in the United States. (Perhaps it should be.) The "Making of the Honda Cog" webisode was also conveniently available shortly after Cog did its rounds. The message to Madison Avenue is so loud and so profound that it is astonishing that it was not picked up earlier: long-form content—whether as a minimovie, a commercial that shatters the 30-second noise barrier, or even the "making of" said commercials—is transforming the overdone, tired, and ineffective gold standard of television advertising.

Unlike elements of branded entertainment, long-form content is up front and explicit in its value proposition. Did consumers feel like they were being sold to when they viewed BMW Films? Did they feel like they were being duped when they watched Jerry Seinfeld and Superman do their thing? Did the man or woman in the street object to the series of episodes telling the story of the iconic brand Napster? No. Nope. *Nein.*

Burger King's debauched chicken, which felt the urge to perform in front of his (her?) Web camera for millions of similarly warped Americans, successfully broke the cardinal rule of the quick service restaurant (QSR) category: Thou shalt not personify that which thou shalt forthwith consume. Subservient Chicken's Web experience was followed up with the chicken-on-chicken caged death match, *broadcast on DirecTV*—an absurdly abstruse WWE-meets-Foghorn-Leghorn-on-acid event, interspersed with several other commercials for Burger King. (Incidentally, the prefight and actual fight footage are available for viewing and download on the Web.)

This example, together with the plethora of product placement and brand integration examples out there, reveals a trend that constitutes a rather astounding sea change. *The*

30-second commercial has assumed a sustaining or reinforcing sup-porting role. It has become the value-add associated with a more substantial media or marketing investment. For instance, in Burger King's TC versus Spicy chicken sandwich campaign, the long-form content functioned like the anchor tenant in a shopping mall, with the spattering of 30-second intrusions being random kiosks found throughout the mall.

In the case of reality programming, most media professionals scoff at brand integration as "nothing new" and something that has been around since P&G put the soap in opera and Texaco Theater graced the living rooms of Americans.

But they're wrong. Again.

Although the appearance and even the execution of brand integration might appear familiar, what we are really witnessing is long-form content, with the 30-second being little more than value added, an unwanted distraction, a necessary evil. Back when everyone loved Lucy, brands were the driving force behind the creation of content; today, the same could be said for an episode of *The Apprentice,* and the 30-second spot is an *unnecessary* by-product. Consumers are wise to the fact that companies like Levi's, Mattel, and M&M/Mars are paying through the nose for Donald "I sold out to Madison Avenue and all I got was this lousy T-shirt" Trump and his gratuitous display of the grandeur and stature of the company he keeps. Did it work? Did scores of consumers rush out to purchase pairs of 501 jeans, conduct local searches on Yahoo!, lather themselves with Dove soap? Some anecdotal evidence says yes:

- According to ePrize, on completion of their *Apprentice* appearance and promotion, Crest received 4.3 million visits to crest.com, 80,000 requests for samples, and 25,000 submissions of marketing ideas at a rate of 25,000 ideas per minute in the first 20 minutes following the show.
- According to Jim Moloshok, senior vice president of entertainment content relationships at Yahoo!, within

three hours of the airing of another episode of *The Apprentice*, Ciao Bella ice cream was the third most searched term on Yahoo!, and by 5:00 P.M. the next day, the product was sold out in all the stores that carried it.

Right now, the smart money is still on a Trump plug compared to 30-second noise, which isn't saying much.

THE INTERRELATIONSHIP BETWEEN BRANDED ENTERTAINMENT AND LONG-FORM CONTENT

Branded entertainment is a tactic, not a strategy, and it works through the strategy of reconnecting and reengaging with disenfranchised consumers with long-form content, which itself is really synonymous with entertainment. In the marketing ring, this constitutes an entertainment and experience one-two punch, and you're on either the sending or the receiving end of it.

Long-form content is the antithesis of the 30-second commercial. Not only do they differ markedly in length, but the perception of one being content and the other a commercial is a vital contrast. Amid this spectrum (content versus commercials), brands play a defined role. In a world where things often seem meaningless, they provide a kind of context that can fill in the gaps and restore order to an otherwise chaotic existence.

As former Coke COO Steven Heyer (in his glory days) once ranted, his carbonated sugar-water brand was a bigger network and had a larger reach than any of the major U.S. networks. That's all well and good, but he didn't explain what to do next. Granted, his insinuation was that brands could be creators and distributors of content, but a slew of songs about Coke ("Real") that became parody fodder for *Saturday Night Live* were about the only creations that appeared. And the fact that the songs were delivered in 30-second commercials was the ultimate failure. Compare that with the success of U2's "Vertigo," which became synonymous with iTunes and iPod (and therefore the Apple brand).

Which Came First: The Creation of Content or Its Distribution?

In defense of the risk-averse marketing populace, long-form content was, for the most part, a series of disjointed promises and visions for the future that in practice were hard to deploy. This is no longer true. The democratization of video has created one of the deepest and most diverse grids for message dissemination, enabling long-form content to be consumed on a number of levels, at several fronts, and within various usage scenarios—home, work, play, on the road, and in the air as well.

The next two chapters discuss how long-form content has been embraced and shared by the "people." In the meantime, some "yadda yadda yaddas" from a man who knows a thing or two about long-form storytelling—to offset my pontifications with his own dose of reality.

The Long and Short of New Media
David Apicella, Senior Partner, Co-Creative Head,
Ogilvy & Mather New York

The 30-second commercial is dead. No it isn't. Yes it is. No it isn't.

That's my considered answer to the industry's favorite question, because I don't believe anyone truly, definitively knows what will become of the 30-second spot. At least not yet.

Sure things are changing, but I also think "new" media has been around for quite a while. The Goodyear blimp is a pretty good "new" media idea. As for content, P&G has been producing "soap operas" for years.

Anyway, the debate rages on, but I do know this: It's a great time to be a creative in an ad agency.

Blogs, webisodes, long-form content, interactive billboards, mobile marketing, content integration—you think it, you can do it. The trick is doing it right. Just because BMW and American Express found success in long-form content doesn't mean its right for everyone.

With the freedom to explore the creative frontiers of new media come dangers to the soul of the brand. None of these "new" forms of advertising work, unless the communication begins with a big idea that at its heart speaks to the essence of the brand. And these days, most brands must constantly reinvent themselves both through their offering and positioning.

At Ogilvy we like to say we are in the brand transformation business.

Increasingly, as the world changes and markets evolve, brands need to evolve, too, to reach consumers in new ways wherever they may be.

Building a brand and tapping into the relationship consumers have with brands has never been just about a TV commercial or a billboard or a coaster. It's all of that and much more, and I don't think that will ever change.

So how does that get us to "new" media and long-form content? Here's one way.

In 1998 we paired Jerry Seinfeld with animated Superman for an American Express Super Bowl commercial (see Figure 15.1). People liked it. They liked the characters together and they liked the brand for bringing them together.

In fact, people liked it so much that they said we should make more of them.

So we did. We made two 5-minute webisodes designed to run exclusively on American Express's web site.

That was so well received that NBC picked up the first webisode and ran it as prime-time sweeps-month content on the network. That's a pretty good new-media story, and it all started with a 30-second TV commercial.

Long-form content is exciting. It's exciting to work on, fun to watch, and a great way to build the brand experience.

Here's another—retail, the oldest brand experience on earth.

Consider the Hershey's store in Times Square. Originally, Hershey's wanted a billboard in Times Square to give them presence at an

Figure 15.1   Seinfeld and Superman team up. *Courtesy:* Ogilvy & Mather;
American Express.

important global crossroad. We said, "How about a real live experience?" Together, we flipped a billboard into a retail store. A billboard
would tell you about Hershey's. The store allows you to experience
the brand. And trust me, when the New York City tourist goes home
to Iowa and is shopping in the local supermarket for a bag of candy,
that Hershey experience filters into the decision process, impacting
the bag of candy they buy hundreds of miles away from New York.

How's that for new media?

What all these examples have in common is that they have
found new, provocative ways for advertisers and marketers to reen-
gage with consumers and continue to transform and build brands.
Not one of the tools in the toolbox can do it alone.

Is long form here to stay? Probably. Billboards, print ads,
posters, and coasters? Sure. Will we someday project a message on
the moon? Who knows? As for the humble 30-second TV commercial, I paraphrase that great wit and sage Mark Twain, who said: "The
reports of my death are greatly exaggerated."

16

Communal Marketing

Al Ries, in his infinite wisdom, is a man I grew up idolizing. As a student of marketing, he and his compatriot, Jack Trout, defined the very concept of positioning. Their vision—despite recently being challenged by the Granddaddy of Cholesterol, McDonald's—is for the most part, still a fundamental principle of Marketing and Advertising 101 today.

Now that I've paid my respects to Mr. Ries, let me say how much I disagree with the central premise of his not-so-new book *The Fall of Advertising and the Rise of PR* (HarperBusiness, 2002). When I saw him speak about two years ago, I witnessed a presentation with slides as old as the concept of positioning itself. To be fair, there was no way he could live up to the godlike stature he had in my mind, and I hope to follow his lead by selling consulting services based on my book, securing speaking engagements based on the book, and selling books based on my consulting and speaking abilities (mention this ad and get a 10 percent discount off my rate card).

Now back to his hypothesis about the role of PR . . .

According to Ries, advertising did not create the mighty Amazon and eBay brands, it did not make Starbucks what it is today, nor did it add any zeros to the market cap of Google. He's right about that; however, I dispute his claim that public relations is the hero in these cases. PR did not build these brands—you did; I did; we all did (and then we screamed for ice cream).

Community built these brands, and PR notably rode the powerful wave of public interest, activity, and involvement that followed. Inarguably, PR created an additional wave of public awareness and interest, but it cannot be credited as the primary factor in the explosive growth of these brands.

The Internet economy uses the term *viral marketing* to indicate the network effects and quantification of the word-of-mouth process. Word of mouth remains the undisputed king of credible and qualified referrals that ultimately lead to a sale. As I proudly remarked to the customer service person who walked me through the setup of my second TiVo box, I have probably sold more TiVo boxes than the most successful salesperson at *any* major department or electronics store.

But I fear that many marketers have underutilized viral marketing while others have overutilized it. That's right, both too little or too much viral marketing can be a bad, bad thing.

COMMUNAL COMES FROM THE WORD *COMMUNITY*

This chapter is not called "Viral Marketing"—if it were, it would be all about trying to get consumers to do the marketing work for you. That should come as a bonus—the cherry on top of a successful campaign. *If you begin with the objective of getting your customers to spread the love without giving them a reason to fall in love in the first place, you'll end up in the same boat as the rest of the me-too marketers who are trying to crack the viral "da Vinci code."*

Viral marketing at its oversimplified worst is simply the ability to refer a friend. It's one of those "just because you *can* do it doesn't mean you *should* do it" adages to which I only wish marketers would take heed. For some reason, the marketing community is often guilty of overdosing on its own Kool-Aid. Touting your own importance is acceptable within the confines of your cubicles, but should not spill over into the consumer domain. Why would you think consumers care so much about what you have to say that they would risk spamming their friends with your propaganda? It's *easy* for consumers to "organically" tell their friends, colleagues, and family members about anything: Cut + paste = voilà! The ability to copy a URL works wonders. *They don't need you or your help!*

That said, I happily contradict myself to prescribe to marketers that the easier they make it for consumers to connect a message, idea, program, or piece of content with others, the better. For example, allowing consumers to download marketing content (read: ads) on their hard drives rather than preventing them from doing so certainly makes it easier for them to "spread the brand love." This probably breaks every fair use statute and intellectual property law on the books, but your consumers are doing it anyway. It's like being told *not* to take photographs at a Disney resort—instead of someone taking away a special memory to share with friends and family, who are ideal prospects for the mighty Mouse empire, this rodent is determined to limit the experience to the geographic confines of the park and officially sanctioned, overpriced retail merchandise (sigh).

Thank your lucky stars for Nike—not only for their tear-jerking commercial (see lifeafter30.com), which somehow reduced the 82-year-old Curse of the Bambino into a one-minute story of perseverance and human triumph, but for explicitly making this downloadable to both PC and Mac formats. This validates several new marketing tenets, from distribution to community to control.

One final point about referrals: They should be rewarded. Technology has given us the means to track and

Nike's Red Sox "Just do It" is arguably the best commercial since Apple's "1984"—Even though it is an anomaly, it demonstrates the most fundamental point of advertising: that creativity will always trump mediocrity. I'm even prepared to overlook the fact that this commercial was apparently made a year earlier, in anticipation of the Cubs winning the World Series and breaking *their* curse!

measure consumer behavior, and therefore offer rewards. Failing to do so must be the result of either laziness or greed.

How do you know when a product has finally become a brand? Or when a brand has finally emerged as a true leader from the throngs of undifferentiated me-toos? One gauge I use is when your customers become your sales force.

How often have you had people tell you they're Mac converts or heard others arguing the merits of the Treo versus the BlackBerry? No, they're not geeks; they're your most loyal customers—true advocates—and they might as well be on payroll when all the business they funnel in through personal endorsements and recommendations is factored into the equation.

A few years back, Palm launched the Palm Champions program online, the purpose of which was to reward customers for recommending Palm to their friends and colleagues. Technology facilitated this value exchange, creating a perfect win-win-win situation: The referring party earned Palm bucks, the referral got free software (and the new Palm), and Palm received an acquisition and retention combo including a wealth of data and goodwill. Not only was this an evolution of the classic referral tactic, it also combined the powerful elements of word of mouth, viral marketing, affiliate marketing, and CRM, while connecting with and rewarding the people most likely to keep coming back. This was a great example of communal marketing and demonstrated an important principle: Rather than "investing" in mass media, invest in your customers instead.

What are the implications for marketers? This Referral v2.0 directly plugs the tactic into a more meaningful business objective and strategy. It rewards your most loyal customers who, let's face it, probably know more about your product than salespeople do. Combine this with the potential to exercise some degree of leverage over word of mouth and viral marketing, and you have a potent marketing weapon to add to your arsenal.

Think about what it means to your business and to your brand to have your customers act independently as your not-so-silent sales force. Surely it tells you that you're doing something right. The question then becomes, What are you going to do about it? Whatever you do, don't take this for granted.

CONTROL: THE CRITICAL "COG"

If there's a common thread that ties together the changes on both the consumer and the marketing sides, it can be summed up in one word: *control.* Consumers have it; marketers don't.

Anything that marketers can do to cede control to their consumers, to acknowledge the power shift, and to recognize the irrevocable changes that have taken place is a step in the right direction. But this is so much easier said than done—because if there's one thing that marketers struggle about relinquishing, it's control. This is the reason a new CMO feels compelled to fire the incumbent agency; it's why a newly named agency of record cannot resist the urge to fix what may not be broken.

The degree of control and the network effects of communal marketing are inversely proportional. Viral success can be somewhat of a hit-and-hope approach—for example, "Subservient Chicken" might have been attempted in the same way for the same brand at a different time, and it would have passed like a ship in the night.

There is a small group of practitioners who seem to get it right more often than not. It might be their willingness to relinquish control, combined with an entrepreneurial and risk-inclined test-learn-test-learn approach that works. Viral success is often the result of throwing a bunch of ideas in various iterations and interpretations against the wall—and when something sticks, it's ready to serve; when it slides off, clean it up and learn from the experience.

Crispin Porter's razor-sharp work for Burger King has produced such hits as "Subservient Chicken," the TC-versus-Spicy chicken fight (in particular contrast to KFC's contrived Chicken Capital USA), Ugoff and his pouch for salads, and the Angus Diet. Can't you tell they're having fun, and don't you think this irreverent pleasure will transfer to their community?

Unfortunately, many marketers who have tried their hands at communal marketing have tried either too hard or not hard enough to create real PR success. Maybe Al Ries should have written a book about community, since it is an almost mandatory precursor to creating publicity buzz.

Keep in mind, though, that communal marketing can be a double-edged sword. If you release your hold on the control button and let things go where they will, you must be prepared to accept and deal with the consequences of uncensored dialogue and esoteric individual expression, in a world where you'll find out pretty quickly whether your perception of reality is, in fact, realistic.

Not Hard Enough

Regarding the "refer a friend" button as a sufficient communal marketing effort is pretty pathetic. Although it's easy to implement and it's certainly better than doing nothing, it is really just a pitiable attempt to reap the rewards of connecting like-minded consumers with marketing messages without having to work too hard.

The "refer a friend" solution is indicative of a bigger problem—it's the manifestation of the same silo mentality that is endemic to the marketing business in general, which holds that sticking to one particular form of distribution is better than using many. But it's not really the marketer's decision to make; the consumer has the right to seek what most appeals to him or her. Whether communal marketing takes the form of an online Web button, a form to completed, an e-mail, short messaging service (SMS), or a telephone call, the easier it is to spread the word, the better it will be for you as a marketer.

AT&T Wireless (now Cingular) got it right with both phone and SMS voting on TV's *American Idol,* but they left out the Web as a vital third venue. Worse still, they restricted the voting to viewers who possessed AT&T wireless phones. If they thought teenagers would switch to AT&T just so they could vote, they were sadly mistaken.

This is the same line of thinking that prompted some airlines to decree that only first-class passengers have the right to eat and that coach class should be left to nibble on trail mix. This is an offense against the basic, inalienable right to not be hungry. (Maslow must be rolling in his grave.) Virgin is one airline that understands this—rather than take the negative approach of withholding entertainment and food, it did something positive, rewarding its premium customers with a true nonessential premium—in the form of perks like a physical bar, massages, and limo service.

In the case of *American Idol,* AT&T could have acquired a lot of goodwill had it opened its phone-in network to everyone and rewarded its own customers with an extra vote or the chance to win a walk-on role in the show's finale (now *that's* reality TV). I can understand that voting was opened up only at the end of the show in order to be fair and balanced to the contestants, but come on—is the real world fair or balanced? (Just ask the folks at Fox News!) Why not real-time voting with real-time scoring to bring a bit of *Showtime at the Apollo* authenticity to the program? *American Idol* is one of the few programs that generates buzz around the watercooler, so it seems a pity that the voting mechanism and extent of interactivity are so linear and not true to the very communal nature of the program itself.

Spreading the Word

The best way to spread any word today is e-mail. It is the single biggest means for sharing the likes of Honda Cog, JibJab, or Consumer Union's "The Drugs I Need" parody, but it is also the least sophisticated, controlled, and complicated. One can only wonder why we're not seeing video clips and highlights of TV programs surreptitiously leaked to the online masses on a more regular basis. One of the real positives of the illegal music file-sharing era was that you could get that live version of "She Bangs" that William Hung butchered or the Clay Aiken masterpiece, "Solitaire," there and then. Content wants to be liberated . . . which is not necessarily saying it needs to be *free*.

This was of course before they were available legally on iTunes, but the point is that Napster, for better and for worse was nothing more than a reflection of the times and a glimpse at the future of marketing. In this vision of the future, communities of consumers will rely on their connections to one another to enhance their lives, often by circumventing—and therefore at the expense of—the notoriously slow and stubborn marketing community.

In 2005, General Motors launched a promotional campaign to spread "a message so important we need the whole country to tell it." GM let out one word every day through a variety of traditional media such as billboards in order to have a riddle solved on www.findthemessage.com. This might sound intriguing—except that consumers solved the riddle before the campaign could even hit its stride.

"This is the last time you will ever have to feel alone on our nation's roadways" crowed the Web, with the consensus being that the answer to the riddle was "OnStar" (the in-car communications linkup).

This is a unique twist on communal marketing. While I'd

like to give GM credit for anticipating the inevitable outcome, I just can't. Its use of traditional billboards, for example, was so retro it was positively Ice Age. That said, I would
argue that the outcome was not exactly a bad one for GM—
the fact that consumers had been nudged into a state of
involvement, to the point that they ended up exactly where
GM had wanted them to be (all roads led to OnStar), could
only be described as a success.

In this case, consumers helped accelerate the delivery
and efficacy of the message from an otherwise inefficient
campaign.

Too Hard

Mazda attempted to emulate the swooshers (described later in
this chapter) with a "false" blog that backfired horribly. Companies like BzzAgent use deliberate and even alleged under-
handed tactics to disseminate viral or communal buzz, with
mixed results. Guerilla marketing, itself a subset of communal
marketing, is really the predecessor of the technology-infused
viral incarnation. Perhaps it should be called *controversial
marketing,* since it is really the buzz generated after the fact
(through PR) rather than the tactic itself that gets the effort
onto the radar screens of the press and various communities of
interest such as in the case of the 2005 Super Bowl ads, or the
fake VW ad featuring a suicide bomber.

Ericsson generated much debate when it recruited a
band of amateur actors as stealth agents to emulate the natural instincts and tendencies of loyalists (like those in the
TiVo and Palm examples mentioned earlier, except fake). By
posing as tourists and real customers, they would bump into

> Communal success is not forced. Nor is it false. Rather, it is
> organic and often—viral or exponential. It is more often than
> not unplanned, but that doesn't mean it cannot be anticipated
> and prepared for.

people on the street and demonstrate the capabilities of the new Ericsson T68i phones.

For what it's worth, I think duping is in the eye of the beholder, and my faith in today's intelligent consumers (tenet 1) tells me that they will make decisions that are right for them. They can sniff a falsehood a mile away—and as long as the information (as opposed to the source or vehicle) is authentic, they should be able to make the right decision. The tactic in this example is no less deceptive than the 30-second commercial equivalent that showed incredibly high-resolution photographs on the cell phone and then a tiny print caveat that says "simulated" underneath. (I know this because I bought the phone in question, and the quality of the pictures sucked!)

Many companies have resorted to subversive means to connect with Malcolm Gladwell's Mavens, Connectors, and Salespeople and Jon Berry's Influentials.

Professor Chrysanthos Dellarocas, of MIT, put out a white paper that measured the economic impact of companies that pay employees or others to seed message boards with comments that are favorable to company products (iMediaconnection.com, November 24, 2004). The research showed that there was some first-mover advantage associated with "conning" the masses, but ultimately, as me-too's jump on the bandwagon, the clutter, lack of authenticity, and suspect motives behind the posts replace any short-term economic gain with inevitable losses.

PLANNING FOR SUCCESS

Being wrong can even be a good thing: A site that crashes is a great testament to excessive demand—if and only if it can be quickly rectified or leveraged to success. Matt Lauer loves the site crash, in that it's fairly newsworthy when demand is so great that a site goes down. This, however, is an extremely risky game of chance to play. In reality, I'd rather be prudent 20 times over (meaning that I'm investing in the bandwidth for the potential upside) in order to be right once (and thus be able to execute seamlessly) when the viral storm rolls in.

Just Right

Communal marketing is what turns a really good idea into a really great campaign. It's as much a part of Hollywood's recipe for blockbuster success nowadays as any form of traditional advertising.

Peter Jackson, now-legendary director of the masterful *Lord of the Rings* trilogy, tapped into the power of community years (that's years!) before the actual release of the first of his three megahits. In fact, the rabid fans of J. R. R. Tolkien's classic tale even weighed in as a community and influenced major directorial decisions, resulting in certain scenes reaching the cutting room floor.

A more perverse example of the power of community is when Marvel Studios chief Avi Arad found out the hard way that a simple deviation from the Hulk bible (failing to put the Hulk in his trademark purple shorts, for example) could lead to disaster (although ultimately, the movie's script took care of that!). Whether they are viewed as an instant and live form of market research or a continuous source of valuable dialogue, Arad conceded that those who troll the Net are now "filmmaking partners" as opposed to just people who steal ideas and download movies illegally.

SPIDEY-SENSE

The 2004 furor over the decision to plaster *Spider-Man 2* logos on first, second, and third base at a series of interleague major league baseball games set message boards, dailies, and trades abuzz with discussion, debate, and disgust.

One of the questions debated was whether major league baseball should get with the times or whether this tactic was messing with a sacred tradition. The former camp (let's call them the pragmatists) essentially argued that advertising has encroached on almost every other facet of baseball (and other games), so why not make a play for the blank canvases of uniforms and plates? The latter camp (the purists) drew the line at the diamond and fought for the right to maintain the dignity and integrity of America's pastime.

I could elaborate on this intriguing case in marketing's tormented history. I would mention inconsistencies in what is considered acceptable and what is considered blasphemous. I would talk about the All-Star Game and the Yankees' little sojourn to the east (and I'm not referring to the Bronx) to kick off the season. I might argue that other sports, such as soccer (the world's number one sport), have been able to seamlessly and successfully integrate advertising into uniforms, fields, and other venues, although some contend that this turns *Field of Dreams* into a nightmare.

But I won't.

I could also spend a considerable amount of time discussing the increasing clutter and the proliferation and fragmentation of media alternatives, as well as the growing challenge of getting noticed in a world governed by empowered and skeptical consumers. I might suggest that, on one hand, marketing and media professionals must fully explore new ways of reaching, connecting, and engaging—particularly with younger audiences, but on the other hand, stepping over the line could create a vicious cycle of backlash (can you say "wardrobe malfunction"?).

But again, I won't.

Instead, I'm going to tell you about an amazing arachnid that broke the box office record for opening weekend sales with a whopping $114,844,116 in receipts—more than Yoda, Gollum, Jesus, Harry Potter, or the Hulk (see Table 16.1). How's that for esteemed company?

I love the story of *Spider-Man*. This movie, quite frankly, should never even have sniffed the kind of money it ended up earning. It wasn't the first superhero flick and it certainly wasn't going to be the last, yet it swept away its competition.

Table 16.1	Opening Weekend Box Office Record Holders	
All time	*Spider-Man*	**$114,844,116**
January	*Star Wars*	$ 35,906,661
February	*Passion of the Christ*	83,848,082
March	*Ice Age*	46,312,454
April	*Anger Management*	42,220,847
May	*Spider-Man*	114,844,116
June	*Harry Potter 3*	93,687,367
July	*Spider-Man 2*	88,156,227
August	*Rush Hour 2*	67,408,222
September	*Sweet Home Alabama*	35,648,740
October	*Scary Movie 3*	48,113,770
November	*Harry Potter*	90,294,621
December	*Lord of the Rings: Return of the King*	72,629,713

Source: Box Office Mojo.

Nontraditional media such as the Web (you can take that pun as intended) played a major role in this movie's success. Not only was *Spider-Man* the number one movie in opening weekend box office receipts, it was also the movie with the highest number of online advertising impressions allocated to it. Coincidence?

Spider-Man is another Avi Arad production and, in this case, the movie studio helped distribute myriads of *Spider-Man* communication paraphernalia such as posters, Web banners, and exclusive movie trailers. The strategy of distributing to and embedding free creative in the multitude of fan sites on the Web became a model for future successes such as *Lord of the Rings*. The studio's awareness of the legions of passionate influencers and fans out there made for the barter deal of the century. Fans wanted display advertising (there's a first), trailers, and information about the upcoming release—and the studio gave it to them (sounds like a Jet-Blue commercial).

Free advertising is one thing, but when consumers and fans actually request and initiate the distribution thereof to highly qualified audiences made up predominantly of influencers and early adopters, the only logical outcome is a great communal marketing success story.

Which brings us back to *Spider-Man 2*. Who in their right mind would want the task of trying to top its predecessor? Forget topping—try for just half of the first *Spider-Man*'s opening weekend sales. If achieved, that would beat January, March, April, September, or October records.

Enter the lamest marketing ploy in history (at least on paper): putting logos on the bases at major league baseball games. That is a surefire way to invoke the essential right-brain response for advertising to do its job of persuasion—*not*.

What seemed like a yawn on paper became an overnight tempest in a teapot, as 79.4 percent of ESPN's 45,000 respondents rapidly voiced their disapproval of the plan to put a six- by six-inch *Spider-Man 2* logo on three out of the four bases.

Here's another stat: 15 stadiums over a three-day period equals 45 games between June 11 and 13. That's 45 out of a season total of 2,429, coming in at a whopping 1.85 percent.

On paper, the value of these impressions wasn't very compelling. But in reality, this was arguably one of the shrewdest media strategies deployed in recent times. I'd like to believe that whomever was responsible for this proposal had no intention whatsoever of going through with it; the outcome (uproar, protest, rebellion) was a sure thing—a racing certainty. If the goal here was to get the word out that *Spider-Man 2* was swinging into theaters in the most impactful and memorable way possible, then this exercise in awareness achieved Super Bowl proportions. The only risk factor here boiled down to a calculated gamble on go or no-go decisions to attend the movie's theater release, namely, consumers boycotting the movie. The pinch hit worked, and on July 2, 2004, the eight-legged freak known as media strategy soundly defeated *Austin Powers* (which had held the previous July record of $73,071,188).

It's ironic that most (outraged) fans, who might not have been able to tell the difference between Derek Jeter and

Tobey Maguire all the way up in the nosebleed seats, felt so strongly about who was on first . . . and second . . . and third. It is not ironic (or surprising) that it was the community (including—but not limited to—the outraged fans) that was once again responsible for this box office home run.

ODE TO BLOGS

George Masters, a school teacher who (in my humble opinion) created a better iPod ad than Apple ever has, had his commercial initially viewed by more than 70,000 people, not to mention prolific press coverage, thanks to its being picked up on a few influential blogs.

Bob Parsons, CEO of GoDaddy.com, has his own blog (www.bobparsons.com), where he talks at length about his company's Super Bowl exploits.

Joseph Jaffe (that would be me) relaunched his branded flavor of commentary—called Jaffe Juice (www .jaffejuice.com)—in blog format, thanks to the expert partnership of the visionaries at Gawker Media.

The name *blog* is really a red herring. It tends to resonate and project the image of a geek, keying away in a musty basement, when in fact it is quite possibly the sexiest thing ever to hit the world of publishing.

Any individual (even you) can set up a blog, but the real power is going to come from the corporate world (you again), where solid relationships will be cultivated based on honest, open dialogue and superior content.

The world is abuzz with the migration of formalized marketing communications from monologue (30-second spot) to dialogue (digital/interactivity) format. Why, then, should the business-to-consumer or business-to-business content or publishing worlds be any different?

The cluttered world desperately needs filters—both quantity (think funnel) and quality (think purification); blogs provide a distilled panacea of byte-size nuggets of value, in a nonlinear format (through the ability to link in and out), and offer you the ability to join the conversation at any time.

Web logs, or blogs, are so much more than online diaries, which are updated as often as the author wishes. Through the power of the hyperlink, any article, web site, or source of information or entertainment that is referenced in the blog connects to a posting with the click of a mouse. In fact, the number of links that connect to and from the blog are instrumental in determining its success in terms of penetration and visibility on everything from search engines to directory listings.

Blogs threaten to destabilize the traditional publisher-editor relationship because they truly democratize the field. Anyone can comment on a posting, so the blog becomes a dynamic open dialogue.

A true brand belongs to the people (its consumers, you and me). If you, as an advertiser or marketer, wholeheart-edly believe this statement, then I think you are well on your way to mastering an evolved state of communication with your audience. By allowing communities of interest or like-minded thinkers who are defined by their values, beliefs, judgments, brands, and even the types of media they con-sume to come together and participate in the brand develop-ment process, a wider, more comprehensive, and credible net can be cast.

However, I caution you about another fundamental aspect of communal marketing that really speaks to the entire process of interactivity and involvement: *Just because you want to talk with consumers doesn't mean they want to talk to you.*

Just Do It Right

Nike executed against this belief using Gawker.com, a trendy, opinion-led blog site for their "Art of Speed" campaign. According to the official blurb on the blog, "For Art of Speed, Nike commissioned 15 talented young filmmakers to interpret the idea of speed. Over the course of 20 days, this weblog will introduce these innovative directors, their short films, and the digital technology behind the scenes" (see Figure 16.1).

Figure 16.1   Art of speed blog. *Courtesy:* Nike, Gawker Media.

The result was a smooth-flowing tribute to journalism meshed seamlessly with the Nike brand that delivered perfectly against a fundamental tenet of new marketing: Reach the *right* people as opposed to simply trying for the most people—or in the case of communal marketing, reach the most people by reaching out first to the right people. (See Chapter 17.)

The Promise of Communal Marketing

For the longest time, Burger King made headlines only for the wrong reasons. In fact, when the account was up for review (*again*), there was a running bet within the advertising industry on how soon the agency would lose an account that had very quickly become a dog (or chicken). Then along came a wacky simulated "underground" site of someone dressed up as a rather eccentric chicken who, thanks to a web cam, ended up reaching quite a few consumers.

The chicken shown in Figure 16.2 lets you have it your way by submitting to your G- or PG-rated desires. R-rated

Figure 16.2   Subservient Chicken. *Courtesy:* Crispin Porter + Bogusky;
Burger King.

whims, I'm afraid, will earn you a wagging finger. If you
haven't yet visited www.subservientchicken.com, then slap
yourself on the wrist (a command to which the chicken in
question responds fairly strangely, I might add).

This viral (but not salmonella!) success story has been
making the rounds of late, from the hallowed pages of the
Wall Street Journal to the underground message boards of
enthusiastic consumers. I was intrigued by the media coverage of this campaign, both in the mainstream papers as well
as in the trade circles. The most frequently asked question
kept coming back to, "But did it sell chicken?"

This is completely the wrong question to ask. More appropriately, you should ask, "Does Burger King sell chicken?" (Hint: think *Burger* King.) The answer is an emphatic *yes*— and if you didn't know it before, you certainly do now.

"Subservient Chicken" is cocky, to be sure, but it's without question a smart and strategic campaign. It almost single-handedly put BK in the news for all the right reasons, when it seemed the only news about this flailing brand was bad news—a time when the only flame-grilled item on the menu was the company itself. Now millions of consumers—especially younger ones who might previously have not cared at all about the brand—have interacted with this frisky rooster. Many people don't know this, but the man in the suit is actually Richard Hatch. (I'm kidding, but I couldn't resist.) Total hits on the Subservient Chicken web site through March 2005 were 398,958,278 (per CP + B). This is an estimated 14,225,675 unique visitors, each of whom spent an average amount of 7:17 minutes per session (that's 7.3 × 30 seconds to equate to commercials, for anyone keeping score).

To suggest that the product was sold as a direct result of this campaign is shortsighted and displays an acute lack of understanding of how advertising and branding work—at least when they are done right.

What if—and this is an out-there thought (sarcasm intended)—the primary goal of the program was not to sell chicken at all? Granted, any successful effort surely will translate into sales; however, when you assess the impact of the free publicity and the message sent to the investment community, press, channel, and consumer base (past, present, future), doesn't the value transcend short-term sales and enter the priceless zone?

The right kind of question to ask is: "Did this bring people closer to the brand?" And the corollary: "Did this move people further away from the brand?" If the answers are yes and no, respectively, then this chicken is no featherbrain.

The degree to which BK was able to give this campaign legs ultimately determined whether this ended up being a one-hit wonder or the makings of an idea with staying power.

Already, the idea of this chicken as the embodiment of Burger King's "Have it your way" value proposition has influenced subsequent BK marketing efforts such as Dr. Angus's Diet (not a real doctor, not a real diet); the bratty and self-important Ugoff with his masterpiece salad pouch and the DirecTV exclusive: Chicken Sandwich World Championship caged fight-to-the-death between TC (aka TenderCrisp) and Spicy (aka Spicy TenderCrisp).

If you're still not convinced, take it directly from the chicken's mouth: "Burger King Corporation . . . announced that its October 2004 results show U.S. system-wide same store sales up 6.9 percent with U.S. franchise sales up 6.4 percent and company restaurant sales up 12.3 percent year-over-year. October marks the ninth consecutive month of positive U.S. same store sales." Also, chicken burger sales were reportedly up 9 percent in the weeks immediately after the campaign launched. (Must have been a zany coincidence.)

Thank God, a Business with No Experts
Charles K. Porter, Chairman, Crispin Porter + Bogusky

Digital viral marketing is still being invented. People are already having seminars and panel discussions about it, but they're mostly just rehashing all the false starts and failed promises. Everybody knows there's an enormously potent medium here. It's just that nobody has figured out how to predictably harness it yet. That's what makes it so exciting, appealing, and just so damn cool.

A lot of people have already thrown a lot of money at this particular monster, however, and we have learned a few things for sure: Even if you build it, they won't necessarily come.

A few years ago, a guy came to talk to our agency about doing a Super Bowl spot. He had only the vaguest idea of a product, no business plan to speak of, and no real economic model. What he had was a suitcase full of venture capital and a really hot Web address which he'd bought for $2 million. He got his spot done (not by us); it ran on the Super Bowl, he got more than a million hits, and by the end of February he was out of business. In retrospect, this was a pretty typical story in the titanic dot-com meltdown of 2000, and it all proved one thing. Just being in the interactive space, even with a wonderful, cannot-fail Web address and a Super Bowl spot, gets you nowhere. Nowhere at all.

Being more intrusive is just being more of a pest.

Remember banners? They just sat there or, if they were really cutting-edge, blinked. And naturally, once the novelty wore off, the much vaunted click-through rates dropped like a dead turkey from a helicopter. So now everyone's trying to figure out ways to get you to notice them again. I can hear the meeting. "Can we make it float across the screen? Can we make it bounce? Can we make it float and then bounce?" Well here's reality. You can make your pop-up float bounce, take its pants off, and sing "Who Let the Dogs Out." All you're doing is annoying people.

What Just Might Work

As I said earlier, there are no experts in this business yet—including me. But so far, the only two ways that I can see to get people to even pay attention to you in the interactive world are to offer information or entertainment. And, if you really have dreams of viral, entertainment will always win. Imagine two sites. One has really useful information on caring for delicate fabrics. The other has the funniest joke you've seen since high school. Which one are you going to send to all your friends?

One Key Thing to Remember

Viral can be funny. Viral can be patriotic. Viral can be poetic and heart warming. Viral can be celebrity gossip. Viral can be anything that's so interesting or captivating that you just have to share it. Viral can even be a bizarre chicken that will do anything you ask it to do. What viral can't be is boring or sell-y. People are very tuned into the fact that whatever you forward to your e-mail list says something about you. And hardly anyone would ever send a salesman over to a friend's house.

◆◆◆◆◆

17

Consumer-Generated Content

Whassup? Check it out at www.whassup.com. You wouldn't be the first to discover some of the legendary spoofs on the iconic Budweiser "Whassup" campaign such as the Superfriends, South Park, Elian Gonzales (remember him?), Wake Up (for the truly uncool), and Shalom (!), as well as the U.K. version (something about beer, tea, and crumpets just doesn't gel). Type the words "Whassup" and "Budweiser" into a search engine and you won't even find the official Budweiser web site.

These and many other tribute sites are freely accessible on the Net for the many thousands of consumers who were enraptured by this fresh and memorable campaign centered around four friends and their iconoclastic greeting ritual.

What happened here was a community-driven expression of interest, which might easily have been quashed by the folks at Anheuser-Busch with a standard cease-and-desist order, but instead was left alone and (who knows?) possibly even encouraged on the quiet. It is rumored that Anheuser-Busch had these commissioned. Apple similarly did not ask George Masters to remove his ad (how kind), when in fact what they should have done was put it on air!

Consumer-generated content (note that I haven't insulted it by calling it "advertising" or "media") is the Mount Everest of the world of advertising accomplishments. While interactivity-induced consumer involvement (through media messaging) is in itself a significant accomplishment considering the advertising norm, it pales compared to the concept of consumers voluntarily creating their own content with a direct or indirect tie-in to a brand. Some refer to it as "open source marketing" or co-creation.

This is what makes Project Greenlight (Matt Damon and Ben Affleck's reality project about bringing an ordinary screenwriter and budding director's dream to life) so intriguing and why MoveOn.org created such a groundswell of consumer-generated expression in the political arena. There's something fresh and unique about normal people creating content, a process that has been subject to mystification and thus relegated to the clutches of a small, elite group of "creatives."

Visa, a brand that positions itself as being "everywhere you want to be," created its "Ideas Happen" campaign (see the commentary at the end of this chapter), which has completed its second successful run. "Ideas Happen" gives 18- to 29-year-olds an opportunity to pitch an idea to win $25,000 to make the idea a reality. Entrants pitch by submitting a short essay plus an optional video and up to 3 JPEGs of their idea. A total of 12 winners are chosen, four in each of these categories: entrepreneur, community, and self-expression (see Figure 17.1).

This initiative promised to make consumers' ideas themselves into reality. In this case the *product* is the credit card and the ability to have it accepted ubiquitously; the *brand* is the ability to empower ordinary people to realize extraordinary aspirations by acting (i.e., using their credit cards); and the *experience* is to "just make it happen." The web site, at

Figure 17.1   Ideas happen. *Courtesy:* Visa; Microsoft Corporation's MSN.

http://ideashappen.msn.com/, became a sought-after destination for dreamers to submit their ideas through a variety
of multimedia creative outlets, as well as a haven for others
to find inspiration vicariously, through the ideas that
sparked the dreamers.

"Subservient Chicken" uses a combination of planned
and perhaps unanticipated techniques to create its experience. Consumers interact with the site itself, challenging the
chicken to perform weird and entertaining actions. But the
real multiplier took the form of hundreds of sites that mush-
roomed virtually overnight and offered exhaustive lists of
what the chicken would do, would not do, and might do,
including doing the Hokey Pokey, playing dead, dancing on
the ceiling (it worked for Lionel Ritchie), eating a Big Mac
(which makes it gag), and some unmentionable acts as well.
With a bit of digging, I found a site that can help you uncen-
sor the censored commands, although I have no clue how to
do that or why anyone would want to. But it is readily conceivable that a cutting-edge agency and a bunch of highly

engaged consumers could pull a fast one on something that is beyond most of us.

When you visit some of Subservient Chicken's fan sites, it's tempting to conclude that there are people out there with way too much time on their hands. I counted over 225 different entries on one such site. But when you consider the level of commitment it takes to compile such an exhaustive list of chicken commands, as well as the possibility that the same folks have both disposable income and curiosity (and are fairly likely to be the target audience), you might be willing to rethink your perspective on the success of this exercise.

HONDA = LOVE

Honda created a terrific commercial based on the well-known truism that people resemble their dogs.* Using their fleet of models and alternatives, Honda matched people to the Honda that best resembled them (or vice versa).

In contrast to the lazy and obvious approach of competitor Toyota—"with so many Toyotas to choose from, the only question is which model is right for you"—Honda's approach was novel. But had it stopped there, it would have been quickly forgotten. However, what they did next made it special.

Honda allowed consumers to submit their own photographs to compare with the Honda model they felt best fit their likeness. The online community then voted for the matches they thought were best (see Figure 17.2).

Honda created a follow-up ad from the best submissions. I call this "reality advertising" because it comes off as more authentic and credible than any kind of advertising.

There's a reason why consumer-generated content is not called "consumer-generated *advertising*." When consumers

---

*Purebred dogs can be matched to their owners by strangers most of the time. But the same does not hold true for mixed-breed dogs, according to Nicholas Christenfeld and Michael Roy, psychologists at the University of California San Diego.

Figure 17.2   Honda's reality advertising hit in the form of "drive = love."
Courtesy: American Honda Motor Co.; Ruben Postaer & Associates (RPA).

are encouraged to participate creatively in a marketing-related messaging, it really ceases to be advertising or commercial content and becomes just plain content. It therefore competes directly with anything from *CSI* to *Seabiscuit.*

Consumer-generated content is a dynamic and organic strategy as well as a proven involvement tactic. It can be employed in a horizontal fashion to bind one communication touch point with others. It has been around in fairly basic forms for a lot longer than you might realize, dating back to the archetypal consumer-packaged-goods-driven sweepstakes competition in which consumers would submit a written entry on why they should be chosen as the grand prize winner.

But it is only now—and specifically through technology—that such content can be created, influenced, and shared on a broad scale. The digitization of video, photography, and audio editing has democratized the process of conceiving and executing movies, short features, collages, and audio essays.

From iPhoto to iTunes and iMovie, Apple's products are the best-integrated suite of tools, allowing consumer amateurs to become reasonably professional content creators. Of course, the ability to create can have both positive and negative aspects. Remember the Neistat brothers and their little film exposé, "iPod's Dirty Secret"? (See Chapter 7.) According to the counter on www.ipodsdirtysecret.com, this example of consumer-generated content has been viewed over 1.8 million times and that doesn't include the number of times it has been e-mailed and otherwise shared.

The other component in the explosion of consumer-generated content is the means to warehouse these creations. The World Wide Web is not only wide but deep, and it offers the perfect opportunity to buy and sell attention, potentially making each of us the artist of the moment.

IMAGINATION AT WORK

After a successful run, GE changed its tagline from "We bring good things to life" to "Imagination at Work." What better way to bring the brand promise to life than to demonstrate it at work by allowing consumers to use their imagination . . . at work. Users could manipulate an online pen with their mouse, sketch the blueprint of the next big thing since Starbucks, and share it with a friend via e-mail.

This campaign set the bar fairly high, so to meet this standard, GE recently came out with "Imagination Cubed," the first *collaborative* form of advertising that I have ever seen. Now, instead of drawing solo and then sharing the idea, users could invite two or three friends or colleagues to create a drawing simultaneously, thus using consumers as both advertising initiators and recipients (see Figure 17.3). We can only hope that some of this rubs off on NBC!

Another example of consumer-generated content is the two waves of original brand films created *for Converse by*

Figure 17.3   G.E.'s Imagination Cubed. *Courtesy:* General Electric.

Converse fans around the country, under the aegis of Butler, Shine, Stern & Partners. According to the web site, consumers were asked to "make a 24-second film—not a commercial—that embodies the values and spirit of Converse." You might consider this to be the agency's job, but this invitation underscores the fundamental belief that a brand belongs to its consumers. Instead of telling consumers what the brand stands for, isn't it so much better (and more authentic) to let consumers tell us? No more disconnects, *only connects.*

The success of this campaign was determined based on the following proof points:

- The decision was made to launch a second wave of films (13 in total) based on more than 200 submissions.
- Traffic to converse.com jumped 66 percent over the previous August.
- Nearly 400,000 visitors went directly to conversegallery .com, the site housing the films, in three weeks during the launch.
- Online shoe orders doubled in just one month.

- Sales in two bellwether accounts were up significantly for the all-important back-to-school season.

Andy Warhol's 15 minutes of fame may very well prove to be a lot longer and more far-reaching.

A Consumer-Generated Content Perspective
Jon Raj, Director of Advertising, Visa

There was certainly nothing innovative about a blue-chip company sponsoring a contest or a promotion. And of course there was nothing new about promoting that contest in traditional and non-traditional avenues. But what was new was the creation of an integrated advertising marketing campaign that relied less on the product that was being showcased and more on the consumers that the advertiser wanted to influence. The power and control had shifted from the advertiser to the consumer in exchange for the final desired result—brand affinity. And furthermore, without this participation of these consumers there would be no campaign. It was risky, but it was the beginning of something very exciting and rewarding.

"Ideas Happen" was born from the belief that although television advertising was still the dominant medium, consumer habits and lifestyles were rapidly changing. No longer was it a slam dunk to create a 30-second TV spot targeted at 18- to 24-year-olds and call it a day.

Our competitors agreed, as they too were searching for that something special in that proverbial outside-the-box campaign, yet I believe they fell short, as they too, like many, followed traditional steps and outdated assumptions. Many of their strategies were simply telling consumers what was important to them and wrapping a contest around that idea. What we knew we needed to do was to create an entirely new paradigm.

"Ideas Happen" was about young adults telling each other (not the advertiser) what was important to them, which in turn built credibility and affinity for the Visa brand.

So how do you convince senior management that by bypassing the traditional avenues of print, radio, and television brand spots, we have a real chance at breaking through the clutter and actually being heard?

The answer I found was building the plan on solid research, gut, and persistence.

The research is key for a few reasons. First, it can justify your decisions with the people in your organization that do not appreciate the use of such new innovative strategies. Also it is essential in building momentum for the approval food chain.

Once the backing is in place, it's time to look beyond the numbers and evaluate your plan from a different perspective—your gut. This doesn't mean taking uncalculated risks but rather doing your homework to have a good understanding of the landscape. That knowledge will allow you to really be guided by a vision rather than pure numbers. This is the best way to see what will be tomorrow rather than what is today.

And then there is the persistence aspect. It's too easy for great ideas to die or be placed in the proverbial parking lot. There needs to be a persistent momentum to keep the ideas alive and fresh. Typically, colleagues will jump on board only if they see that you yourself are behind it 110 percent.

Finally, keeping the plan under the radar long enough to bypass the "traditional killer," as I like to call them—the folks in any organization who only know the old proven ways to do things and rarely try anything new that may jeopardize their own standing. Also, it did not hurt to call it a "pilot project" until the positive results started flowing in.

The intrinsic gamble of course was creating a program that did not rely on an A-list director or a top-notch designer but rather on the creativity and ambition of the target, 18- to 29-year-olds. The idea of the consumer leading the marketing was of course a dangerous proposition in itself, but it was that risk that made the reward so much more gratifying.

We needed these consumers to understand and embrace the concept that Visa was not trying to pull a fast one on them ("post an idea as you sign up for a new credit card"), but rather to simply and very gently get across that Visa was the company that enabled young people to make their ideas, their dreams, a reality. We knew that if we struck the right balance of branding and consumer benefit we would be able to shift certain key brand attributes that we know grow our brand. We never imagined, though, that the program would yield such amazing results.

The role of the Internet was essential. It is the only medium that allowed for the interaction and database necessary to pull off the complicated program. The pilot year there were over 13,000 entries to view and rank for consumers. The second year that number was at 21,000. Through a partnership with MSN consumers, we're not only able to upload their ideas but also add videos and photos, as well supporting their entries. Those who decided to stay on the sidelines and not enter came to the site in the millions and ranked ideas and eventually voted for their favorites. But most important, the success of the campaign was not to be measured by the millions of visitors or the thousands of entrants but rather by the impact the campaign had on those who were aware of the promotion and their feelings toward the brand. Our research indicated that after the initial pilot year there was over 33 percent awareness of "Ideas Happen" among the target audience, and core attributes were lifted considerably.

Visa was the enabler. Visa made it all happen. Visa was the one that created the program allowing young adults to participate and get their ideas up there to share with their peers. Those were the themes that prevailed. It was much stronger than a flat print ad, a clever banner, or even a moving or entertaining 30-second spot.

The greatest challenge in this arena, and similar ones of course, is all about finding the right media mix. Advertisers for far too long have relied on the "proven" (i.e., television). As a great fan of television I certainly wouldn't count it out by any stretch of the imagination, yet we all must learn to rely on it less and look at other, newer channels and strategies to fulfill our objectives.

"Ideas Happen" is a great example of consumer-generated content (CGC). I believe it is a model that definitely has some staying power, especially in an age of infinite marketing clutter. As advertisers are constantly looking for new ways to reach their targets, consumers are becoming inundated with ads. Many have become so numb and blinded to even the most intrusive advertising that getting a positive response has become extremely difficult. What CGC promises is by handing over some of the control that we advertisers are so used to, we will be able to make a more relevant and lasting impression.

That loss of control is really the essence of the strategy. It demonstrates to the consumer that we not only understand them and value them but we actually trust them to come through. It's a very different way of approaching the marketing puzzle, but if we are willing to step up to the challenge and recognize the changing landscape, then I believe we will be able to move our brands into a very different century.

18

Search

We are surely living through exciting times when brands, devices, and technologies revolutionize the way we work, play, and buy, transforming entire markets in the process. The iPod, the BlackBerry, and perhaps the king of them all, "the Google" are three of the most influential.

Online search has transformed our personal and professional lives in ways that we never dreamt were possible. So it may be a surprise that I say the search bubble is most definitely going to burst. It has to. In fact, it already has!

Search is no longer the sole domain of the search engine. Google, for example, has diversified itself quicker than a bunch of overheated rabbits looking to do what they do best. Today you will find yourself Googling or being Googled way beyond google.com—you will find it on your desktop; you will find it in your e-mail; you will find it on your browser; you will find it embedded into the Web pages of the leading Web publishers as well as perhaps your own

home page. You already find unbranded search on your
TiVos and sometime soon perhaps you'll see Google power-
ing your entire television search experience.

But this chapter is not about Google—although it would
be fun if it were. Rather, it is about search and how marketers should be thinking about it.

The beauty of search is in its simplicity. The lowly text
link is the great leveler of playing fields. It displaces the
mightest Goliath with a nimble and dexterous David. It has
spawned an entire industry of SEOs—search engine operators or optimizers—that will dumbfound you with the depth
of their insight into a subject you thought you had mastered.

Here's an exercise: Try to create a text link to sell your
brand, product, or service using the following guidelines:

> Title: 25 characters or less
> Line 1: 35 characters or less
> Line 2: 35 characters or less

You may not use exaggerations no matter how devoutly you
think your product or service is the bee's knees; you may not
use a single exclamation point; no excessive capitalization;
no repetition; no incorrect spelling or grammar. (But how
will I "think different"?)

Here's my attempt to sell this book:

> *Life After the 30-Second Spot*
> Find out how to energize your brand
> with bold new marketing approaches

I thought I did a pretty good job—it's concise, it's to the
point, it mentions the title, and it's action-oriented.

I ran this by several experts in search marketing and
here's what they had to say about it.

Warning: What follows is at times quite technical, but (to
borrow the PGA Tour tagline) *these guys are good!*

If advertising as an art is the process of compressing
complex facts, proof points, and insights into a singular and

Kevin Lee: CEO, Did-It.com

Every test we have done shows that title creativity must take a backseat to the use of the search keyword in the ad itself in order to keep click-throughs high enough in Google (ads get disabled or your ad is farther down given the CPC you are willing to pay). In Overture a more creative approach can work, even going so far as to prequalify the clicker, but even Overture bounces ads with a boor CTR (they call it a Click Index).

My guess is you should custom-write the creative for all your important keywords that also have decent volume (power keywords). Alternatively, you could use the Google DKI to parse the search term into the creative automatically.

By tuning your creative to the individual keywords, your overall efficiency goes up. Also, the better the match (synergy) between the keyword, creative, and landing page the better the conversion rate.

> Keyword *brand*
> Is Your Brand Dead?
> *Life after the 30-Second Spot*
> Energize your brand
> Proven marketing approaches

> Keyword *advertising*
> The New Brand Advertising
> *Life after the 30-Second Spot*
> Free book excerpts, advertising
> Author Joseph Jaffe. Get the Juice.

distilled message and you thought that was hard enough to do in 30 seconds, try it out on a text link. Marketers who insist on doing this themselves (there should be a warning: "Do *not* attempt this on your own") and agencies dabbling in search need to train their creatives to draw on an entirely

Ron Belanger, VP, Performance Marketing, Carat Interactive

The challenge with search is not only that marketers are limited to text, but also that searchers themselves are in a very literal, rather than abstract, mind-set. In other words, the copy *Life after the 30-Second Spot* is a great title for a book and will resonate well with readers browsing business books at their local Borders. Searchers, however, give clear input for which they want an answer. The problem (search query) may be something like "marketing strategy" or "advertising trends." What would incent a user to click on the term? Something like "Learn the latest strategies in marketing from a leading interactive marketer. Click here to read reviews." It's boring, admittedly. But when your message is competing against 10 to 20 other search listings, you cannot afford to be cute or clever. This type of direct answer to a direct query gets the best response rates.

Marketing taglines and Madison Ave–speak do not work well at search. Always try to think more like a librarian than a copywriter when writing search copy.

New Marketing Secrets Revealed
Learn the latest marketing trends
from Joseph Jaffe, brand strategist

different bank of skills to successfully break through the clutter in a world governed by search.

This task is not as alien as it might seem, however. Is it really that different from constructing a memorable and meaningful tagline? I envision a creative explosion within search that recognizes search as the window to a brand's soul (i.e., the access point to a brand web site). It is the perfect foot in the door, and with the injection of humor, irony, and wit, search could potentially be deployed for uses other than "*Buy now!*"

Note to Marketers:
Search and Ye Shall Find

Search or pull marketing banks on consumers' newfound gift of control. It is the epitome of empowerment where they can immediately seek out a broadly or narrowly defined subset of information, choice, brands, or anything else. On the consumer adoption continuum, search fits somewhere among interest, desire, and action. Search presupposes a certain level of awareness and at least a minimal amount of interest. It is, in effect, the reward for awareness done well.

Search does not and should not replace any form of awareness-based advertising or communication, although it would be foolish to presume that search cannot play a role in the awareness process. Consider, for example, the marketing of this book. I will gleefully purchase a landfill of keywords as broad as "marketing" and "advertising," as focused as "marketing + ideas + book," or as specific as "jaffe" + "book." I'd be delusional to think that anyone looking for anything on the subject of marketing would have any kind of awareness through intent to purchase my book, but I suspect that a well-crafted, provocative lead-in, teaser, or call to action might tempt the curious to make the best investment of their professional lives.

In a second possible scenario, I'll be talking to a defined group of potential buyers, researchers, and even journalists who are looking for books on marketing, of which mine is one. It is conceivable that they might overhear someone mention a great book on marketing by some Young Turk whose name escapes them.

In a third case, search plays the perfect matchmaker. Based on focus, specificity, and relevance, my book's web site or the appropriate place to purchase it on Amazon.com should "organically" (meaning I never paid for it) or with a bit of help (meaning I did) come up trump.

In the first situation, search plays the reluctant role of mass-media distributor, one in which it does not naturally perform that well. However, savvy marketers (that's you) can deliberately place their presence in a top-of-mind (or above-the-fold) position. The consumer's subset of viable choices is the largest in this case, and while the likelihood of an impulse purchase is lower, it is still possible (like when Jim Carrey's character in *Dumb & Dumber* is told that the chance of his dream girl ever considering him is one in a million, he immediately rejoices, saying, "So you're saying there *is* a chance!"). The definition of Google is 10 to the power of 10, which is *a lot*. The next time you do a search on Google, take a second to view the number of responses to your query—it will blow you away. It's also a delicious microcosmic expression of the world in which we live today—a world consumed with clutter. The message to marketers is quite simple (Messrs. Ries and Trout would rejoice): If you're not one or two or three, you're out of luck.

In the second example, search finds a home and its sweet spot by creating market conditions in which marketers and consumers can harmoniously coexist. Any preexisting awareness is duly rewarded with instant recognition and (hopefully) inevitable action. But it is also a place for surprise and a golden opportunity for a new player to stake its claim on the consumer's fixed amount of money, attention, and consideration. In this case, the subset of viable alternatives in the searcher's mind is a lot smaller and more targeted, and therefore his or her expectations are correspondingly in line with these criteria. They still can be influenced in terms of *what* book they might buy.

In the final example, search is a hot knife slicing through butter. It is the straight line, the shortest distance between A (question) and B (answer). With limited information, an intelligent and resourceful searcher can immediately find Jaffe's new book on life after the 30-second spot.

Of course, this searcher could also have simply gone to Amazon.com and typed "jaffe" in the book search field. This explains why the search bubble burst a long time ago. Search is pervasive across the Web today and constitutes the definitive reason why Amazon and eBay (and Google) are what they are today. Without the ability to search, the overall proposition is flat.

One additional search scenario is possible: A business professional is reading an article in *Adweek* in which I am quoted or the theme closely matches that of this book. Adjacent to this article would be a link to purchase the book from a variety of blessed e-commerce web sites.

WHERE TO SEARCH

The search space is innovating faster than most. Here are a few trends or predictions about what we might expect in the not too distant future.

Search within Ads

The diffusion of search has not only spread throughout the publishing Web, but indeed is present within advertisements themselves. On some levels, this dials fairly nicely into the utility component of RUE, with emphasis on "R", "U", *and* "E".

In this example, the consumer gets a chance to interact with an online creative, which allows the consumer to fine-tune the selection criteria of someone for whom they might be thinking of purchasing a gift. In this case I'm looking for a gift for a 32-year-old female who likes food and travel and has been nice (the angel becomes the devil once the slider is moved too close to the "naughty" extreme—which might be construed as nice to others!).

As the search results reveal (see Figure 18.1), I get a host of relevant/related/real gift suggestions that I could purchase (using my Discover card, no doubt) there and then. How's that for convenience?

A Role for Branding

There are tactical implications necessary to plug in the gaps or disconnects that might arise from ambiguous 30-second fallout. In other words, a simple keyword-based campaign

Figure 18.1   Search and advertising become one. *Courtesy:* Discover Financial Services; Goodby, Silverstein & Partners.

would make sure that if consumers are searching for an advertising-initiated web site but can't remember the brand or URL, they would find it through an organic or paid link.

To find Burger King's chicken fight, I typed in "burger king spicy tender chicken direct tv" and got a variety of Los Angeles restaurant listings, as well as a Las Vegas listing (I'm not going there) and two news articles about BK's promotion, but no www.chickenfight.com. A simple and extremely efficient paid listing would have prevented this disconnect from happening.

A Search Experience

Right now search has been all about getting in and getting out as fast as you can. It presupposes a state of interest, but does not really address the awareness or preawareness phases of the consumer adoption process. Expect to see this change, especially as the Web becomes more of an entertainment medium. Expect to see a search experience that rewards the casual visitor with a bit of extra time on his or her hands.

Search and the 30-Second Spot

Another lifeline to the terminally ill 30-second spot could come from search. Imagine typing in "honda new car SUV" and getting a host of thumbnails for relevant television commercials. Better still, marketers would only pay for the commercials that were viewed.

Thoughts on Search Engine Marketing
Kevin Ryan, Executive Vice President, Did-it.com

The first evolution of the search engine as we know it today appeared in the early 1990s—named after a comic book character, Archie.

Around the time people began to search online, search engines began using automated robots (natural search) to "crawl" web sites and index information. Later, amid the dot-com boom coming and going, search sites started selling listings (paid search) to augment the revenues heretofore known as "advertising."

Let the games begin! Search engine marketing (SEM) today is a multi-billion-dollar industry that has experienced astronomical growth. Its specialized architecture has demanded an entire online advertising industry segment. Web sites have to be optimized for natural search. Advertisers will benefit from buying into paid search. The processes are complicated, so here are some things to keep in mind as you head down the search integration trail.

1. *The search marketing universe.* Search engine marketing providers have become divided into firms specializing in natural search and paid search.

   Paid search is known as the artistic portion of search marketing, while natural search engine optimization (SEO) is known as the scientific portion of search.

2. *Who will be responsible for the search assignment?* Here are your choices: you can either train your techs to build search

engine–friendly web sites and assign paid search to the marketing department, or you can hire an optimization specialist to work on natural search and pay them to tell you how to build Web pages and manage paid search programs. There is a third option—you can assign the task to your agency and they will execute some combination of the second option for natural search and attempt to manage the paid search portion on their own.

Agencies, while maintaining an acute understanding of your business and how to communicate your message to the world, may have just a basic understanding of search and may lack the necessary search tools in house.

The most important thing you can do here is research your options and understand your own needs.

3. *The hard truth about natural search.* Appearing in natural search results might possibly be the most important aspect of search engine marketing. It is also the most misunderstood. There is no way to cheat or trick a search engine into giving you better rankings. You can, however, optimize your web site for search result inclusion or hire an expert to do so for you.

The practice of web site search optimization primarily takes into account the following two factors: *relevance* (content) and *popularity* (visits).

4. *Agency, advertiser, and developer harmony.* Site optimizers and site developers will never see eye to eye. Developers want to create a rich media experiential interaction between the site and the user. Optimizers, on the other hand, will want to rip the site apart so that search engines can find and rank each page well. The only way out of this mess is through effective stewardship of the natural search process and recognizing how users prefer to interact with your site. Small tweaks to site architecture will often yield great natural search results.

Your agency will most likely want control of paid search components. Specialized tools are required to manage paid search, so be careful or you may end up paying an agency for search management while they pay for said tools, which means you are paying double.

Above all remember this: If you plan to hire multiple firms to manage natural search, paid search, and online media, make certain that each firm knows exactly what their role is.

5. *Build search budget independence.* Search demands its own budget. All too often, marketers cannibalize online advertising budgets in order to pour more money into paid search because it may appear to perform better.

There are plenty of places (other than an online ad budget) to find the comparatively small investment required to build a solid search initiative.

6. *Manage paid search with an iron fist.* The measurement of online and offline desired action information is critical in search, and it should come as no surprise that it can be quite different from other online marketing initiatives. You will be measuring positioning effectiveness: studying bid-costs trends, the impact of search activity, and latent action activity, in addition to existing online measurement criteria.

7. *Think like a searcher.* The disconnect in how language is actually used and how brands would like it to be used is common in search as well. Using natural language whenever possible in search-listing copywriting while avoiding using productspeak or technical terms will go a long way toward building a solid search program.

In many cases you may already have a list of keywords that surfers use to find your web site—just ask your site manager or information technology providers to run a referring keyword list from your site log.

In searching for your brand, searchers will not necessarily use the terms you want them to. They will search for whatever they've become accustomed to saying and *you* have to meet them in a search result in their own words, not the other way around.

8. *Search around the world.* But before you rush out to sell your widgets through Denmark's top search site remember the following.

Don't rely on automated translation tools to interpret search terms and phrases. Just as you study user behavior in your country of origin, you must apply the same disciplines to search. Hire a local or specialized translator to help you with this process. Often, site providers will help you along.

Don't forget to translate the landing pages. Landing pages consideration or optimization is a critical component of any search initiative, and this is no time to slouch.

Ask about the rules and local laws. Be familiar with the local culture.

Happy searching.

19

Music, Mobile, and Things That Make You Go Mmmm

Take an extra point if you correctly identified C&C Music Factory.

Music has long been the X factor that has the ability to unite, divide, and galvanize people because of its power to emote. And yet it has been largely left off the marketing table or at best relegated to a portion of the budget tagged "nice to have but . . ."

Coming from South Africa, I was stunned at the absence of recognizable lyrics in the typical U.S. 30-second commercial. To the day I die, I'll never forget "When a Man Loves a Woman," which was used by TBWA Hunt Lascaris to help Cardies (South Africa's version of Hallmark) aim straight for the heart. The spot showed an elderly (er, mature) country bumpkin trying to win the heart of his similarly graying sweetheart. He treks to her farm in a horse-drawn cart, on a bicycle, and eventually on foot (as he gets more desperate), bearing an array of appropriate gifts, such as freshly laid eggs and even a pig. Nothing breaks through the woman's resistance until, as a last resort, he arrives with nothing more than a card. This might as well have been from Cupid himself because it hits the bull's-eye, and the rest as they say, is history.

I take the pains to reenact this commercial for a couple of reasons. The song is obviously one of them, but the other is that I remember it as if it were yesterday, when in fact the commercial came out well over 10 years ago. I committed it to memory and heart then, and it still resonates today. Clearly, the song had a lot to do with it.

Segue to the United States, where marketers opt to send their agencies to the far corners of the globe to produce over-the-top commercials, but when it comes to music, they turn to the archives, dusting the cobwebs off some stock material or, worse still, paying some subway wannabe to create an "original" score. At the opposite end of the spectrum are those who pick cool songs (read: expensive) that are so far from being on strategy that they are about as memorable as the 2003 Detroit Tigers, who were one game away from being the losingest baseball team in history (hey, if *winningest* is a word, then its opposite should be, too).

Now let me lead you on a journey that will take you far from the previous two scenarios. Picture yourself on a train, bus, or plane. You're sitting opposite someone wearing headphones, but all you see are two white wires leading from their ears to their jacket pockets. What are they listening to? What device are they using?

It's an iPod, of course—the sole salvation of the decaying Apple dynasty. On the terms of the recent "iPod economy," this is one device to rule them all. To call the iPod an MP3 player is to call Wayne Gretzky a mere hockey player.

If you visit the iTunes web site, you will get a glimpse of the future of mobile applications, music, movies, photographs, audio, micropayments, and whatever else you can cram into your very own iPod. My iPod has everything from Queen to Latifah, from Dire Straits to George Strait (not really) to

George Michael. I also have the 9/11 Commission tapes, the presidential debates, Sun Tzu's *The Art of War*, and Dan Brown's *Angels & Demons*. (N.B.: Audiobooks are a great cure for insomnia, but I was curious. Be sure to download mine when I go "audio" if for no other reason than the accent.)

The iPod doubles as a hard drive and is quickly diversifying into photos (with the launch of iPod Photo), video, and anything else that Microsoft is likewise bundling into its Media Center. (Isn't it interesting how these rivals are in effect doing the same thing, albeit on different devices?)

IPOD AND U2'S "VERTIGO"

This is an accolade, despite the abusive frequency with which we have been subjected to this commercial. Despite my loathing for the excessive repetition in this campaign (let's blame media for a change), it still remains one of the brightest stars in recent times upon which we can gaze for direction and inspiration.

Music is such an amazing trigger because it has built-in context: You remember where you were and what you were doing when you heard a certain song for the first time. This being the case, the marriage between U2 and iPod/iTunes makes all the sense in the world.

Apple's iPod/U2 campaign is, on one level, nothing more than a U2 song overlaid on the iPod/iTunes template. But it's also a pretty shrewd example of the unification and integration of two like-minded brands. U2 embodies everything that Apple stands for (or wants to stand for): independence, creativity, self-expression, authenticity, an edge (excuse the pun) without the taint of being perceived as overly commercial (excuse the pun). They are in essence two peas in an iPod (this time intended). The "integration" in terms of the exclusive release on iTunes and the iPod U2 Special Edition makes for an even more powerful means of fulfillment.

Had Apple partnered with Britney Spears, I suspect we would not be talking about this campaign in these terms.

The 30-second commercial featuring U2 is in many respects no different from a commercial for an upcoming movie—that is, it's like a trailer. It is entertaining above everything else. This is a prime example of the "experience" economy whereby advertisers have to earn the right to secure a consumer's attention for 30 seconds (and if you've been following the other approaches, hopefully more).

The iPod has become the guiding light for music's shift from passive participant to active player. The iPod combines two M's—mobile and music—that have demonstrated their media staying power and remained true to the much maligned, misunderstood, and misinterpreted third dimension (after work and home): *on the road.*

Let's face it, home is no longer a sanctuary; it is a cluttered playground for annoying marketers—the incessant telemarketing parasites (which, by the way, include the spooky taped "reminders" to vote from Al Gore, Curt Schilling, and Rudy Giuliani prior to the 2004 presidential election), the spyware and spam that invade our computers, and the standard 30-second drivel, which takes us back to the problem at hand. Consumers have blatantly voiced their disapproval by using antispyware applications, pop-up blockers, do-not-call lists and TiVo.

At work, the situation is a lot less cluttered, and besides the muted television in the corner of the cafeteria and the restroom reading material, the Internet really does rule the roost. However, the cubicle at work is not exactly the time or place to consume media, other than what I call the *moments of truth:* prework (bagel time), lunch hour, and prehome (just the time when clients *start* calling with last-minute requests).

The environment on the road can be fairly cluttered at times as well, but it's one of those underused opportunities that are substantial in terms of both quantity (length of time) and quality (captive audiences). On-the-road time includes the commute to and from work, and would be a boon for radio if it weren't for little plug-ins like iTrip, which allows your iPod to be played through your car radio, and the propitious advent of satellite radio.

This new era is being heralded by Howard Stern, and like his subject matter (porn intended), he is often first to seize and even create a new category and a subsequent new wave of growth. Stern's announcement that he had signed with Sirius and effectively thumbed his nose at Michael Powell's FCC was without question one of the biggest media news items I have ever witnessed. It signifies the beginning of the end for commercial-endorsed "free" radio content—and it is not that different from network television's woes. In the face of this, marketers will, of course, grip their security blankets even tighter and, in a woefully inadequate display of bravado, will repeat the song and dance with which they greeted TiVo: Satellite radio has no critical *mass;* people won't pay for it, blah-blah-blah.

Right now if I were one of those Detroit auto execs who eats, sleeps, and breathes automotive fumes and must find a way to differentiate the forgettable products coming off the assembly line, I would make sure that every car comes standard with satellite radio, a DVD player, GPS, and even Internet capability. At the least, I would give consumers the option to add these features at an ever-lower price. Ultimately, that's what will help them stake out a position against their competitors—not the APR (most consumers don't even know what that means) or the glut of 30-second commercials that are really just 29 seconds of lead-up to a 1-second hackneyed punch line. (This will work, of course, only until everyone's doing it.)

So, marketers, tell me now how you feel about consumers adopting satellite radio? (Hint: Before you open your mouth, think back to the beginnings of HBO and whether you ever doubted *its* ability to take off; if so, then this would be the time to just shut up.) Your moment of truth is coming sooner than you might expect, and together with the DVR could deliver a one-two punch that you may very well never recover from.

You might think I'm heading in a tangential direction, but you would be wrong, because I'm coming right "back to Doe," not a deer but the BMW which comes with a built-in iPod, integrated into the design of the car. Similarly, VW and Apple have formed the Pods Unite partnership. The new VW Beetles include an iPod car kit. In both cases, two dynamic brand synergies have been created.

So, marketers, do you see the light? The circuit connecting marketing to technology is then complete.

Captive Audiences

Just as I believe music is underused by marketers, so too is the potential to serve captive audiences. Movie houses are a good example. Marketers have been treading on eggshells here because of the tidal wave of consumer backlash, when the golden goose (back to egg analogies) is staring at them in the face. This could be an ideal backdrop for long-form content.

On the business front, well-traveled professionals, including everyone from jet-setters to those living out of a suitcase, are ruled by a single device that supersedes even the iPod: the BlackBerry. Because of its addictiveness, it's frequently referred to as the Crackberry, aka the Blueberry.

This simple gadget has arguably left the Palm and Treo in its wake. The BlackBerry burst onto the scene with essentially one value proposition: persistent, or push, e-mail (the ability to receive your e-mail dynamically, in real time, without having to dial or log in). Although the BlackBerry is good at e-mail (at the time of writing this book, HTML e-mail was not available) it is below average at pretty much everything else, from its phone service to its sole game, BrickBreaker. (I recently sat next to a CEO from a public company whose BrickBreaker record was an enviable 7,565. Mine is 7,450.) The point is that these captive audiences will do anything to pass the time when they are stuck on the tarmac—and that includes reading their e-mail, of course.

I'm stunned at how long it has taken marketers to wake up and smell the berries when it comes to reaching this elusive and ultradesirable segment. Most marketers have just finished patting themselves on the back for having made the migration to HTML; however, in all irony, it is the text e-mail that prevails on the BlackBerry.

When people sign up to receive e-mails, they should be given three choices: HTML, text, or BlackBerry "byte." By electing the BlackBerry option, they would receive executive summaries, or BlackBerry bytes, containing the highlights/headlines or, most important, sound bites, bullet points, or proof points of any given mailing. It's just another way to break through the clutter we've created, without having to rely on the same-shit-different-day (SSDD) approach of traditional marketing.

DOESN'T MOBILE = WIRELESS = CELL PHONES AND PDAS?

Before I'm chased into oblivion by impassioned wireless aficionados, let me just say "yes, yes, and yes." Of course cell phones, PDAs, and other mobile devices are included in the mix. I left them out until now for several reasons: First, I wanted to make the point about mobility (on the road) being the third (untapped) proving ground for marketers to connect with their customers, and second, wireless has been poorly understood, merchandised, and utilized to date. Furthermore, I hope you've picked up on the references to wireless from previous chapters—for example in the *American Idol* discussion in Chapter 16.

Imagine walking past a Starbucks and receiving an alert or SMS informing you that your 25¢ off coupon for a latte is waiting for you inside. This *Enemy of the State* nightmare is being made possible due to all cell phones needing to be GPS-enabled for "security" purposes. The GPS proposition might work out really well for marketers, provided they let consumers control the flow of messaging—or *pull* the relevant content based on their unique needs. For example, before entering a shopping mall, you could request your own customized list of offers and specials. If you're walking into a car dealership, this would be an ideal time to download a list of available pricing options or promotional deals. Anything less would lead to my last Grande Skim Latte ever purchased.

Mobile really delivers on "right place" (as in the right message to the right consumer at the right time) like no other medium, and it should be made use of with that in mind.

Stewart Cheifet, managing editor of *Computer Chronicles* on PBS, told me, "*It is important to understand that the so-called mobile phone is not really a mobile phone anymore. It is literally an external chip which allows us to be beamed,* Star Trek *style, to virtually anywhere in the world.*" The mobile phone (BlackBerry included) is *the* most ubiquitous device—most people carry it with them 100 percent of the time, whether they're at home, at work, or on the road. Marketers should be salivating at that prospect!

Cheifet refers to the mobile phone as an economic extension of oneself—it's a business avatar, a transaction device, safer than a credit card, more trustworthy than a check, and more convenient than cash. He describes a recent trip to Singapore, where he used his mobile phone to pay for a cup of coffee, buy a Coke from a vending machine, book two tickets to the movies, pay for a gadget at an electronics store, rent a car, and get a message from the library reminding him that his book was due. It should be patently obvious how far behind the United States is in this department *and* that marketing communication and m-commerce opportunities are lying in wait.

As a viable new marketing approach, mobile phone advertising is still lagging behind the other alternatives (such as Internet advertising and product placement). In fact, 76 percent of an In-Stat/MDR sample believed mobile phone advertising would have minor to no impact on TV advertising. This might imply that many see it is a complement to TV advertising (although I would argue that in this case, it still impacts TV advertising, albeit positively).

But don't be fooled by this data. Cell phone penetration is heavy around the globe—in fact it is the United States that is surprisingly backward in terms of the latest innovations and advances in the field, despite 171.2 million (according to CTIA) wireless subscribers. SMS is still being used in a gimmicky fashion by marketers; however, expect to see far richer and deeper programs developing through the singular and combined use of video, camera phone photography, and MMS (custom multimedia), as well as a range of customizable accessories such as ring tones, wallpaper, and screen savers.

What makes mobile so important to marketers is that it comes equipped with an advanced level of consumer acceptance of premium content/products/services. Ring tones, for example, are the fastest-growing segment in *all of music* (including music downloads), and they were estimated to bring in sales of around $300 million (CTIA estimate) in 2004. *Billboard* introduced a "Hot Ringtones" chart, and the 2004 inaugural ring tone of the year went to 50 Cent's "In Da Club."

Mobile obviously dials into the wireless benefit (no wires), and similarly it is likely to make good on the promises of broadband, search, and network(ed) connectedness (the "perfect storm"). With increasing screen sizes, resolution, video capabilities, Wi-Fi access, and bandwidth, the mobile device is truly "the third screen." Nokia and Samsung Electronics phones will stream video from Major League Baseball and the NBA, while subscriptions to MobiTV (from a company called Idetic) will deliver live television to cell phones from channels including Fox Sports, MSNBC, and TLC.

Interoperability (i.e., communication between networks) will be a key variable in the mainstreaming of mobile.

On the marketing innovation side, Motorola sponsored an entry at the 2004 International Documentary Film Festival in Amsterdam called "Cell Stories," which was shot entirely with the video camera in a new Motorola cell phone. Similarly, Motorola launched its V710 camera phone with a series of short films, shot by Edward Lachman, the cinematographer behind movies such as *Erin Brockovich* and *The Virgin Suicides* (www.hellomoto.com/mobilegallery).

Murphy's Brewery created the Murphy's Limerick Challenge to promote brand awareness as a ramp-up for Saint

Patrick's Day, to engage consumers at the point of purchase (pubs, liquor stores), and to leverage the viral aspects of mobile. Using a cross-carrier Short Code on various point-of-sale (POS) and out-of-home (OOH) materials, participants could text in their endings to a limerick that began "There was a young bar maid from Cork" (I guess "Nantucket" was taken). The best responses were displayed on a branded minisite (with thanks to Enpocket).

In association with Disney, McDonald's UK launched a mobile "text and win" campaign to promote the movie *The Incredibles*. Customers could text in an eight-digit code to win a variety of mobile content prizes including ring tones, logos, and Java games (with thanks to Joshua Cooper at ClearMessage).

The third season of *American Idol* proved to be a watershed event in text messaging history. Through a host of SMS applications,* AT&T Wireless viewers could use text messaging to cast votes for their favorite *Idol* contestants, enter a $50,000 sweepstakes, send fan mail to their favorite finalists, and play trivia games, as well as receive behind-the-scenes information. Fans sent 13.5 million text messages over the course of the season, an 80 percent increase from the previous season. The learning and engagement curves were evident in that the number of text messages increased by nearly 700 percent from the first episode to the last. In addition, 40 percent of the AT&T Wireless subscribers who sent *Idol*-related text messages had never sent text messages before.

A Mobile Perspective
Jason Devitt, CEO and President, Vindigo, Inc.

When you forget your phone at home, you go back and get it. In fact it's the thing that you are now most likely to go back for, next to your keys and wallet.

*A partnership between Mobliss, AT&T Wireless, Fox Broadcasting Company, and FremantleMedia.

A mobile phone is tremendously empowering. When you have it with you, you're connected—to people, information, music, entertainment. Today's mobile generation, and the rest of us who are being swept along with it, are said to be disconnected. But I don't think that's accurate; instead, mobility makes information pervasive, and consumers are still connected, but only how and when they want to be.

Five years ago, when we created Vindigo, it was a truly mobile, location-specific experience; you downloaded it to your Palm and when you were in San Francisco, finishing a dinner, you'd look up the best tiramisu in the city, and the next thing you knew, you'd be off to Trattoria Contadina. Now, mobile consumers can be spontaneous in their decision making, looking up whatever individual, company, or information they need, whenever they need it.

As marketers, we need to keep in mind this different adjustment in consumption patterns. Consumers may use the phone for only a minute or two at a time, making them an entirely different type of audience—active and captive, coming for brief visits, to snack on information, to find what they need only to disconnect minutes later.

It may be used for only a moment, but it's the exact moment it's needed. Many times, it will be at the point of purchase or decision. The mobile phone, this device that holds precious contacts and information critical to people's daily lives, is the ultimate form of one-to-one marketing. In fact, it's already possible to target a specific individual, based on where she is and her past history with the brand.

The phone, now called the "third screen" (after PCs and television) is unlike a PC or television. A mobile phone is an intensely personal device; it's an extension of a person's personality and an expression of lifestyle. It's a fashion accessory, a repository of your friends, a means of personal entertainment. One young woman described her phone as her "best friend."

And because the phone is intensely personal and unique to each individual, there are cries that this device cannot and should not be used for marketing. However, there has never been a successful communications or entertainment device that did not have a strong marketing component.

Just today as I walked to work, thousands of tourists and locals in Times Square were voting on their phones for their idea of beauty in a Dove campaign. A large billboard showed the real-time results of the poll. As a communications device, smart marketers know that this is not one-way marketing. This is a new way to let consumers interact with brands. But the consumer is in control, and if the brand isn't relevant, consumers will disconnect.

And it's more than a way to deliver your message; as phones become faster, smarter, more intuitive, they can also be a fulfillment channel. Smart marketers such as Kodak are working with Vindigo and using the mobile medium to excite, sell, and fulfill demand for their products. Wallpaper based on a new movie is both a marketing tool and a revenue opportunity.

This medium offers up opportunities for new branded content, interactive games, sweepstakes, and coupons. It is incumbent upon marketers to keep messages timely, topical, and relevant.

In many ways this device fulfills the original one-to-one, location-specific marketing promise that Vindigo developed to address. With the GPS that is already available, mobile phones become the ultimate local advertising medium. When you or I walk around, we are bombarded with all of the ways marketers are trying to reach us. But now consumers have all the power of the Web in the palm of their hand, so your product better be the best or closest or most relevant. Anyone with a mobile phone can find out immediately who everyone agrees has the best tiramisu.

While today it may feel that the mobile generation is just young people, it's leaving nobody behind. Today, in the United States, consumers are sending more than 1 billion text messages per month, and in 2004 consumers will spend between $500 million and $1 billion on mobile content—ring tones, wallpaper, news, games. There is clearly a marketing opportunity here.

So the 30-second spot will evolve, and I predict that soon every television commercial will end with a short code, consumers will respond, vote, sign up for more information, receive coupons. It will extend the reach of the television, print, outdoor, and the Web. Picture your brand in the pocket of your target consumer.

20

Branded Entertainment

Star Jones's self-proclaimed fairy-tale wedding—the first of its kind in world history—was overblown with a queasy amount of corporate commercial shenanigans. Believe it or not, the event (or at least the gift bag) was sponsored in part by the following companies:

- Armani Fragrance and Body Lotion Gift Set (Giorgio Armani)
- Aromatherapy Candles (Henri Bendel Home Collection)
- Baby Phat Gift Set (Kimora Lee Simmons and Baby Phat)
- Bally's Gym Membership (Bally's Total Fitness)
- Bibles (Zondervan)
- Custom Designed Evening Shoes (Starlet by Star Jones for Payless)
- Custom Designed Silk Shawls (Cecilia DeBucourt)
- Custom Designed Swarovski Key Chains (Key to My Heart)

- Custom Designed Tee Shirts (Honey Child by Tracy Mourning)
- Custom Makeup Kits (Giorgio Armani)
- Diamond Star Pendants and Earrings (Simmons Jewelry)
- DuWop Gift Pack (DuWop)
- Engraved Cufflinks (TheKnot.com)
- Fendi Sunglasses (Fendi)
- Game Boy Advance Console and Game (Nintendo)
- Harlequin Romance Novel Gift Set (Harlequin)
- King of Shaves Gift Pack (King of Shaves)
- Lancôme Resurface Peel Treatment (Lancôme)
- Lingerie (Victoria's Secret)
- Matrix Gift Set (Matrix)
- Men's Leather Shoes (Moreschi)
- Pajamas (Karen Neuberger)
- Personalized Tote Bags (L. L. Bean)
- Polo Gift Pack (Polo/Ralph Lauren)
- Silver Kissing Bells (TheKnot.com)
- Sweat Suits (RocaWear)
- Takeouts (Better Boob Job)

And if you don't believe me, you can read it for yourself on www.starandal.com ("blending two hearts and souls into one.") There was even an official airline for the wedding—Continental.

Branded entertainment—also called *product placement* and, most recently branded, *Madison+Vine*™—is partly a bubble that, I think, has already burst. It's been misunderstood and misapplied, and in many respects the reason for this is the incremental transplantation of branded entertainment into the good old 30-second spot.

DaimlerChrysler found out the hard way that the only winners in the hiring of Celine Dion to promote their new line of Chryslers were Celine herself and, of course, Peter Arnell, the "agent" (a natural leap for the "agency") who made it all happen. But don't blame it all on Arnell; ultimately, this campaign was doomed to fail because of a lack of integration. Did new buyers receive any tie-in perks or incentives such as concert tickets or free CDs? No. Pray tell, what drove this investment other than the overpowering fumes of ego?

The Celine Dion fiasco was the victim of several strategic miscues, but it was ultimately the product of the kind of panic and desperation for a quick-fix solution that would also feel the most comfortable and remain closest to the status quo. This was nothing more than a celebrity endorsement that played itself out through a series of 30-second commercials, with an occasional personal appearance at an auto show and DaimlerChrysler's headquarters. That's one hell of a price to pay for a personal appearance—*I* would have done it for less.

On the surface it appears that mixing brands with the entertainment world (Hollywood, television, sports, and music) is like mixing oil and water—the result is not very integrated at all. I don't know that brands even need the crutch of overpaid and reclusive stars in order to offer their consumers an experience that both engages and entertains. Napster never needed it. Nike can do with or without it. Buick knew how to leverage it and turn it into something that outperformed its potential, with Tiger Trap.

COMMERCIAL-FREE TV

If by now you're still not convinced about where the 30-second is heading, look no further than the proliferation of media-free media. Commercial-free TV—such as Ford's sponsorship of the season premiere of Fox's *24*—could be seen as an admission that one chapter is ending and the next is beginning. This is, in effect, what HBO is—minus the nudity, expletives, raunch, debauchery, and gratuitous violence. In other words, the 30-second spot is a toothless, starving lion on the prowl—very desperate and woefully ineffective.

The only way commercial-free programming can survive is through subscription or premium viewing. This is happening—through pay-TV, on-demand viewing, and DVD. My concern is that if brands stick their proverbial foot in this door, whether consumers won't slam the door too hard in return.

Product Placement: The Lazy Man's Guide to Branded Entertainment

If commercials aren't doing it, how about the content?

I am regally stumped at how smart people continue to make stupid decisions because they are motivated by fear, desperation, laziness, or ego. Nowhere is this more evident than on television (with network TV at the head of the class), where product placement has become so blatant it is telegraphed from miles away to wary and savvy consumers.

Despite a new marketing landscape, marketers remain skeptical about the efficacy of bold and innovative formats and approaches, and product placement is the quick fix to which they turn again and again. In 2004, 34 percent of advertising industry executives felt that product placement would have a major impact on television advertising over the next three years. And it is doing just that. Product placement revenues spiked, from Tyson Foods' paltry $0.6 billion in 2003 to Citibank's rich $2.0 billion in 2004, and is estimated to hit a Hershey's whopping $13.3 billion in 2009, growing by a factor of 22 in just six years. (Statistics are from In-Stat/MDR.) According to Viacom's Les Moonves, 75 percent of all CBS prime-time broadcasts will incorporate product placement by 2008. On the other hand, media mogul Barry Diller does not think "advertainment" is particularly effective. He'll be pleased to know I agree with him.

My concern with product placement is largely based on overuse and abuse by marketers that has led to the flat-out rejection by consumers. I also have an instinctive belief that product placement is relatively largely ineffectual. *The Apprentice* has become the quintisential branded entertainment vehicle of choice. Entire episodes have been built around brands such as Levi's, M&M's, Crest, and Mattel.

They're often gratuitous and transparent. When Donald Trump says his show is the best, his buildings are the tallest, and his developments the most successful in history, we are willing to believe him, but when he does the same for his brand buddies, it doesn't ring true anymore. Furthermore, I'm not sure there's any substance there other than the benefits associated with "presence" — *"choose me because I'm here"* is the message of episodes that feature Levi's catalogs being compiled and candy bars being produced and sold. There are no functional, utilitarian, or emotional drivers or proof points being communicated. It almost makes me long for the 30-second again in order to eradicate the gratuitous brand invasion of content. In the advertising world, we call it "reasons to believe" — I don't recall a single one in *The Apprentice.* If I appear to be speaking out both sides of my mouth, I apologize. Earlier in this book, I sang the praises of *The Apprentice,* and now I lambaste it. It's a catch-22 all right. Perhaps I can resolve the two points of view with the following official statement: There is a continuum of desperation, at the bottom of which sits the 30-second spot. One peg higher in the food chain is branded entertainment, but there is still a long way to go before we see the light of day.

Granted, initial investments in *The Apprentice* (which is one of the better-executed reality shows) have led to short-term spikes, but these are due to first-mover advantage. At present, I have to query both the long-term benefits of participating brands *and* the sustainability and scalability of this kind of format beyond the next few years. Does this fad have staying power, and if not, what comes next? It is *not* too early to be asking these questions.

There are, of course, good, bad, and ugly ways to do this (e.g., Yahoo! ties in its participation "beyond" the episode with drive-to-Web benefits), but fundamentally there is something wrong with the methodology and assumptions that are responsible for growing this cancer, which may destroy, from the inside out, the remaining equity that exists in television content. I have a simple litmus test to gauge the subtlety of product placement and brand integration: If it looks paid, it probably is. It sticks out like a sore thumb. However, if it leaves a viewer guessing whether it was paid or, even better, elicits no response at all from consumers, then it's likely to have been smartly integrated and built into the script.

"Absolut Hunk," the deal between the Vodka producer and *Sex and the City*, which proved that size does matter, was one of those instances in which the fine line between subtle and blatant was crossed again . . . and again . . . and again. Such overexposure of any brand, especially within content, is inexcusable. I find it odd that we make the church-state argument about editorial content and commercialism, but when it comes to entertainment content and the very worst kind of commercialism, the kind that comes without full disclosure, nobody says anything.

American Idol is a classic example of the best (or at least, better) and the worst aspects of product placement and branded entertainment rolled into one program. I would place Coca-Cola in the "better" camp for their immersive and holistic brand-wrapping on *AI*. For starters, they have first-mover advantage. In addition, there's the deliberate and desirable association with all things musical, especially for a younger demographic. In other words, Coke's sponsorship of *American Idol* is consistent with its brand positioning, its strategy, and its ("real," self expression) advertising mantra. Finally—and it's nothing to sneeze at—is the fact that Coke did this carefully and with consideration:

- The Red Room, formerly known as the green room, was a clever touch, as was the red sofa (except that in season 4, it is now adorned by an obvious and contrived white swoosh).
- The judges' opaque glasses of Coke (which I'm sure contain anything *but*) are another subtle touch (except when the camera lingers a little too long).

Ford—bless 'em for continuing to try harder—is just plain bad, or maybe *sad* is a little more accurate. The musical videos of wannabes cavorting in a Ford ("Ford Moments") are in reality moments of shame.

And in dead last place would be Subway, which put together what can only be described as a humiliating skit in which the finalists served up some kind of sub in a feeble attempt to romanticize chipotle chicken (hold the shame).

The tragedy here is that the subpar Subway effort drags down any glimmer of hope for branded entertainment that came with Coke's efforts. (Demand your money back!) Furthermore, its transparent commercialism is going to be sniffed out—and subsequently rejected—by the savviest of demographics, which is the very audience of *American Idol*. If I were Madison Avenue, I'd be trying to digitally force the Clapper, Oxford HealthCare, or some denture product into an old rerun of *Murder, She Wrote*—not contaminating *American Idol*. Not that I'm comparing Subway to dentures, but in terms of the coolness factor, it's probably close.

THE FUTURE OF BRANDED ENTERTAINMENT

Don't throw in the Ralph Lauren towels just yet. There is hope.

For one thing, product placement will always serve a higher branding purpose if it's done smartly and in such a way that it keeps the integrity (a word unknown on Madison Avenue) of the content and the intelligence of the consumer intact.

Sir Ian Fleming knew what he was doing when he seamlessly integrated like-minded product branding into the fabric of his James Bond umbrella brand. Lotus, Aston Martin, Rolex, and martinis "shaken not stirred" (sort of a brand) have become icons representing the sophisticated Bond style. I wouldn't be surprised if the brand guardians of 007 had fought off (or worse, agonized and deliberated about) the advances of Ford, Swatch, and, sorry to say, Absolut (sadly, no longer the premium choice).

Proving that big things can come in small packages, the

Mini Cooper had its day in *The Italian Job,* which although pretty obvious, was a whole lot more digestible than the repellant GM orgy in the *Matrix* sequel. (By the way, it seems like a funny way to promote a car by showing it getting totally annihilated and shot to pieces.)

Home Depot is, in my opinion, one of the top marketers today and the best example of how to integrate a brand into content. The company has practically written the book on how to stand for an "experience," how to be a brand catalyst and not just a brand destination, and it has done exceptionally well in a highly competitive category by owning practically all "branded" content on programs such as *Trading Spaces.*

Survivor was a great way for a home improvement, do-it-yourself-empowering brand to move beyond gratuitously serving as the challenge "reward." In one particular task, Home Depot was the pivot around which an entire reward was structured. The tribes had to build their own shelters using a toolkit of products from the Depot. The challenge demonstrated both Home Depot's primary functional *and* its emotional value propositions: the ability to build things for yourself and the benefits, such as personal satisfaction and creating unique things, associated with being given the means to do so, not to mention the importance of having a roof over your head! Compare that with the Snickers bar that was split between a winning tribe, whose members proceeded to slobber over the bar as if it were a sexual object. Viewers didn't have a shadow of a doubt that the tribe members had been coached by the vulturelike producers.

Home Depot has also dominated the entire home improvement genre on television, maintaining a lock on reality shows such as *Trading Spaces* and targeted channels such as HGTV. Finally, how about branded entertainment in the form of a toy (see Figure 20.1) which works wonderfully, compared to the McDonald's kit available at your nearest Toys "Я" Us that I'm sure every responsible parent would cringe to purchase for their child.

Figure 20.1   Who wouldn't want to buy this well-branded toy for their kids? *Source:* jaffe, LLC.

SCHIZOPHRENIC BRANDS

If the ability to smartly weave a brand into the fabric of content has enhancing properties, then likewise the ability to do so poorly must have the opposite—detracting—qualities. Such is the case with branded entertainment, but I would take this one step further to delineate between old and new marketing, between traditional and nontraditional approaches.

A case in point is FedEx, whose weak Super Bowl attempt in 2004 and insulting follow-up in 2005 made me wonder what Brown could do for me. If you continually feed from the trough of mass swill, that's what your output will be, too. Nontraditional methods like branded entertainment (when done right) are an entirely different story.

A good example is the one-liner that appeared in the movie *Runaway Bride,* when Julia Roberts flees her wedding and hitches a ride on a FedEx truck. "Where is she going?"

asks one guest. "I don't know," says another, "but she will definitely be there before 10.30 A.M."

A more substantial instance occurred in the movie *Castaway*. Forget the 30-second; try a 90-minute commercial for FedEx. This story incorporated the brand in a manner that was completely on target. Do you remember the scene at the end when Tom Hanks delivers the one unopened package to its intended recipient? What does that say about a corporate culture that prides itself on perseverance and follow-through and ultimately delivers (in every sense)?

I challenge anyone reading this book to tell me that when you watched this movie, you were thinking "product placement"—and if so, whether it detracted from your enjoyment of the movie. The audience actually groaned during the screening of *The Matrix* that I attended. But was it really product placement in *Castaway?* Actually it was, but that doesn't really matter, at least as far as consumers were concerned. Interestingly enough, FedEx did this deal for a steal, bartering in kind for brand placement by graciously donating aircraft, shipping, and storage facilities, and the like—wish it were that easy today! Contrast this with the astronomical fees that the studios are commanding today for weaker plots, vulnerable tie-ins, and lesser benefits and then compound it with a skeptical audience who is in on the joke. Help, I'm trapped in a circular hell. Let's move on. . . .

CELEBRITY ENDORSEMENT: A DIFFERENT KIND OF BRANDED ENTERTAINMENT

The previous section addressed the existence of schizophrenic brands—both effective and ineffective marketing for the same brand, indicating that the company itself is far from integrated. The reason for hit-and-miss efforts coming from the same brand is the same reason you see hit-and-miss attempts from a single advertising campaign—because different people are working on the business and are not communicating. Otherwise you'd probably see FedEx using fewer Super Bowl commercials and replacing them with smarter nontraditional efforts.

This principle likewise applies to another favorite technique of lazy marketers and greedy agencies: the celebrity endorsement, the quintessential expression of borrowed interest.

Take Buick and its tie-in with one of the most marketable commodities in sports—Tiger Woods. The brand's 30-second commercials are ho-hum at best and, quite frankly, a waste of time and good money. Sure, I'm going to purchase a Buick just because Tiger Woods was behind the wheel.

Now segue to one of my favorite examples of new marketing and nontraditional heaven: "Tiger Trap"—a *Candid Camera* moment of genius that encompasses so many of this book's 10 new-marketing approaches that it is practically a road map for the future of advertising.

Think about it, golf lovers. You're hacking—er, playing—around with three of your buddies on the golf course when you get to a par 3 and notice that some schmuck has left his wedge on the tee. You may or may not notice that it says "Tiger," but you sure as hell notice when he inconspicuously pops out of a bush and asks if anyone has seen his club.

And as if this moment couldn't get any more surreal, Tiger then, on a whim, challenges the four to a nearest-the-pin competition and "jokingly" offers a new Buick as the prize. Of course, the prize is very real, and after he tosses the keys to the amateurish winner, camera crews "spontaneously" burst on the scene and account executives gleefully collect consent forms from the four participants.

This series of minimovies was digitized and delivered primarily via the Web. They were promoted through a variety of media, from print to online advertising. *But* what actually got my attention and "informed" and "persuaded" me to take a gander online was actually a segment on ESPN's *SportsCenter.* Now *that's* branded entertainment.

Not only had Buick succeeded in creating a four-minute ad, but the creation had actually elevated itself to the sacrosanct status of editorial content. I'll probably find out after this book is published that the segment was paid for, but it doesn't really matter. When I viewed it, I was wearing both my consumer and my marketer hats, and the *SportsCenter* segment sailed through both B2B and B2C BS tests.

One other fantastic example of celebrity endorsement is Reebok's "Whodunit?," which created an entertainment and experience extravaganza, fully leveraging its association with NBA stars like Kenyon Martin or Steve Francis to create an on-brand experience around a crime—the figurative murder of a player's career by another player, who was wearing a pair of Reeboks (which puts a new spin on the statement "It was murder out there"). This was a truly integrated program, with television ads being time-released in a specific sequence to drive interest and even drop a clue or two along the way (horizontal integration).

A REALITY CHECK

Nothing will ever replace smart thinking and the ability to pair the right brands with the right forms of entertainment or opportunities.

Macy's Thanksgiving Day Parade is a fitting example of the ultimate form of branded entertainment. Not only does it provide umbrella visibility for the famous department store, but it also provides it for the multiple brands that appear in the parade—including the Ask Jeeves butler, the brandosaurus that is Barney, Ronald McDonald, M&M's, and the Grand Old Sponge himself, Mr. SquarePants, who in 2004 conveniently flew in to promote his new movie.

Another glowing example is the now-famous car giveaway on *The Oprah Winfrey Show*, when Oprah gave away 276 Pontiac G6s to flabbergasted audience members. This was one hell of a way to kick off her nineteenth season in style.

It is tricky to even attempt to calculate ROI from such an ambitious stunt. From a media-value standpoint, however, an appropriate apples-to-apples comparison is to contrast a typical 30-second spot on *Oprah*, which typically sells for around \$70,000, with the tons of airtime (estimated at half the episode) dedicated to the Pontiac brand, not to mention all the publicity generated in all sorts of media outlets, from *People* to ESPN's *SportsCenter*. But did it sell cars? Initial returns showed the G6 outselling its most direct competitor, Ford's new Five Hundred, by 20 percent," according to *Business 2.0* magazine. That said, with just 27,000 G6's sold in its first five months, it can only be summed up as tantamount to metaphorically stalling the car. (Wonder if they counted the 276 cars that were given away as part of that total?)

Branded entertainment is not and should not be synonymous with big-budget product placement, content integration deals, or sponsorship by celebrities. It is about *brands as entertainers*, using their network of relationships with their customers to become this. As the name suggests, this is entertainment that happens to have a brand associated with it. For some reason, we've been convinced that we need the networks to help us with this task, when in reality we already have the silver bullet—our web sites.

At a 2005 conference on Branded Entertainment, Motorola's chief marketing officer, Geoffrey Frost, said: "We need to recognize there's a third person in our marital bed—technology. Let's rename our union Madison + Vine + Valley and recognize that technology is enabling our audiences to do what they really want to do whenever, wherever."

Sounds impressive enough, except that I said the same thing two years prior to that in one of my "Jaffe Juice" pieces. It's taken two years for mainstream marketing to come to terms with the fact that Madison and Vine was just a pit stop in the middle of nowhere.

"Valley" isn't just a third street that meets the intersection of Madison and Vine, it's actually *the* street. Whereas Madison and Vine are both one-way streets, Valley runs both ways.

Perhaps the most fitting conclusion to this book (which begins with "Jacksonville, we have a problem" and ends with the hit-and-miss infestation of content by commercials) can be found in an episode of *The Apprentice*'s third season in 2005, which aptly demonstrated the mass confusion and uncertain future of the 30-second spot.

In that particular episode, teams Magna Corp. and Net Worth were tasked to create 30-second spots for branded-sponsor Dove. Their efforts were so dismal that judge-and-jury Donny Deutsch thought *both* sucked and promptly declared a mistrial. Executioner Donald Trump did what he did best. Ironic? No doubt. Surprising? Not at all.

Thirty-second spot: "You're fired!"

I leave you in the capable hands of R/GA's Bob Greenberg, who presents a thoughtful perspective on the notion of swimming with the brand, which delivers significantly on the goals of engaging, experiencing, and ultimately entertaining.

Swimming with the Brand: How Can Advertisers Create Experiences That Engage Consumers?
Bob Greenberg, Chairman, CEO, Chief Creative Officer, R/GA

There is a technology convergence brewing right now that threatens not only the advertising industry, but the entire infrastructure of television, both advertising-supported and subscription-supported. Right now, there are peer-to-peer networks like BitTorrent that enable users to trade massive digital files—like the entire final season of *Friends* or the entire last season of *Six Feet Under*. Using DVRs, users are downloading these shows to hard drives and editing out commercials, if they exist. Then they are placed on the peer-to-peer networks for download by anyone with a fast Internet connection.

Once the content is downloaded to a computer, consumers are no longer limited to watching it on a small PC screen. Wireless home networking and entertainment convergence devices allow consumers to stream the files right onto the television set. These files approach DVD and HD in terms of quality, with no more grainy postage-stamp-sized images.

The increase in bandwidth opens the way for new forms of advertising and marketing programs that are richer and truly interactive. They can take the form of either informational or experiential, but in both cases experiences are delivered to consumers in a targeted fashion.

Creating online experiences where consumers "swim with the brand" are becoming increasingly common. One way to achieve this is through online games, such as we did for Nike in www.nikegridiron.com, a game based on football using Nike players as the focus. Campaigns are being influenced by games either through viral contests and live events competitions or in-game product placement and custom brand-building multiplayer experiences.

Broadband adoption also allows for richer online content in the form of viral e-mails, newsletter programs, and personalization. In the area of personalization, there are many examples, from creating game avatars that have a user's likeness (such as with EyeToy) to www.nikeid.com, where consumers can build personalized Nike products. The bandwidth also permits the use of Web-based demos for B2B, such as the Software at Work ones created for IBM, explaining complex systems more simply.

Experiences may also be designed that are informational. One example is the online mentoring program created for Nestlé Purina, encouraging extended interaction with the brand through the used of robust content on pet care. Another area where content presentation is pivotal is for e-commerce. Consumers have access to more information at their fingertips, and they are spending more time considering purchases, through the use of comparison shopping, insisting on detailed descriptions, product reviews, and so forth. They expect that the messages will be specifically targeted to them through "opt-in," local online advertising, and online merchandizing that ultimately meets their needs. Consumers are receiving information that is useful to them and helpful in making purchase decisions.

The technology advances have allowed the production of content to become digital, opening a range of possibilities. By originating marketing concepts in the digital format, whether it is for commercials, outdoor signage, online marketing, print campaigns, or direct mail, the result is that the assets can be reused and repurposed for other aspects of the campaign. Through the creation of a digital database, the same images can be shared among agencies. The ultimate outcome is that there is consistent branding, lower costs for the clients, and a library of images for future use.

Another medium that is rapidly growing is *pervasive*. Pervasive technologies allow consumers to communicate, but also to learn and shop on multiple devices, whenever and wherever inspiration strikes. The full extent of mobile has not yet been felt in the United States. One example is the game R/GA developed for Yahoo! that was played on a 23-story sign on the Reuters building in Times Square and accessed through passersby's mobile phones.

Mobile technology is being used in other ways. Phones are becoming wireless wallets used as prepaid electronic cash, tickets, membership cards for clubs, and loyalty programs. Phones are increasingly being used for multiple uses and have marketing potential way beyond communications.

Consumers are expecting more engaging experiences on all the devices with which they interact. The size of the device is less relevant, with convenience being a key component. The long-term implications are that creators of advertising need to develop new skill sets to architect truly immersible online experiences, not linear stories as is done in traditional media. The experiences should marry design, graphics, and architecture while integrating sound effects and music, full-motion video, games, entertainment, and database-driven technology. There is the need for a new language and copywriters who can create online writing standards.

Ultimately, the successful online experience should be 2 minutes × 120 minutes wide. The 2 minutes represents a short-subject video or game, and the 120 minutes, the multiplicity of links that emanate from online ads or sites to additional content and information. Constructing this type of digital experience entails very different requirements from those needed to create a linear 30-second television spot. Innovation and inspiration are the key drivers today.

◆◆◆◆◆

Epilogue: Why Should You Care?

What should you do about this?

The 30-second spot in its prime (time) was the homecoming king. Today, some 65 years after it was first used, it is like Sean Connery—still sexy as hell but not much of a long-term prospect. I contend (and I hope I've given you enough food for thought that you share my contention) that the 30-second spot has outlived its usefulness. Rumors of its demise may very well be exaggerated, but they are irrelevant. Using the 30-second spot today is like taking a wooden sword to fight a fire-breathing dragon. You better have fire insurance.

In a bizarre twist of fate, the 30-second has been thrown a lifeline from the most unlikely of rescuers: the Internet. The ability to deploy (and extend) the life of the 30-second spot on the Web is a short-term solution to a long-term problem. Ultimately, there needs to be something else, and fortunately, there is—in the form of the 10 bold new approaches discussed in this book, which are revolutionizing and transforming the marketing and advertising games.

Those marketers who have been searching in vain for "big ideas" and ways to extend their brands will probably find that the answers have been right there in front of their very noses. Every brand—and I mean *every* brand—has the potential and the means to execute an involving experience, the ability to break the monotony of traditional marketing and deploy bold new alternatives in counterpoint to Einstein's definition of *insanity* (continuing to repeat the same thing over and over, hoping for different results).

Some marketers and agencies have started down this one-way street. Amazon.com Theater is one example. Let's see how many of the 10 new approaches discussed in Part 3 are in fact in play at the same time in this particular case:

1. Internet — (duh) check
2. Gaming — Not applicable
3. On-demand viewing — check
4. Experiential marketing — check
5. Long-form content — check
6. Communal marketing — check
7. Consumer-generated content — there was a link "Attention filmmakers: Give us your e-mail address to hear more about future Amazon Theater programs"
8. Search — in time . . .
9. Music, mobile, and things that make you go Mmmm — in time . . .
10. Branded entertainment — check

Seven out of ten ain't too bad. (Gee, I wonder how many books they sold?)

Then there's George Masters and his 60-second ode to Apple iPod. This is an excellent example of several of the approaches coming together — primarily interactive + long-form (hey, it's no 30-second spot) + communal + consumer-generated content. And here's the thing: The client and agency were pretty much nowhere to be found. There is an entirely independent brand conversation going on, and agencies are in danger of being completely removed from the loop through their inaction (or consumer "pro-action").

In theory, emblazing new marketing is easier than you think, but in reality it's a little tougher because it starts with the realization that you've been doing things suboptimally (read: wrong) or, to be a little kinder, you can expiate missed opportunities by:

- **R**ejecting the status quo and objectively discarding staid and failing paradigms
- **E**mbracing change by entertaining a suite of new tools/options
- **A**ccepting responsibility and a higher level of accountability or marketing efficacy
- **C**hallenging your external partners to adapt . . . or die

- **H**iring or investing in talent that can adapt to—*welcome and capitalize on*—the rapidly occurring sea changes in marketing

Reject the status quo and question everything. Look inward and outward in an attempt to objectively determine the efficiency and effectiveness of your current marketing communications efforts. Accepting things because that's how they've always been or resisting change "on your watch" is ultimately going to cost you your job and result in holding back your brand. You're losing touch with consumers who have gained the ultimate power—to choose and control their media-consumption experiences. Flawed methodologies that are adopted by everyone will result in gains for no one. It is time to retire the Wanamaker concession and surge forward with a precise, informed, and carefully considered point of view on the comparative efficiencies and effectiveness of your integrated efforts.

Embrace the full suite of new marketing options and alternatives that are open to you. Dipping your toe in the water isn't exactly going to win you the triathlon that lies ahead. You need to move beyond lip service and tests, and if you are going to experiment, then it needs to be a substantial effort—one that comes from the top as a corporate directive and precipitates a massive cultural shift. This is what P&G did, calling an "all stop" and turning its battleship around before it ran aground (or into an iceberg).

Accept a new level of accountability—a higher standard that not only eliminates the guesswork, legacy assumptions, and hypotheses simplified to the causal relationship between investment and return, but goes several levels deeper to help separate and compare all touch points. It's important to understand which communication touch points are overdelivering (and all things being equal, should be increased) and which ones are underdelivering (and need to be cut). It is also important to maintain a firm grip on the reality of brand versus business or long-term branding versus short-term sales. This is an age of "and," not "or," and your ability to balance your often contradictory objectives will become increasingly an art *and* a science.

Challenge your marketing, advertising, and/or media partners to get with the program . . . or get out. This is the time to focus your efforts on getting the most out of your partners, not paying the least for them. This is the time to be ensuring that you're getting their best *new* ideas, not repurposed ones, and certainly not window dressing, in order to help sell through the more familiar recommendation of 30-second spots. This is the time to evaluate your partners' ability to *generate* (ideate) and *integrate* (execute) in an objective and collaborative fashion. It's also the time to ensure that you're with the best of the best, as opposed to the rest of the rest. In an age of consolidation and generalization, you need experts, not jacks-of-all-trades.

And finally, *hire* like there's no tomorrow, because there may not be (at least for you). Ask yourself this: If today purchasing people handle the procurement and selection of a communications partner agency, tomorrow could they be handling the output as well? Stop shaking your head and look around you—your marketing department used to be a lot bigger than it is today; you used to have a lot more responsibility than you do today. The only thing you have to fall back on is arguably your weakest ally—a tired and ineffectual 30-second spot. You must weed out those who continue to resist change and bring in an entirely new suite of talent. To the extent you are able to train and migrate old marketing managers into new ones, you will be able to maintain a degree of continuity, but ultimately what is required is a major disruptive schism in the fabric of your operating ethos.

BBDO and JWT are two of the largest Goliath agencies that have turned to the two great hopes—the creator of BMW Films, David Lubars, and the source of various Nike experiences, Ty Montague. In doing so, they're both reinventing and repurposing the wheel. Time will tell whether it is possible to teach an old dog new tricks. The message ringing out to creative directors is a mixed one: Create a different solution or experiment (à la P&G) and you'll get your one-way ticket to a cushy job at a dinosaur. Can a leopard change its spots, though? Even if change does come from the top, how exactly will you handle the decay occurring in the middle?

I called this book *Life after the 30-Second Spot* and played on the fact that you could interpret this in several ways:

- The 30-second spot is dead (thus, life after death).
- There *is* life after the 30-second spot.
- The 30-second spot is no longer the gold standard (whether dead or alive) and in its place is a whole host of possibilities and exciting alternatives that both can and will energize your brand by reestablishing, maintaining, and ultimately strengthening the connection, context, and relationship with your customers.
- The 30-second spot can survive (or be saved) only with the help of technology. Corralling, Commercials Frozen in Time, Behavioral Targeting, and/or Advertising on Demand all sound appetizing enough . . . but the $58 billion question* will be, *"Is it too little, too late?"*

We're entering a golden age in marketing that may look nothing like traditional advertising. Television is becoming richer than it has ever been before—from surround sound to high definition—and is also in the process of digitization resulting in a suite of on-demand options, from video on demand to the digital video recorder. Gaming has usurped much of today's available content to bring forth a movie- or television-like experience that is being *immersively* consumed by communities of people who concede that it's no fun playing alone. (Watching television, in contrast, has become an act of viewing alone.†) Radio ascended into the heavens (via satellite) and will undergo a transformation from free to fee.

---

*Full year 2004 ad spending for network, spot, cable, and syndication television, as reported by TNS Media Intelligence.

†According to Knowledge Networks (December 2004), 45 percent of prime-time TV viewers are watching TV by themselves, versus 31 percent a decade ago.

Print will limp along and play to niche audiences unless it is able to deeply integrate and leverage its online and mobile properties. As printers and printing continue to decrease in cost and increase in productivity, expect consumers to print their own magazines from home, using a selective binding process that may incorporate a superrefined degree of targeting. The tablet PC will come with packs of $3 \times 100MB$ screens that consumers will preload with content and dock at home or at work. The Web will look both more and less like television each day, as consumers will switch back and forth from an active to a passive stance depending on their posture and the degree of arc between themselves and their screens.

Technology will be the great ally and lurking enemy. For every threat it raises, it will also bring an accompanying opportunity for those who wish to see the possibilities. *Skipping ads may prove to be the norm, but avoiding experiences could be the exception.* Above all, content will remain king—now more than ever. Great content will be consumed and shared among like-minded communities of interest, and everyone will be welcome to participate, create, and comment.

The winds of change have begun to blow. PepsiCo's announcement to reintroduce Pepsi One diet cola with a myriad of new marketing touch points and tactics—and nary a hint of television advertising—has no doubt upgraded this gentle breeze to gale force winds. Do you *still* think news of the 30-second spot's demise has been greatly exaggerated?

There is a glorious life ahead after the 30-second has been put to bed. I just hope you'll be around to see it.

Index